Historical Significance

of the

First Successful Colt Experiment

The Colt Paterson Revolver

by Michael R. Desparte

iUniverse®

HISTORICAL SIGNIFICANCE OF THE FIRST SUCCESSFUL COLT EXPERIMENT
THE COLT PATERSON REVOLVER

iUniverse books may be ordered through booksellers or by contacting:

iUniverse
1663 Liberty Drive
Bloomington, IN 47403
www.iuniverse.com
1-800-Authors (1-800-288-4677)

ISBN: 978-1-5320-3928-7 (sc)
ISBN: 978-1-5320-3927-0 (e)

Library of Congress Control Number: 2018905894

Print information available on the last page.

iUniverse rev. date: 10/10/2019

Historical Significance of the Colt Paterson Experiment

SPIRIT OF THE TIMES NEWSPAPER

NEW YORK-SATURDAY MORNING, JULY 7, 1838

Samuel Colt, was the recipient of a Gold Medal from the Committee of Learned and Practical Mechanics of the American Institute.

"The most important of the Colt patents, insofar as Paterson manufacture is concerned, is (patent) number 1304, dated August 29, 1839. This patent records the improvements brought about by (the) Paterson (plant), mostly prior to the start of any actual production."

"No production pistols have been found of the 1836 patent design, whereas the earliest Paterson pistols produced conform to the drawings of 1839. It is certain that pistols of the 1839 pattern were in actual production prior to the dating of the patent. (However), Pistols of the belt size in 1839 pattern are shown in (this) 1838 illustration."

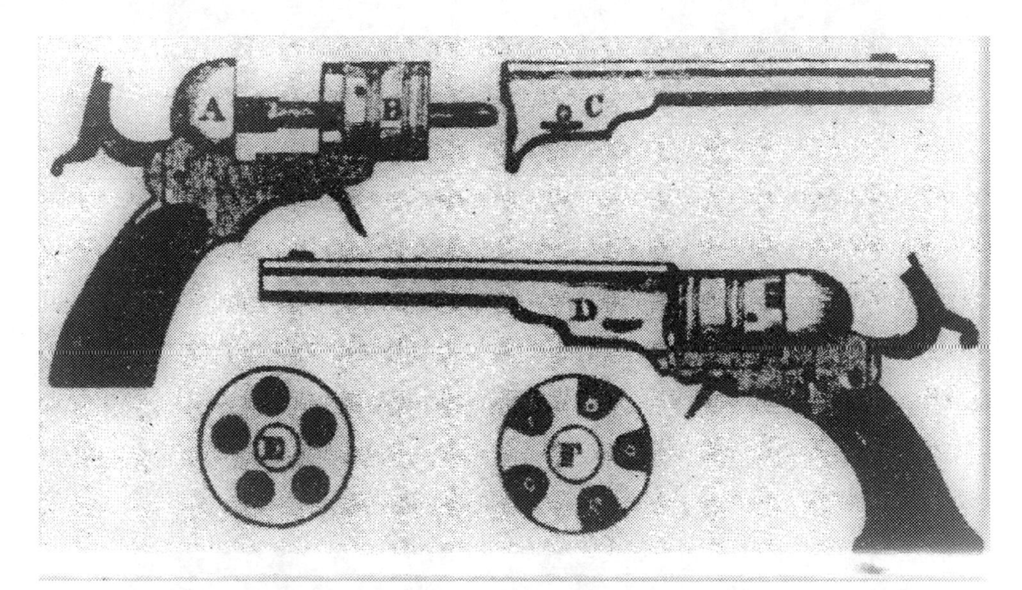

The above pistols are Belt Models built prior to the 1839 patent. They are shown on the cover and throughout the following Research Paper. The illustration identifies the pistol in the upper left corner, with a normal sized receiver, is a No 2 Belt Model having a straight hand grip. The pistol in the lower right corner, with an extra-long receiver, is a Belt Type Experiment, having a flared hand grip, and may be the exact same Colt Pistol written about in the following pages in this Research Paper, i.e., the Colt537.

The statements in quotes are the comments of James E. Servin, author of , "Colt Firearms 1836 - 1938" found on page 10, colum 2, paragraph 10.

Michael R. Desparte, Author

Table of Contents

Acknowledgments

No work of this magnitude could be thorough and reasonably complete without the help from so many. Their assistance has been indispensable. Whatever acclaim this research paper may receive, the value of that acclaim is due to the unselfish contributions of my family, friends, and acquaintances.

This Research Paper is dedicated to late R.L. Wilson, Author of so many books on the Colt Revolver. He was my inspiration and the reason I pushed on in this research project. It was with his support, his encouragement, and his suggestions that make this paper what it is. It was his recommendation that I acquire, "The Paterson Colt Book." This was a joint effort of collector Dennis LeVett and R.L. Wilson. Without their combined contribution, I would not have been able to compare Mr. LeVett's collection of production revolvers to my Colt537, the experiment.

Roy Markot, Author of Colt Brevete Revolvers, provided encouragement, and guidance on how to approach writing this paper, and generally pointing me in the right direction on firearm editing and publishing.

Bruce Balistrieri, Curator, Paterson Museum, Paterson, N.J., who dedicated one complete day providing me with various sundry of important bits of information on the Colt Paterson Revolver. His information was important in understanding the construction of the revolver, including the identification of various persons with expertise in the field of early percussion revolvers.

My gunsmith, Raymond Booze, for his tireless assistance in Colt537's dismantling, inspection and analysis, in making this research paper as thorough as it is. Without his countless hours of help, it would not have given this paper the impact it has.

My editor, Carol Crawford, provided general guidance, and supportive editing.

No work of this type could be thorough and reasonably complete without the help of my family. I am indebted to my wife, Lois, who painstakingly went through this paper, making repeated editorial reviews over the past eight years.

My son Joseph for his extremely valuable contributions in chart preparation.

My other three children Lisa, Jeff, and Mary were also contributory with their constructive comments.

Then there were friends and neighbors, most provided editorial reviews of my preliminary work on this paper. Col. Robert Brookshire, Ted Gaudette, Walter Shiel, Tony Van Dyke, Jerry Hemphill, Mark Spykerman, Scott Riddle, Peter Barron, Rouven Forbes, Sonny Freeman, to name a few..

Author's Note

My quest to find the origin and the significance of the Colt537 is the result of a life-long fascination with arms. It began with my uncle, Nicholas Vucalich. His name in Croatian means Son of the Wolf. He lived up to the characteristics of that name. As a young man, I tried to live up to that name as well. He ran away from home and joined the army at the age of fifteen, fought in World War I at the Battle of Belleau Wood. When his unit was being overrun by the Germans he realized how bad his situation was and began to pray. At that moment an artillery shell burst above his machine gun emplacement. It knocked him out, and when he came to, the battle was over. From that point on he was a God fearing man. As the story goes, words directly from my Uncle, he eventually received a Battlefield Commission as a 2nd Lieutenant. Being proud of what he accomplished, he wrote home to his mother, my Grandmother, telling her the good news. His mother, thankful that he was alive, wrote to the Army, relating that her son was under age and joined the Army without parent consent. The Army, in turn, discharged 2nd Lt. Vucalich and sent him home.

In his later years he lived with us, and as a young boy I listened to these and other stories, about his hunting and fishing trips in Upper Michigan and Canada. We became very close. What really warmed my heart was when he told me I was the son he never had. How lucky can a kid be, having two great fathers?

When I was about thirteen years old, my uncle purchased a .22 automatic rifle for me, the Winchester 63. I added it to the two BB guns on my gun rack in my bedroom. Since my uncle joined the army when he was fifteen, I saw no reason why I couldn't join the Army National Guard at seventeen. While still in high school I joined the National Guard rifle match team and won a few medals, and became proficient in shooting the M1 Garand and the M1 Carbine. I guess, in a way, I was trying to follow in my uncle's footsteps. That same year I won a $50 prize for selling a few chance books for a school raffle. My school, the Mount Carmel Catholic High School, was run by priests. Instead of giving me the $50, I asked my priest friend if he could get me a Marlin 30-30 rifle. I had never before heard a priest exclaim "Jumpin Jehoshaphat!" He indicated he would see what he could do. He also mentioned that he needed a letter from my mother giving me the permission to have the gun. That's how my gun rack acquired its first deer rifle, A Marlin 30-30, lever action.

In 1953 I gave $3.00 to a friend for a broken chrome plated revolver. It looked like a nice gun, but it didn't work. All the interior pieces were missing. It was an 1874 Colt Lightning, the first double action revolver the Colt Company produced. I asked my Dad to help me pay for its repair. Instead, he suggested I go to the library and see if I could find a gun book illustrating the parts I needed, and fix it myself. I did that, but was never able to make it work satisfactorily. In helping to restore its appearance, I used a little wood filler on the hand grip where a piece was missing, then stained the filled-in piece with black shoe polish. It blended in well with the black rubber hand grips on the frame. Since much of the chrome on the gun had peeled off, its appearance left a lot to be desired. I brought the gun to an upscale gun store in downtown Chicago, the VL&A sportsman's store. The cost for stripping of the chrome and re-bluing the gun was $35.00. This was back in 1954, and at that time, it was a lot of money for a senior high school student. Two weeks later, I went back to the store, gave the gunsmith my ticket, waited, and worried, wondering what it was going to look like. When he came back from his work area, I couldn't believe he was holding my gun. It looked so beautiful. Now I really had something I was proud of. The gun fit in the drawer on the bottom of my gun rack. I lay there on my bed at night looking up at my gun rack smiling to myself.

In 1954, I was on the high school football team. We did well that year. We won the City of Chicago Catholic League Tournament. The school's notoriety in winning was a great benefit to me; I received a football scholarship to the University of Wisconsin, and majored in science, with minors in geology and environmental issues. Graduating with Bachelor of Science Degree wasn't enough for me. I later went on to acquire a Master of Arts Degree.

My first real job was working on an off-shore drilling rig in the Gulf of Mexico. I guess I wanted to see if I had the right stuff for hard work. My first career type job was in City Planning, and within a few years I became the Regional Planner for the Northeastern Part of the State of Wisconsin. A few years after that, I became Chief of Planning for the Minnesota Pollution Control Agency and later promoted to State Director for Minnesota Environmental Programs. Having an urge to teach, I made my way back to the university setting and eventually became an Associate Professor with the University of Wisconsin. Thirteen years later, I retired. Realizing that may have been a mistake, I accepted an offer to take the position of Planning and Development Manager for the State of Florida in the Florida Keys. In an attempt to put all these experiences to practice, I became County Commissioner for Flagler County Florida. Six years later, I retired for the last time.

I enjoyed deer and squirrel hunting with my old roommates from the University. We had become life-long friends. I was surprised as to how well we all fit in with each other, me being from a big city and them from small towns in Upper Wisconsin. We still communicate.

Over the years, my collection and my interest in antique firearms grew. Then I discovered the Colt537 which evolved into this research paper. It took eight years of research to reveal what this gun really was. I hope you enjoy this research paper as much as I enjoyed writing it.

Part One

A Case Study

of

The Colt537 Story

Chapter One

The God Element and DNA

The God Element and Deoxyribonucleic Acid (DNA)

Recently scientists believe that they discovered the God element. Many times we hear the comment of an idea or a thought originated in our DNA. Was a new revolver concept in Samuel Colt's DNA? I do not believe that the development of repeating guns was, but it is reasonable to believe that the young man was interested in guns. The spark that ignites an idea develops into a never ending series of branching thoughts and ideas on through the ages.

So let's start at the beginning with gunpowder. It is recorded that gunpowder or black powder was invented somewhere around the ninth century by the Chinese. Wikipedia tells us sulfur is an element found near hot springs and volcanic regions in many parts of the world, particularly along the volcanic China Rim of islands, in the Western Pacific. Sulfur can be found in the volcanic active areas of our world. And crystallized potassium nitrate is formed from bat guano, a bat product found in caves. Think about that for a moment. When this composition is dampened with water, then dehydrated, it becomes crystallized potassium nitrate. Charcoal, the remains of a fire, can also be found in caves. Man originally lived in caves, a most secure habitat at that time. His earliest tool was fire. The cave dweller used fire to keep warm, prepare food, and a host of other uses. It isn't unlikely that the combination of these three elements, sulfur, potassium nitrate, and charcoal could have randomly found their way into the fire pit at the same time, prior to ignition. One can bet, he or she really got a bang out of this random collection of products. We will never know who it was that asked, "how did that happen?" If he or she was able to replicate that bang again, that is the person that discovered black powder. It all started by accident.

Was the revolver concept in Samuel's Colt's DNA? Like I said before, I do not believe that the development of a repeating gun was continually on his mind, but it is reasonable to believe that the young man was interested in guns and the idea of a revolver was picked up from somewhere or something.

Young Sam was a crew member on board the sailing ship Corvo bound for Calcutta. The ship eventually landed in London.

Historical Significance of the Colt Paterson Experiment

> "Nearly every street in the old town had at least one small shop where pistols and fowling pieces were sold and/or repaired, and good shops were as plentiful as locksmiths; an iron worker often combining all three trades in one. The fancy dress shops and gentleman's tailors were far less of an attraction to young Colt than the gun stores, and he stopped at every shop window. An agent of Corvo's owner, who was assigned to look after Colt, gave him the latitude to gaze inside at rows on rows of every conceivable type of gun. There were beautifully cased pairs of flintlock dueling pistols." 1

Young Colt's eyes centered on a specific primitive revolver, it was flintlock, made in 1813, having a cylinder that is manually rotated to the next firing chamber, **Image 1.**

Image 1

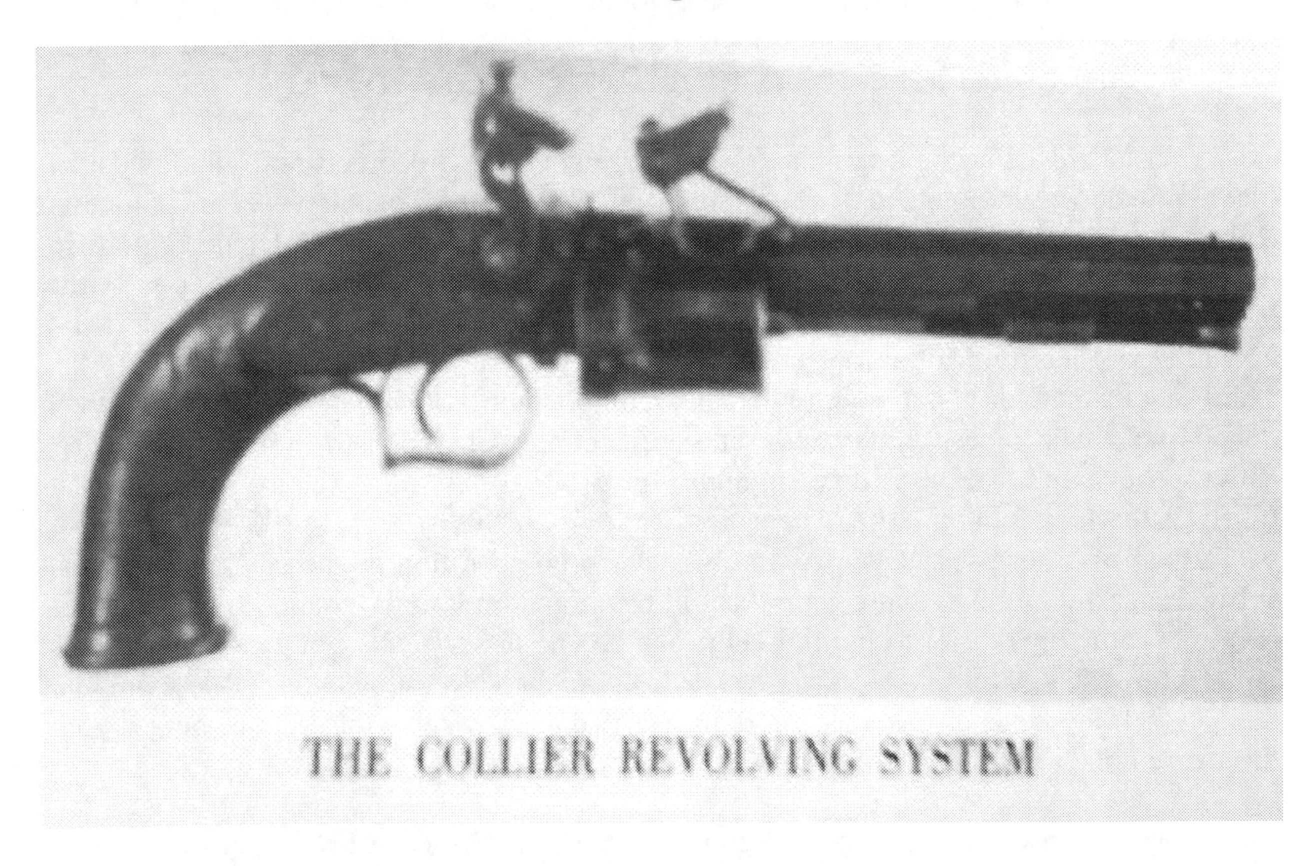

Source: The Colt Revover, C. J. Hven and Belden, Page13

---

1. Collier, through contributing some of his own inventive ability to the design, patented his gun in England. A recent examination of this gun indicates that the model was made by Artemus Wheeler, an American, who communicated his designs to Elisha Collier, then living in London. Page 65 (Ca. 1819)

Colt's Concept

Elisha Collier was the inventive gentleman of Boston who had devised a repeating flintlock firearm using a rotating chambered breech. Lack of public interest in the United States is supposed to have caused him to seek patronage in England. In 1813 the U.S. was far from a manufacturing nation. Colt took great interest in this flintlock. Back on board ship, he had the opportunity to whittle a concept of his first model pistol, **Image 2**. The six-chambered cylinder, with holes bored with a hot wire, which was based on what he had seen of the Collier pistol. Sam felt he could do better in making a truly revolutionary revolver.

Image 2

Image 3

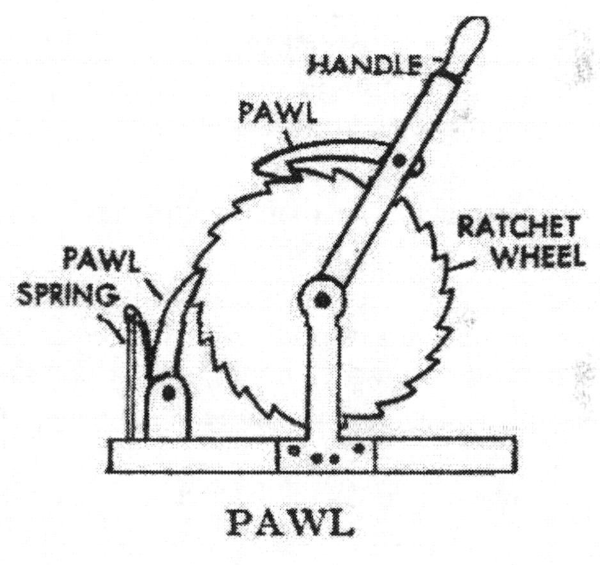

Picture the ratchet wheel, **Image 3,** physically attached flatly against the left side or rear of the Colt's wood cylinder in **Image 2**. The idea of a ratcheted rotation of the cylinder came to him as the ship was being unloaded with cargo. A windlass serrated at the foot, or ratchet cut with a stationary pivoted pawl to lock and hold the capstan firm. Then when the pressure was eased up on the levers of the capstan, it could rotate to the next fixed position. In his mind, these concepts represented the cocking of the hammer of a percussion type revolver. During the cocking process the cylinder would rotate to the next position, and stop when the next firing chamber was aligned with the bore of the barrel. It would be locked in that position by a bolt, and the hammer would end up cocked and ready to fire.

Anson Chase, Gunsmith

Anson worked in the North Schenerard Gunsmith Shop. He had recently come to Hartford from Enfield, Massachusetts. Anson was recommended to Colt, possibly because his prices were cheaper than most competitors. Sam and Anson met to discuss his ideas for the development of a revolver, based on the concept he developed while on board the Corvo. He was a cabin boy on his first voyage to and from Calcutta. Sam took to Chase's ideas and planned to work on Colt guns, off and on, for several years. The first pistol, however, was a rush job and pushed through as fast as it could be put together. When finished, Colt brought the pistol, with a letter of introduction from a well-known Hartford family, to the Washington Patent Office in D.C. The Commissioner of Patents, Mr. Ellsworth, provided an important step in Sam Colt's climb to fame. Ellsworth gently dissuaded Colt from an immediate application for a patent. The Commissioner knew that the crudely finished specimen of a firearm Sam had shown him was not a mechanical marvel. But, with a little time and money spent in smoothing out the rough edges, it could become something worth a patent. Ellsworth did provide him with an, affidavit of claim of invention, establishing priority of invention, and this initial firearm was deposited in the secret archives of the Patent Office. As time went on Sam accumulated the financial resources and knowledge with which to develop his pistol.

John P. Pearson, Gunsmith and Watchmaker Extraordinaire

Baltimore was a friendly town to Sam; he found his recurrent billings as a lecturer at a museum profitable, and when he was not performing on stage with his laughing gas exhibitions, which continued to fund the development of his repeating revolver, he would be found wandering about the streets down to the harbor looking for a good gunsmith.

> "A. T. Baxter's skill and craftsman as a gunsmith was well known and enabled him to prosper, to the point of employing a few extra hands. He was always glad to take on a little more work. He detailed one of his men, a John Pearson, to take care of all of Sam's needs, and left the problem pretty much to themselves."[2]

John worked on several pistols, including one in brass, and two rifles. The Colt Cabinet of Arms in the Wadsworth Atheneum, Hartford, CT, has what is thought to be a complete line of Colt experimental weapons. Although missing certain pieces, the collection proves that Colt was responsible for the design of the firearms patented by him in 1836. What was unique about John Pearson was he had training as a watchmaker. He was someone who was familiar with the intricacies of watch-like mechanisms, and had the perfect experience for designing similar mechanisms for Colt's experimental pistols.

---

[2] The Story of Colts Revolver, Wm Edwards, Page 31, Col 2, Par 2, L 1

Image 4

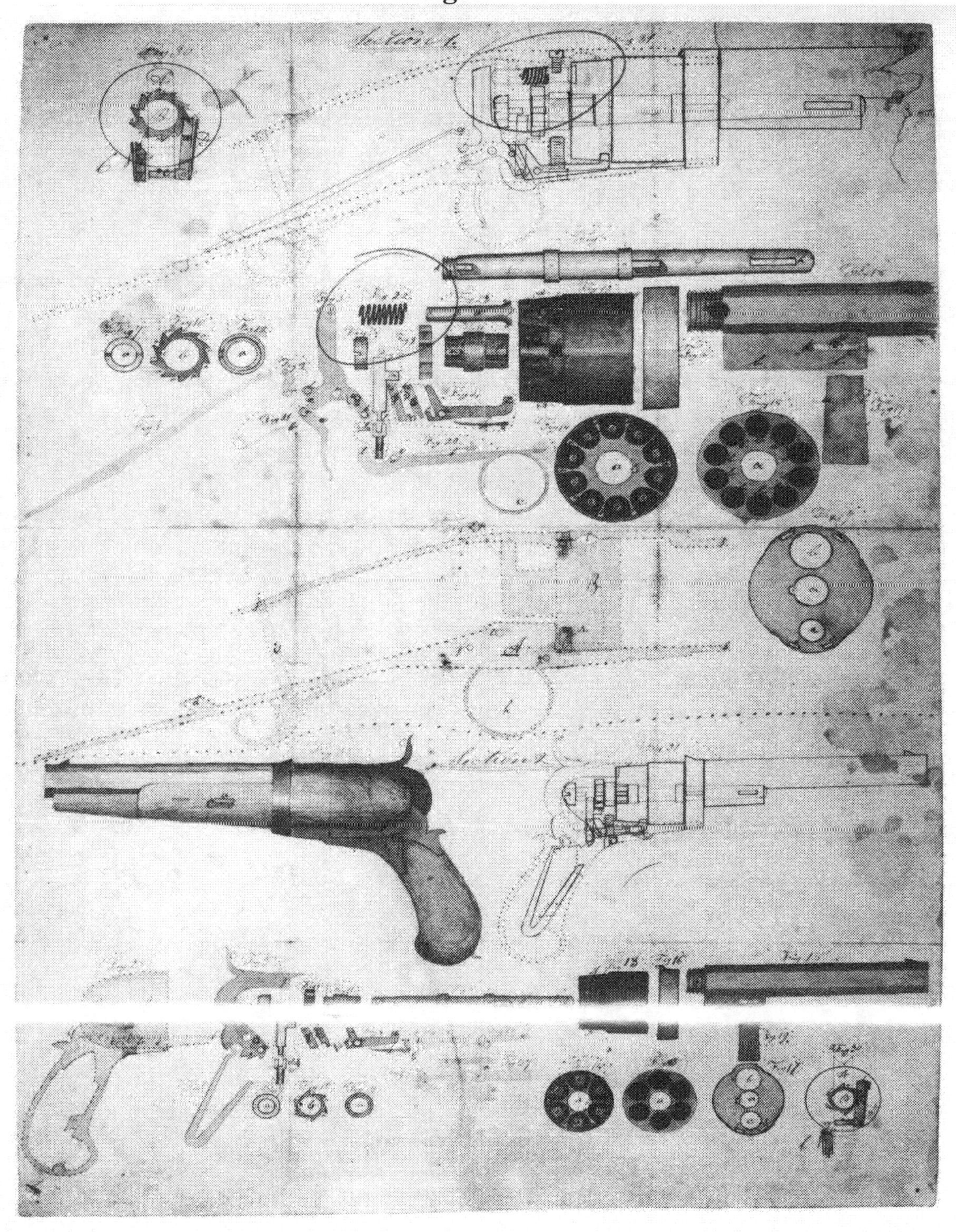

Source: Paterson Colt Pistol Variations, R.L.Wilson

The first Colt Patent in England and France, 1835, and the United States, 1836 New Patent Arms Mfg. Company Activities

Historical Significance of the Colt Paterson Experiment

John Pearson and Samuel Colt worked collaboratively in making minute improvements throughout the series of sixteen experimental revolvers. Eventually, in late 1835, Pearson made for Colt what was called the deluxe sample revolver. Although it was a small gun, a .33 caliber, with an overall length of close to 8 inches, it was extremely attractive showing a floral engraving and highly finished hand-grip. **See Image 4 on the previous page**.

Watercolor drawings were made of this deluxe sample to be submitted along with the first Colt patent applications in England and France in 1835. He later submitted his application for patent to the United States Patent Department on February 25, 1836. There were certain advantages in submitting the patents in this order. During the organization of the Patent Arms Mfg. Co. and its initial operations, the stockholders learned that the designs were not at a point which allows for quickly entering into production and swift profits.

The focus of initial factory operations was on two revolvers designed, **See Image 6 and Image 7, on pages 8 and 9**, and built at the Colt Factory under the supervision of Pliny Lawton and Sam Colt. Pliny was the plant supervisor. These revolvers were to be used as the final experiments and/or prototypes.

After an experiment was determined feasible, it is transferred to the prototype phase. Here measurements are taken and incorporated into the production machinery. Flaws in this final phase of development were sought prior to the development of models made for sale.

The Advanced Stage of Design Sketch for the No. 2 Belt Model Paterson Revolver

During Colt's trip to England and France to obtain patents from each of these countries, Pliny Lawton developed an advanced design sketch, named the No. 2 Belt Model revolver, **Image 5.**

Image 5

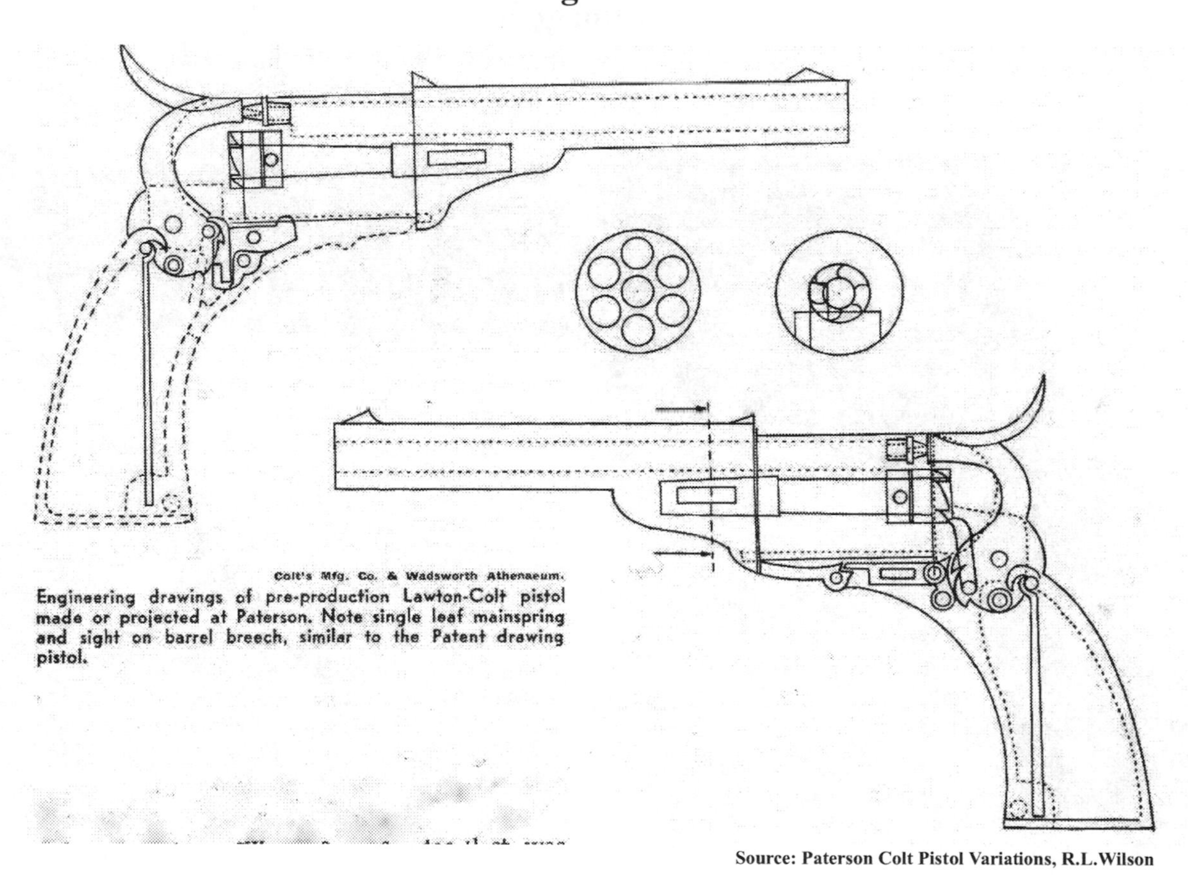

Source: Paterson Colt Pistol Variations, R.L.Wilson

Engineering Drawings of Pre-production Lawton-Colt Pistol

It has six firing chambers and a straight grip with a single leaf mainspring. It also had a rear sight on the breech end of the barrel and a high hammer spur. This high hammer spur is also found on Prototype experiment six-shot version of the No. 2 Belt Model revolver. There are similarities in the two handmade experimental models that follow. They are essentially take offs from the above design sketch that illustrate continuity in design development. They are found in the actual revolvers fabricated from the above drawing.

The First Lawton-Colt No. 2 Prototype/Experiment

The first is the actual No. 2 Prototype, experiment six-shot Belt Model revolver. Not much is said about its competence as a six shooter; however, there must have been a few inadequacies due to the limited amount of attention that was garnered from any of the source material. This model lacked a frame plate, disallowing access to the internal firing system.

Image 6

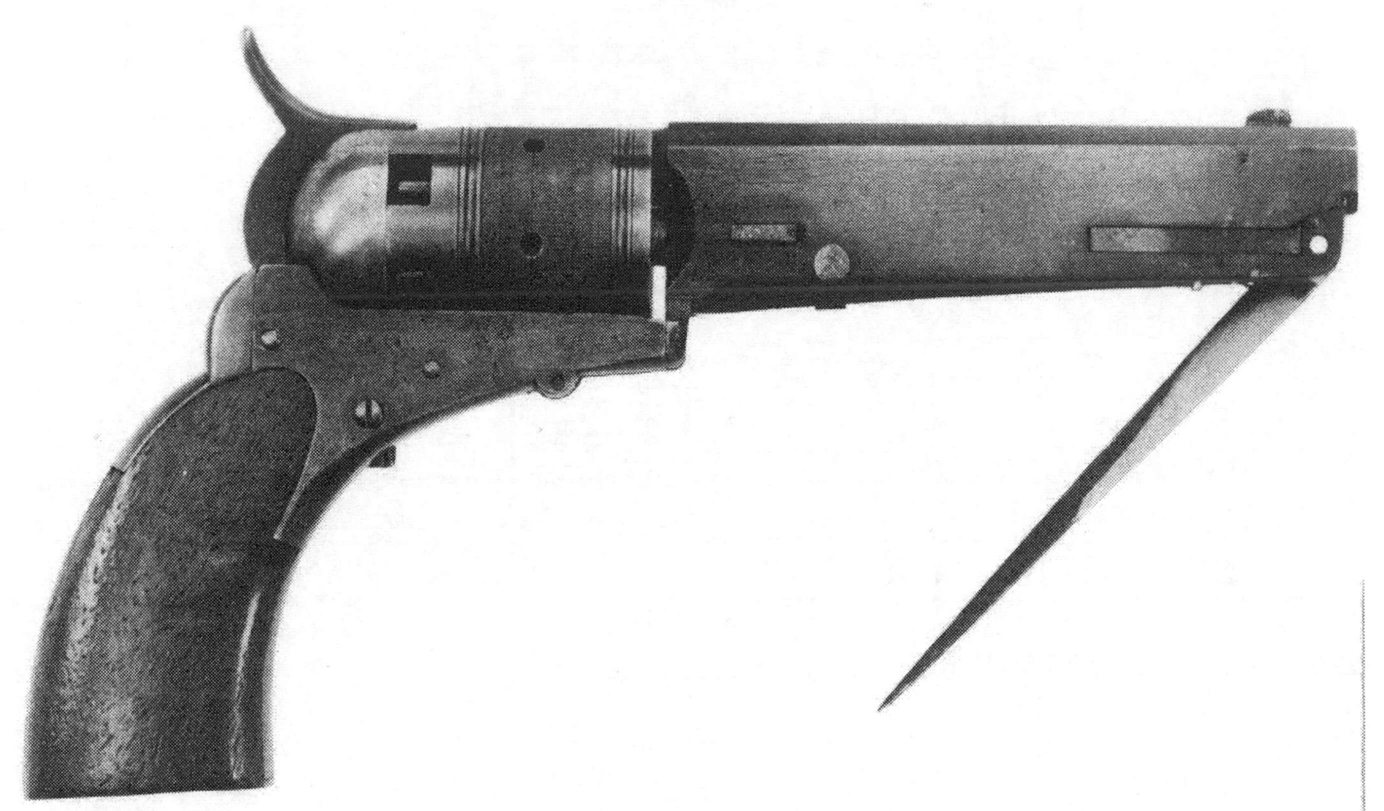

Source: Paterson Colt Pistol Variations, R.L.Wilson

Prototype Experimental Six-Shot Version of the No. 2 Belt Model

This No. 2 prototype/experimental is a six-shot version of the No. 2 Belt Model pistol. It was the first model developed from the design sketch, **Image 5**, **on page 7**, made by Pliny Lawton, Factory Supervisor. This six-shot version has an extra-long cylinder, similar to Colt537. It is a .29 caliber powered by a straight main spring.

Throughout this manuscript, I will illustrate the similarities that prove, without a doubt, that Colt537 is the last hand-made product prior to the development of the Nos. 1, 2, 3 and 5 production models. Hence, Colt537 is the genesis of the Colt Paterson Model revolvers.

The Second Lawton-Colt Prototype/Experiment a Combination of the No.3 and No. 5 Production Models

The second experimental/prototype, really considered a semi-prototype, is Colt537, **Image 7**. This model was also built under the supervision of Pliny Lawton and Colt. However, this one was a five-shot version of the experimental/prototype used in designing the four production models of the Colt Paterson Revolver. Those were the No. 1 Pocket Model, Nos. 2 and 3 of the Belt Model and the No. 5 Holster Model, later Identified as the Holster or Texas Model. Below is an image of the Colt537. When I examined this revolver, it became obvious that most of its parts were hand made. Check out the resemblance of **Image 7 with its image on pages 31 and 32.**

Image 7

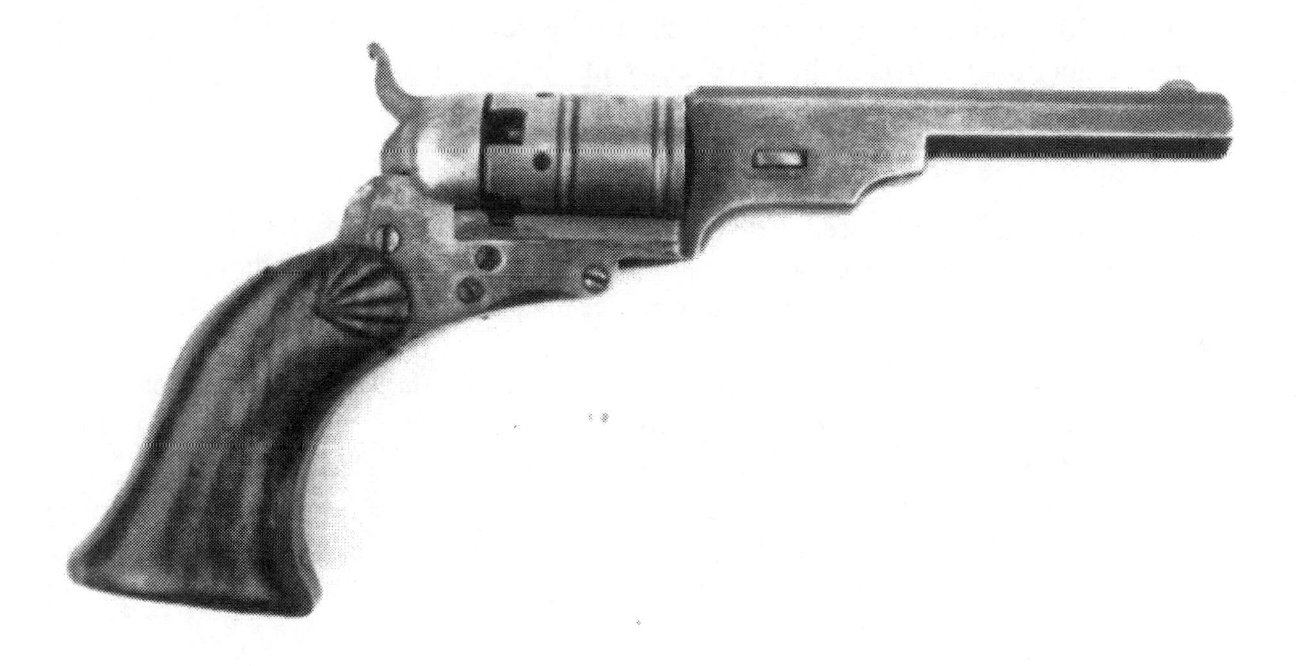

Source: M. Desparte

It is believed that this is the first flared handle made for colt firearms.

Colt537 Experiment

This exact revolver is also shown in **Images 14 and 15 on page 31 and 32**. A copy of an advertisement shown in the Spirit of the Times-News Release, New York, Saturday Morning, July 1838 is found in **Appendix 5**

Chapter Two
The Acquisition

The Acquisition of Colt537

Late in 2011, an internet auction relating to this revolver, i.e., Colt537, came to my attention. The auction advertised the revolver as an:

"Early copy of a Colt Paterson Belt Model"[3]

There were three key words that seemed to be odd about the description, the word, "copy" and the words, "Belt Model." I was willing to take a gamble on these words due to the image of the gun which seemed to contradict the description.

Upon further research on the revolver, it was obvious the revolver was not a Colt Paterson Belt Model. The frame and cylinder are longer in length than the normal Paterson Belt Model cylinder and frame. It did not have the correct Belt Model screw arrangement, observable on the right exterior side of the frame. This arrangement is indicative of a modified internal mechanical design of the firing system. Due to the size of the frame and cylinder, it could be considered a Holster or Texas Model, if it were a .36 caliber revolver.[4] The ad stated it was a .31 caliber.

A copy of the auction ad, obtained at the onset of the auction, relating to the subject revolver, is provided in Appendix 1. During that auction, the revolver was identified as, Lot # 537. In order to reduce confusion as to which revolver is under discussion, in this manuscript, auction lot # 537, will be identified as "Colt537." Since many of the records of the Patent Arms Manufacturing Company are non-existent, a logical progression of factual and circumstantial evidence will be used to prove the authenticity of Colt537. To reiterate the words found in the book *Paterson Colt Pistol Variations* by R.L. Wilson, Wilson states

---

3. Dakota Plains Auction Co. Result 572 of 574, Lot #537 Information
4. Paterson Colt Pistol Variations, R.L. Wilson, Page 5, Par 2, L 1

Historical Significance of the Colt Paterson Experiment

> "I am aware of the danger of making very positive statements regarding Patersons. The records are not complete enough to tell all the facts, and much of what is known is the result of careful study of known pistols and the few records that have survived from the factory days. Because of my research and studies, in this discussion the statements made are my opinions and I will often say "known to me."[5]

> And,

> "While I doubt that a factory production pistol variation not described and photographed will ever appear, it may be possible that variations exist unknown to me."[6]

Mr. Wilson does not say anything about experimental models. His focus is on factory production models. To my thinking, there are the experimental revolvers, made for Colt, by John Pearson, as well as the two that were designed and developed in-house by Pliny Lawton, under Colt's direction, **Images 6 and 7**. Both sources played a key role in leading up to the development of all four production models.

The Dakota Plains Auction House ad indicated that Colt537 was a Belt Model. On further inspection, it is evident that the cylinders of the Belt Model and Colt537 are not the same. Colt537 has a longer cylinder. Also, the firing chambers in the cylinder have a greater gunpowder capacity than those of the Belt Model. Therefore, the amount of charge in each of the firing chambers can be manipulated, from the normal .31 caliber charge, up to the amount used to fire a .44 caliber ball or bullet. This gives the experimenter a full range of alternatives as to the amount of power or energy the new frame is capable of sustaining.

The facts that are known are: The subject revolver is a .31 caliber, black powder percussion, five shot revolver. By virtue of its construction, the differences from the norm, i.e. the Colt537 Experiment, was mostly hand-made and considered to be an experimental version. However, some parts may be considered a prototype. There is a difference. The prototype is the template used in manufacturing the final product for eventual sale. Prototypes may or may not have a serial number. A manufactured product will usually have a serial number. While attending the 2015 Las Vegas Antique Arms Show, I had an opportunity to get a cursory inspection of Colt537 by Mr. R.L. Wilson, the noted authority on Colt Paterson Pistols. He mentioned that some exterior parts may be of Colt Paterson Prototype. He did feel it was not a manufactured product, i.e., it was hand made. It had features somewhat similar to the Pocket, Belt or Holster or Texas production models. He didn't go much further than that in our discussion. Due to time and the

---

5. Paterson Colt Pistol Variations, R.L. Wilson, Page 5, Par 2, L1
6. Paterson Colt Pistol Variations, R.L. Wilson, Page 5, Par 2, L6

presence of other attendees wishing to speak with him, our discussion was short. I felt that Mr. Wilson's statement was consistent in terms regarding the danger of making positive statements. Positive statements were exactly what I was attempting to extract from our conversation. Be that as it may, none were received. Consequently, I have spent a considerable amount of time and effort to determine the true nature of the Colt537 experiment. The style, overall design, and type of internal workings guided the U.S. Patent No. 1304 set of nine claims on how the revolver was to be constructed. I discovered a whole host of innovations by Pliny Lawton and Colt in the fabrication and experimentation of Colt537 which were carried over to the development of the four production models. In performing this research, it is extremely difficult to discuss one part of Colt537 without discussing its relationship with other parts or sections of the gun. For instance, when discussing the frame of the revolver, there is a need to incorporate its relationship to the hand grip and/or the firing system. Part of the reason is that the caliber of the firing cylinders determine the caliber of the bore, and for that matter, the size of the frame. At times, it may get very confusing to the reader. One must discipline themselves to review associated sections until the concept is understood. Given the machinery the company purchased to make the four production models, making a revolver exactly like the Colt537 with those machines would have been next to impossible. The machinery had limits as to cutting curves, grooves and other geometrical entities, either due to the gunsmith's ability in manipulating a curve, etc. or the machine's inability to meet the commands of the gunsmith and or machinist. The ability or flexibility just wasn't there.

The Four Production Models and How to Tell Them Apart

First consideration is the size. The No. 1 Pocket or Baby Model is the smallest. The medium sized revolvers are Nos. 2 and 3 Belt Models. Both of these frames are the same size. And the largest is the No. 5 Holster model. However, if you don't have all four in front of you to compare, the most assured method is by analyzing their frame screw arrangement. This is done by viewing the right side of the frame of the revolver. Each model has a set of four screws under the cylinder, on the frame. The nearest to the back end of the revolver is the hammer screw. Moving toward the muzzle of the revolver are two screws that are always close to each other in the middle of the frame. They are the bolt screw (upper) and the actuating bar screw, commonly known as the sear screw (lower). And moving further toward the muzzle end of the frame is the trigger screw. These two screws in the middle of the frame are the tell-all screws. The Belt models exhibit the bolt screw above and behind the lower sear screw. The Pocket and Holster models exhibit the bolt screw above and ahead of the lower sear screw. To differentiate between these last two screws, the Pocket model is somewhat smaller than the Holster model. Further detail is found in viewing **Image 17, Items 22, and 23 on page 46.**

The .28 Caliber No. 1 Pocket or Baby Model

This revolver generally has a 4 ½-inch barrel, eleven lands and grooves in the bore with varnished walnut straight grips. The bolt and sear screws are the two center screws located on the right side of the frame. The upper center screw, i.e., bolt screw, is forward of the sear screw/actuating bar screw. The only other revolver of the four production models with this screw arrangement is the No. 5 Holster or Texas Model, which is the largest frame of the four production models. This model has the dash mark for a finial before and after the company's address, located on the top of the barrel. Reading toward the muzzle, **see Finial Chart on page 94**.

Image 8

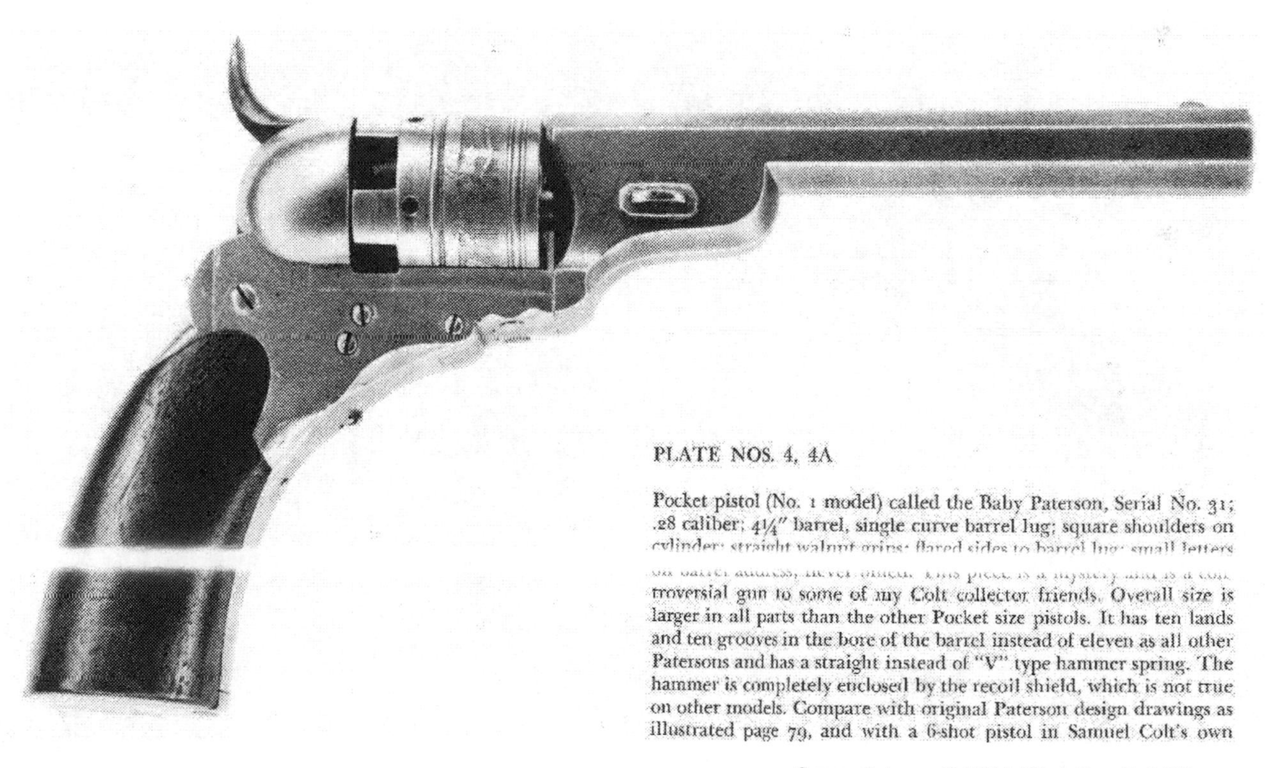

PLATE NOS. 4, 4A

Pocket pistol (No. 1 model) called the Baby Paterson, Serial No. 31; .28 caliber; 4¼″ barrel, single curve barrel lug; square shoulders on cylinder; straight walnut grips; flared sides to barrel lug; small letters [illegible] troversial gun to some of my Colt collector friends. Overall size is larger in all parts than the other Pocket size pistols. It has ten lands and ten grooves in the bore of the barrel instead of eleven as all other Patersons and has a straight instead of "V" type hammer spring. The hammer is completely enclosed by the recoil shield, which is not true on other models. Compare with original Paterson design drawings as illustrated page 79, and with a 6-shot pistol in Samuel Colt's own

Source: Paterson Colt Pistol Variations, R. L Wilson

No. 1 Pocket or Baby Model

The .31 Caliber No. 2 Belt Model with Straight Hand-Grips

The revolver generally has a 4 ½-inch barrel, varnished walnut straight-grips and a blued finish. The bolt and sear screws are the two center screws located on the right side of the frame. The bolt screw is above and slightly behind the sear screw, indicating a change on the way the parts are situated inside the frame. This model has a double diamond finial before and after the company's address located on the top of the barrel, reading toward the muzzle. **see Finial Chart on page 94.** **Compare the length of this cylinder with the the cylinder of Colt537, shown in Image 7 on page 9.**

Image 9

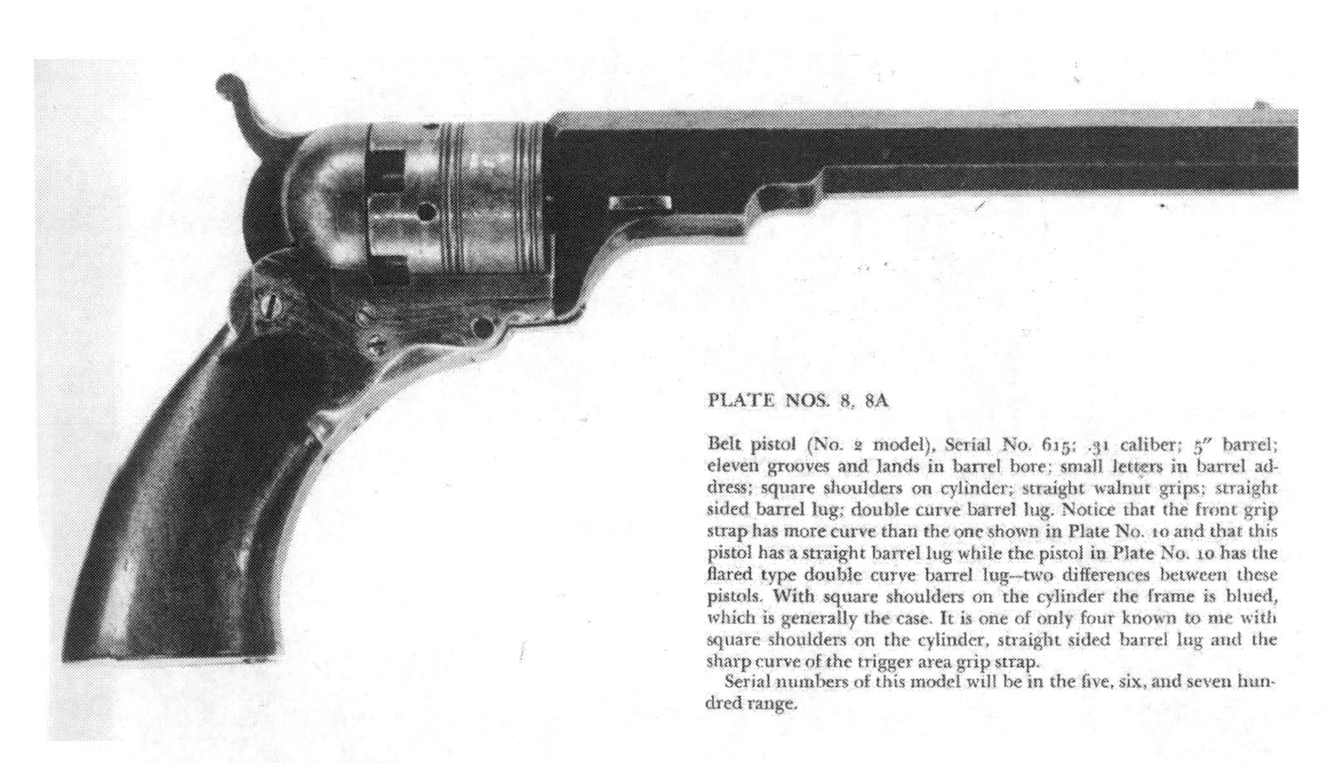

PLATE NOS. 8, 8A

Belt pistol (No. 2 model), Serial No. 615; .31 caliber; 5″ barrel; eleven grooves and lands in barrel bore; small letters in barrel address; square shoulders on cylinder; straight walnut grips; straight sided barrel lug; double curve barrel lug. Notice that the front grip strap has more curve than the one shown in Plate No. 10 and that this pistol has a straight barrel lug while the pistol in Plate No. 10 has the flared type double curve barrel lug--two differences between these pistols. With square shoulders on the cylinder the frame is blued, which is generally the case. It is one of only four known to me with square shoulders on the cylinder, straight sided barrel lug and the sharp curve of the trigger area grip strap.

Serial numbers of this model will be in the five, six, and seven hundred range.

Source: R.L.Wilson

Notice the location of the Bolt Screw and Sear Screw (Actuating Bar Screw)
No. 2 Colt Belt Model-Straight Grip

The .31 and Rare .34 Caliber No. 3 Belt Model with Flared Hand-Grips

The revolver generally has a 5 ½-inch barrel, blued finish, and varnished flared hand-grips. The bolt and sear screws are the two center screws located on the right side of the frame. It has the bolt screw above and behind the lower sear screw, indicating a change on how the parts are situated inside the frame of the No. 2 and No. 3 models. This model has a double diamond finial before and after the company's address located on the top of the barrel, reading toward the muzzle. The principal difference between the No. 2 and the No. 3 is the No. 3 has the flared hand-grip. **See Finial Chart on page 94**. **Compare the length of this cylinder with the cylinder of Colt537, shown in Image 7 on page 9.**

Image 10

Notice location of the Bolt Screw and Sear Screw (Actuating Bar Screw

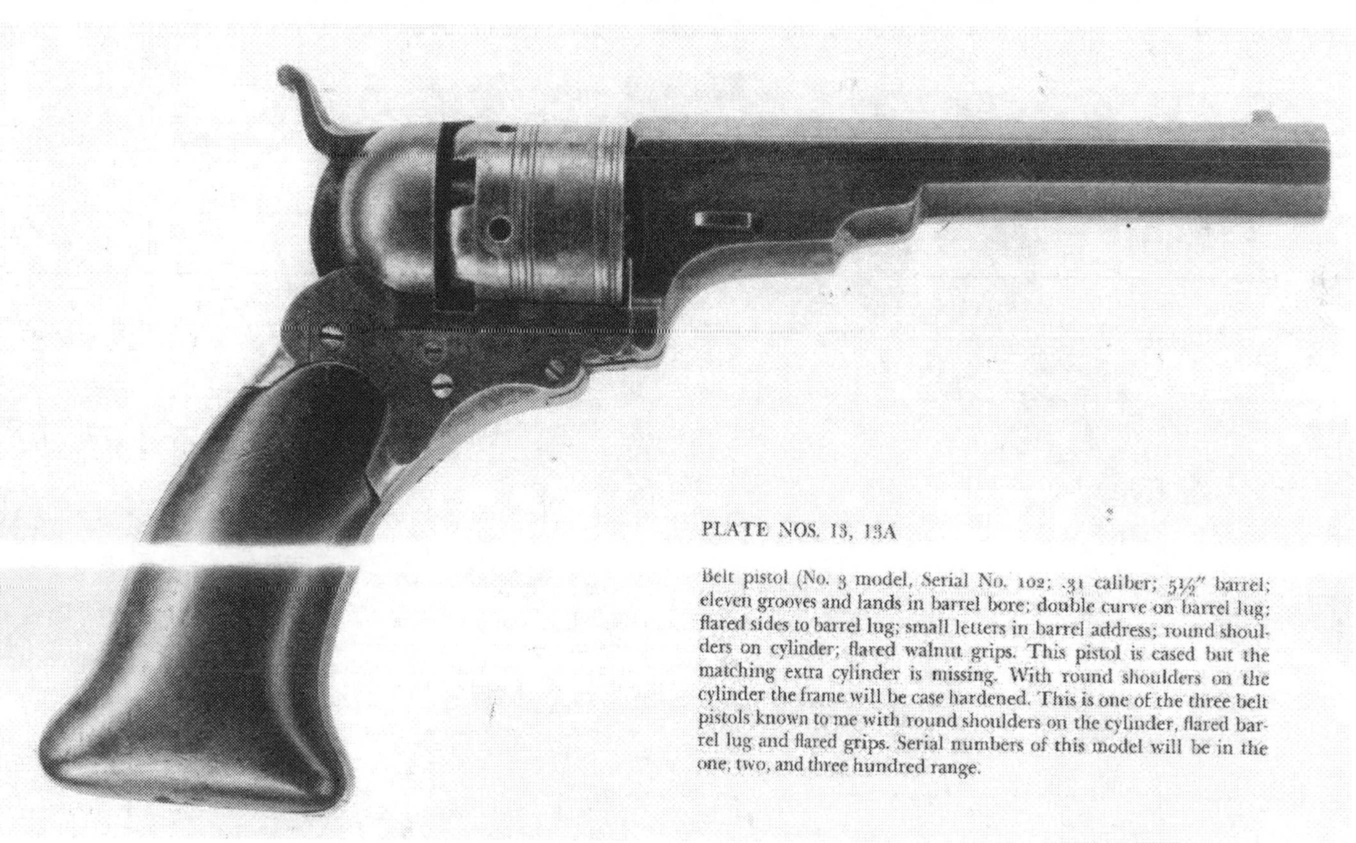

PLATE NOS. 13, 13A

Belt pistol (No. 3 model, Serial No. 102; .31 caliber; 5½" barrel; eleven grooves and lands in barrel bore; double curve on barrel lug; flared sides to barrel lug; small letters in barrel address; round shoulders on cylinder; flared walnut grips. This pistol is cased but the matching extra cylinder is missing. With round shoulders on the cylinder the frame will be case hardened. This is one of the three belt pistols known to me with round shoulders on the cylinder, flared barrel lug and flared grips. Serial numbers of this model will be in the one, two, and three hundred range.

Source: Paterson Pistol Variations, Colt **R. L.Wilson**

No. 3 Colt Belt Model-Flared Grip

The .36 Caliber No. 5 Holster Model, Later Called the Holster or Texas Model

This has the large frame, similar in size to the Colt537 experimental revolver. The barrel ranged from 4 inches to 12 inches in length. It has large flared hand-grips and barrel finials before and after the company's address on the barrel; a bursting star attached to a snake tail configuration. It is interesting to note the bolt screw is above and slightly forward of the sear screw, signifying a change in how the internal parts in the frame are organized from those of the Nos. 2 and 3 of the Belt Model. **See Finial Chart on page 94**.

Image 11

Notice Location of the Bolt Screw and Actuating Bar Screw (Sear Screw)

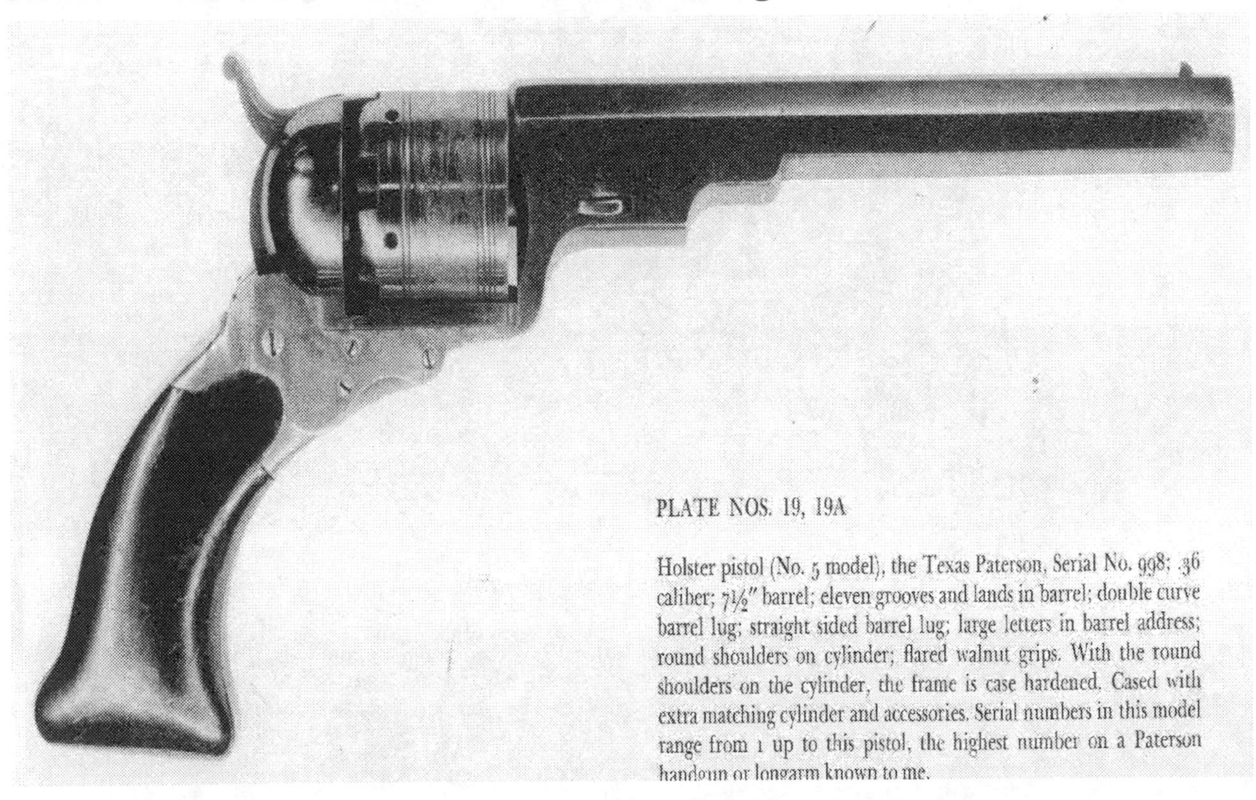

PLATE NOS. 19, 19A

Holster pistol (No. 5 model), the Texas Paterson, Serial No. 998; .36 caliber; 7½" barrel; eleven grooves and lands in barrel; double curve barrel lug; straight sided barrel lug; large letters in barrel address; round shoulders on cylinder; flared walnut grips. With the round shoulders on the cylinder, the frame is case hardened. Cased with extra matching cylinder and accessories. Serial numbers in this model range from 1 up to this pistol, the highest number on a Paterson handgun or longarm known to me.

Source: Paterson Colt Pistol Variations, R. L. Wilson

No. 5 Holster or Texas Model-Flared Grip

Regarding the Parts of the Revolvers

The parts of the No. 1 Pocket or Baby Model, the Nos. 2 and No. 3 Belt Models, in addition to the No. 5 Holster or Texas Model are, not quite, but similar in design to the original Colt537. But due to the differences in size of the four models, their internal parts were scaled to fit the size of their specific cylinder, its firing chambers, powder capacity and caliber of the ball, just about everything is dictated by the size or caliber of the ball.

The ball, in order to have sufficient killing power, requires a specific amount of gun powder. The quantity is controlled by the size of the firing chamber. It must be capable of holding the powder and ball, without the ball obstructing the rotation of the cylinder. The size of the firing chambers controls the size of the cylinder. The size of the cylinder determines the size and mass of the frame, etc. Lastly the size of the internal components would correspond to the size of the frame and their respective function with other internal and external parts. In the case of the Paterson revolver models, the recoil shield would have the capacity to take up any excess space remaining between the breech of the barrel and the face of the recoil shield. For instance, parts associated with the No. 5 Holster or Texas Model (**Image 11 on page 16**) would be scaled in size to fit the size needed for a cylinder having five .36 caliber chambers.

Colt537 has a frame similar to the size needed for the No. 5 Holster or Texas Model. However, the Colt537 was set up with a .31 caliber elongated cylinder and the appropriate internal parts, **see Appendix 2**. The reason or purpose will become apparent.

Estimated Time Line of Development

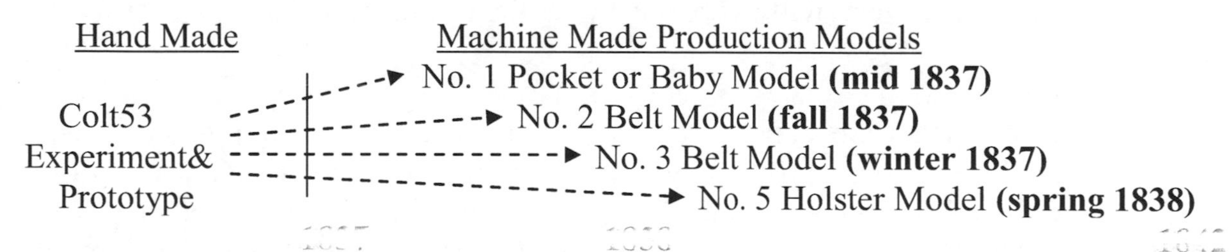

The Colt537 design was used in all four of these models, development slightly overlapped each. As time went on, more parts were machine made. Never completely machine made, and therefore, most parts were not interchangeable.

Conflicts among Corporate Members

Time was moving on and Seldon, the Company Treasurer, was getting extremely upset. Lawton, by this time, was as thin as a ghost from worrying about labor costs (the workforce had been lately reduced from twenty men to only thirteen at the plant). Seldon, realizing the situation, did not want to tax Lawton more than necessary. There were too few workmen to get anything ready in time for future testing with the military. Colt was planning to put on a display for graduates from West Point to show them what was now available if they wanted to purchase a gun. Dudley Seldon disapproved of Sam's suggestions as to the number of weapons to display and test at the graduation. He felt Sam's preferred quantity was "wholly unnecessary." To Seldon, "one musket, one rifle, one large, and one small pistol" may have been enough.

The Levels of Perfection and Timing

> "The senior class at the West Point Military Academy was nearing graduation, and it was thought that participation in this trial might give these future officers some good experience. The board was to convene at West Point on the 16th of June, 1837."[7]

Catastrophic Trial Exhibit in Front of West Point Review Board

The demonstration resulted in simultaneous double discharges. In evaluating the cause, the damaged musket was examined by West Point Review Board. It was determined that a cylinder made of cast steel would be preferable to one made of iron, the iron being more liable to have flaws and seams than a iron cast cylinder. It would appear that these flaws, in the seams in the iron, would have a tendency to ignite each of the adjacent chambers by the passage of a spark from the interior of one firing chamber to another adjacent firing chamber within the cylinder. The Board felt that this is exactly what happened in this instance. It is proper to remark that the cost of the cast steel will probably be more than counter balance the reduction of cost by employing iron cylinders. (the cost of the cast steel will probably more than counter balance the cost of iron cylinders.).[8]

These comments are extremely important in that when attempting to determine whether or not the cylinder of Colt537 was made from cast steel. We can date production of specific parts of the revolver prior to, or after, the use of the Bessemer process in making steel. The Bessemer process was patented in 1856. Cast steel was being used in the making of guns as early as, and possibly before 1837. The Bessemer Process for making steel was patented in 1856. It is believed Colt turned to making cylinders of cast steel in 1837.

---

7. Paterson Colt Pistol Variations, R. L. Wilson, Page 95, Col 1, Para 5, L 1
8. The Story of Colt's Revolver, Wm Edwards, Page 55, Col 1, Par 3, L 1

Introduction to this Manuscript's Gunsmith

This is a good time to introduce the gunsmith who assisted in the evaluation of this revolver. His name is Raymond Booze. He has been a full-time Gunsmith for over forty years. He has held a Federal Firearms License continuously since 1983. At that time, he was employed by a full-time retail firearm and gunsmith establishment. He performed full-service activities in repairs, bluing, woodworking, and machining. He has serviced, repaired, examined and studied a wide range of firearms dating from before the Civil War era to the present day. Rifles, shotguns, and handguns, both foreign and domestic, have been his passion. Early in the 1990s, he was awarded a U.S. Patent for a rifle sight system of his own design and manufacture. He finds all manner of firearms to be particularly interesting, especially those that were designed before computers, or manufactured before "Do-it-yourself CNC machines," the ones that were fit and finished by hand. Antique firearms are the ones that required imagination, inspiration, a touch of genius, coupled with skilled craftsmanship, all of which helped forge the direction of history in some small way.

Image 12

Source: M. Desparte

Raymond Booze, Gunsmith-Antique Revolvers

Historical Significance of the Colt Paterson Experiment

Due to its experimental nature, the Colt537 Experiment, which appears to be mostly handmade, never went into production. It represents the physical concept or theory that had to be proven in a step by step process. The reader will find this proof in the following pages of this manuscript through the familiarization of the revolver's many parts, most still in crude form.

Patent No. 1304 is, in fact, the initial design of the gun that in no small way assisted in building our nation. Specifically, it was the linchpin in opening the southwest region of our nation for the acceleration of economic growth and development. That acceleration started in the early 1840s, resulting in the expansive growth of the West.

Mr. Booze indicated that it isn't every day that someone comes to a gunsmith with an authentic Colt Paterson. After reviewing some of the common characteristics of the Colt Paterson, found in several publications on the subject, it was decided to inspect the inner workings for further authentication. This was a rare opportunity, to have someone approach a gunsmith with a piece of real history, as Mr. Booze indicated. He was filled with a combination of excitement and trepidation. There is always a risk in dismantling any one-hundred and eighty-some-year-old firearm. It is the fear of breaking screws and unfamiliar parts.

In his lifetime of work, he has become very familiar with the Colt 1860 Army revolver, and to a lesser degree, the more common cap and ball revolvers, such as the Colt Walker, Colt Dragoons, and the Colt Navy revolvers.

Using the schematic illustrations found on **pages 48 and 49** in this manuscript, depicting the complete set of parts of a Colt Holster or Texas Model, Mr. Booze maintained we adopt the Schematic Drawing's terminology (when applicable) to be used in describing Colt537's makeup. What is really interesting is that the interior parts (of Colt Paterson models) remained consistent in design for all four production models throughout their manufacture. This means that although parts may vary somewhat in size due to frame differences and fitting requirements, the design and function would "remain consistent to the claims made in U.S. Patent No. 1304 of August 28, 1839."

Although, parts design remained consistent, the parts from any one model were not interchangeable with that same part in another similar model. The reason being, most of the interior parts were hand made. That being said, each of the four models had the same parts as those found in Colt537. Due to the differences in size of the four models, there were slight changes in size or shape, but they still remained true to the claims found in Patent 1304, August 29, 1839.

Comparative Features of Belt Model, Colt537 Experiment and Holster/Texas Model

Holster/ Texas	Production Model No. 3 Belt	Hand-Made Colt537 Experiment	Production Model No. 5
Caliber	.31	.31	.36
Recoil Shield	.31	.31	.36
Cylinders	.31	.31	.36
Length	Normal	Elongated for caliber length of Cylinder	Same length as Colt537 .31 cal.
Bore Ballel	.31	.31	.36
Frame Size	.31	.36	.36
Finials	.31	.36	.36
Internal Parts makeup	.31	.36 ?	.36

It Would Appear That Colt537 Is One Half Belt Model & One Half Holster Model, See Image 85 on page 102, and Appendix 2 on page 142.

Where Does Colt537 Fit in the Scheme of Things?

The previous chart suggests that Colt537 Experiment has a balanced mixture of both the No. 3 Belt and the No. 5 Holster or Texas Model characteristics. Due to its elongated cylinder it could have been developed into a high velocity .31 caliber revolver. In the present day that would have been called a Magnum. But why would Colt go that route when the No. 5 Holster model was having immediate success? And, Selton, the company Treasurer is pressing Colt to get on with production and generate some income.

Perfection was not at hand

The amount of research placed on Colt537 was staggering. New ideas and concepts emerged that went into the development of the four production models, as well as later models.

1. Colt537 employed recent inventions that had not yet proven themselves in the heat of battle, such as the internal use of coil springs which were prone to breakage, as opposed to flat springs that were less prone to breakage and less expensive to fabricate. The addition of the loading lever which increased the speed with which the revolver could be reloaded caused the development of an invention within an invention. There was an improvement in the type of metal used in the larger cylinders, and an increased reliability in the usage of the "V" type mainspring.

2. Some of the internal parts were too complex to be involved in the manufacturing process and would be difficult to reproduce. For example, the complex structure of the sear and trigger extension arm, **see Images 15 on page 32, Image 16 on page 38, Image 57 on page 75, and Image 58 on page 77**. The arbor on which the cylinder of Colt537 rotated was faulty and required attention. This issue led to significantly improving the accuracy of Colt537.

3. An increase in the size/flare of the hand grip was needed. This improved the vertical stability of the shooter during firing the gun, which increased the accuracy of the revolver.

4. Rifling in a handgun needed to be proven before the .36 caliber No. 5 Holster or Texas Model was manufactured. This issue was contributory to the completion of experimentation with the Colt537. However, the knowledge gained from this experiment was eventually applied to the development of all four of the Colt Paterson production models. From the No. 1 Pocket or Baby Model, the No. 2 and No. 3 Belt Models, and the No. 5 Holster or Texas Model, starts with the smallest, the .28 caliber to the largest, the .36 caliber.

5. As to a No. 5 Holster or Texas Model, some of the military still thought, a .36 caliber might be under powered for the military role it was to play. And consequently in 1847 the Colt .44 caliber Walker came into being; and that is another interesting story.

Chapter Three
The Battle of Bandera Pass

Little is known about the exact details of the Battle of Bandera Pass, or for that matter, the Battle of Walker's Creek. These are two of the more significant battles recounted by the Texas Rangers in their efforts to protect the inhabitants in and around the San Antonio area of the Texas Republic, as it was known at that time.

This story is one which stands out from all the other battles that memorialized the significance as to who was gaining the upper hand in the southwest expansion of our nation. Was it the Comanche Indians, in their effort to protect their homeland, **Image 13,** the Comancheria, or the settlers, in their efforts to reduce the size of the Comancheria? The Comancheria was an area of the west occupied by the Comanche Indian Nation. San Antonio and its surrounding area remained in the southern outskirts of the Comancheria. Bandera Pass is approximately ten to twenty miles northwest of the town of Bandera, Texas. This area also fell within the Kiowa Apache Indian Nation.

Image 13

Source: Wikipedia the free encyclopedia and others

Comancheria and Environs

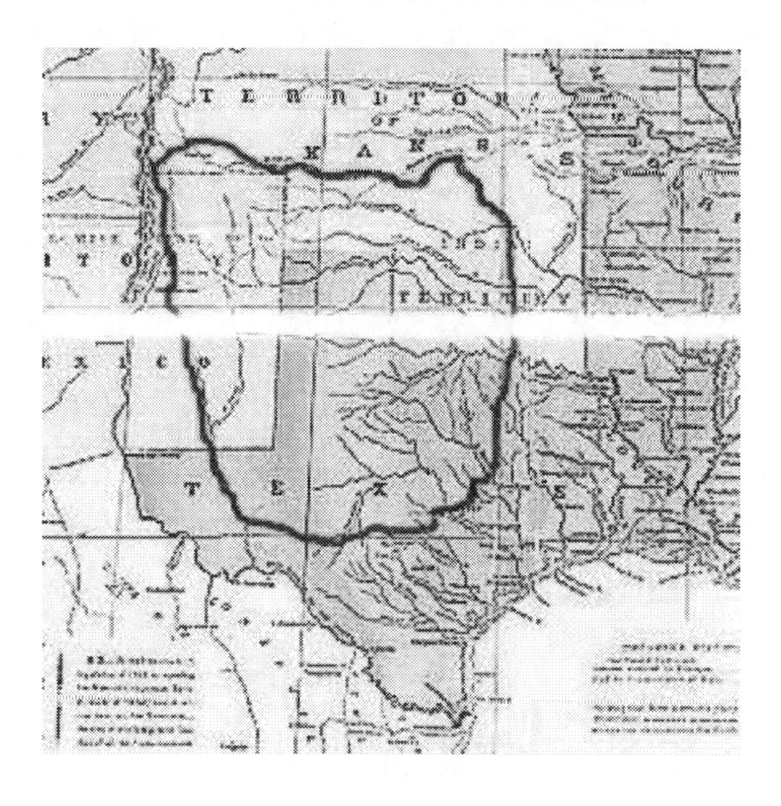

Historical Significance of the Colt Paterson Experiment

This story begins in 1838, with Sam Colt attempting to interest the United States Army in purchasing his new repeating revolvers. At that time, it may have been the Colt Paterson No. 3 Belt Model, which was a .31 caliber revolver. It was rejected by the military, being too impractical, and a bit under-powered in terms of an offensive or defensive weapon. The .36 caliber Paterson No. 5 Holster model, having greater stopping power, was just entering the market. In addition, military staff thought, would need a gun that could fire five times without reloading after each shot. Apparently, none of these high-ranking officers, which Colt attempted to sell his invention to, had the opportunity to fight, hand to hand, in a pitched battle, with Comanche or Kiowa Apache Indians, known for their horsemanship and abilities with a bow and arrow.

The Comanche and Kiowa Indians, having been practically born in the saddle, were excellent horsemen In terms of fighting, they were able to string and accurately shoot five or six arrows while attacking, on a horse, at full tilt. While at the same time, the defending Soldier, Ranger, or Settler was trying to remain cool, taking the needed time to reload his single-shot musket and in doing so, in the back of his mind, having fearful thoughts of ending up as a scalped pincushion.

One must understand, the Comanche was doing what no other indigenous Indian nation had managed to accomplish. They were succeeding in defending their homeland, even expanding it at times, while facing the best Spanish military forces of the Mexican Army, the Texas Rangers and the influx of new settlers combined. Up until the introduction of repeating revolvers and rifles, weapons and tactics were definitely on the side of the Plains Indians. Disease, the Texas Rangers, and U.S. Cavalry were on the side of the Texans. The outbreak of smallpox may have decimated more of the Indian population than anything else in the mid-1800s, but don't discount the Colt Paterson.

In a bold move, late in 1838, Sam Colt sent a pair of Colt .36 Caliber, No. 5 Holster Models to Sam Houston, the then President of the Republic of Texas. After acceptance of the five shot revolvers, Houston passed them on to the army for analysis. They were slow in recognizing their true battle worth and eventually rejected the weapon, thinking the barrel would get too hot to handle and the whole revolver was a bit too complicated for use in the field.

About the same time, late in 1838 or in the first month of 1839, a Washington, DC hotel owner who had a son who was serving in the U.S. Navy wrote to the Secretary of the Navy, praising the capabilities of the Colt No. 5 revolver. It motivated the Secretary to order 180 of the new Paterson revolvers. These unused revolvers, for some unknown reason, languished in a Galveston, Texas, warehouse.[9]

---

[9] Pioneer History by J. J. Starkey, Terryville Times, Wed. Dec 24, 1952

Historical Significance of the Colt Paterson Experiment

On January 16, 1841, The Texas Congress authorized the establishment of a new company of Texas Rangers. Its Captain was to be a Ranger by the name of Jack "Coffee Hays. His responsibility was to raise a company of forty privates to operate in the region surrounding San Antonio, which included Kerr and Bexar Counties. Hays, while discussing his assignment with President Houston, were informed that the US Navy had received 180 new Colt five-shot repeating revolvers, and they were located at a specific warehouse in Galveston, Texas. It was suggested that he could place a request to the Secretary of War for the acquisition of said revolvers. Approval was granted, and Captain Hays returned to San Antonio with a sufficient number of these revolvers to arm each member of the new company with two revolvers, each with an extra cylinder. Therefore, each Ranger would be able to have two revolvers with ten ready-to-fire shots for each of his revolvers. Since there was to be a complement of forty-one Rangers, i.e., forty rangers to a platoon, including Captain Hays, the Company would have an immediate firing capacity of 410 shots. They would be capable of a quick reload, using the second cylinder for another 410 shots, a total of 820 ready-to-shoot rounds of ammunition. This is quite a formidable defense, and, for that matter, a formidable offense as well.

Understanding how serious Hays was about training, one would suspect experience was gained during their down time as well as when they were involved in other, possibly smaller skirmishes with the Indians and outlaws of the region. This paid off in spades during their later, more difficult engagements. What is known is that Hays did train his Company on various offensive and defensive riding techniques, as well as how to fire and quickly replace the cylinders of their new Colt Paterson Revolvers, while attacking on horseback.

In June of 1842 or 1844, the argument of the year continues, Captain Hays was notified of a sizable Comanche war party, led by Chief Yellow Wolf, raiding settlements in the north and west reaches of Bexar County. This being a serious challenge, Hays and his Rangers were eager to try out new battle plans based on the use of their new revolvers. Hays and a squadron of fourteen Rangers were mustered up with the intention to proceed up the Medina River Valley and on through Bandera Pass to patrol along the Guadalupe River Valley. A contingent of Comanche Indians under the command of Chief Yellow Wolf was at the same time coming south on a raiding expedition, possibly heading toward some little settlement north of San Antonio. The Indians reached Bandera Pass before the Rangers. Seeing their approach from a few miles distance, Yellow Wolf and his Indians laid a well-planned ambush and straddled up high on both sides of the pass.

It would be hard to believe that the Rangers were not aware of the potential of an ambush as they went through the Pass. It would be a perfect setup for such an action. The Rangers had made it through approximately a third of the pass when they were attacked. Shots, arrows, lances, and war hoots filled the air. Prepared as they were for anything, the Rangers were still startled. Men and horses, both being hit by these flying missiles, caused instantaneous confusion among the Rangers. Some of them were shot from their saddles, while others tried to manage their frightened rearing and plunging horses. Captain Hayes, while maintaining his composure, commanded his troops to:

> "Steady yourselves, we can whip em, no doubt about it. Dismount, tie up the horses and find cover, we're gonna fight em on foot."[10]

A few Indians came out in the open to goad the Rangers to come out and fight. From their hiding places, other warriors taunted the Rangers, hoping to get them to mistakenly make a frontal charge, against the Indians who were in well-fortified positions behind rocks, trees, and bushes.

Being an experienced Indian fighter, Hays knew what the Indians were hoping to accomplish. He, however, waited until the entire war party emerged from the thickets and formed a line of battle on both sides of the Pass. As the battle ensued, the bewildered Comanche fell back, thinking to themselves, how can they shoot so many times from one gun and not reload after each shot? The Rangers, fifteen in total, each had two pistols with an extra loaded cylinder for each revolver, totaling three hundred ready-to-fire rounds of ammunition. Hayes tactically took the fight to the Indians. At times it was a hand-to-hand, rough and tumble, fierce fight. After approximately five hours of back and forth fighting, with darkness approaching, the Comanche realized a loss of thirty to forty dead from their total complement of seventy to eighty, and ceded the loss of the battle to the Rangers.[11] Although outnumbered now by roughly three to one, the Rangers drove off additional counterattacks with the use of their newly acquired Colt revolvers.

Hays and his Rangers pursued them for an additional three miles, keeping them under continuous fire. During the three-mile chase and Indian retreat, their Chief Yellow Wolf pressed three separate counterattacks. The Rangers countered with alternating activity of some men fighting, others replacing cylinders or reloading. On the last counterattack by the Indians, Yellow Wolf received a bullet in the head. Stunned by his death, the remaining Comanche lost their will to fight and disappeared into the landscape.

Not many Rangers, Indians, or inhabitants of the area actually realized the significance of this little known happening. The Battle of Bandera Pass occurred in June of 1842 or 1844, approximately fifty-five miles north of the present City of San Antonio. It involved protecting the inhabitants of the then Republic of Texas, by the newly formed San Antonio Company of Texas Rangers. They were an addition to the other Ranger units assigned to various districts throughout the then established territorial boarders of the young Republic.

---

10. Pioneer History by J.J. Starkey, Terryville Times, Wed. Dec 24, 1952, page 7, on reprint, page 2, par 5, L 1
11. Paterson Colt Pistol Variations, R.L. Wilson, Page 189, col 1, par 3, L 9

Historical Significance of the Colt Paterson Experiment

Who was at fault for the pillaging Indians, the Texans on one hand, and the Indians on the other? Texans wanted the freedom of the west and essentially, title to the land they had taken from the Indians. Who were these Indians? Comanche and Kiowa Apache tribes, who in times past fought other tribes to acquire the range of lands used in their effort to survive, all were interested in a better life, and so, at that time, fought to survive.

This marks the first time that there was a clear indication that the new revolver, i.e., the .36 caliber, No. 5 Colt Paterson Holster or Texas Model, later called the Texas Arm, was the device that aided in turning the tide against Indian raids. As time went on fewer raids occurred, more revolving rifles and pistols were acquired by inhabitants. More military became involved. And, as a consequence, more and more Indian land was given up through repeated defeats. The crowning blow was the construction of the railroads crossing the plains on previously held Indian lands. This enabled and encouraged the spread of commerce and industry, more settlers, more guns, more protection.

The real beginning of Western Expansion was entirely due to the development and use of the Colt Paterson No. 5 Holster or Texas Model revolver. There were others that designed rotary cylinder firing mechanisms, but Colt perfected the product. How this model was developed is only a part of the story. Understanding what really happened during these battles is the most significant issue. The tide was turning against the Indian and the way he lived. The growth of the United States ensued.[12]

12. Battle of Bandera Pass, Wikipedia, the free press

Chapter Four
Reference Material & Definitions

Reference Material on Colt Paterson Pistols

In order to perform an in-depth research effort, I needed to educate myself on the characteristics of each of the models of Colt Paterson revolvers, as well as Colt Paterson Brevete revolvers. There is no better way to perform this analysis than conducting an in-depth review of the following manuscripts. These authors exhibit the highest level of authority in the field of early black powder percussion revolvers. They are to be applauded for their contributions'.

The Folding-Trigger Paterson Colt, (William G. Renwick), 1934

This book traces the various evolutionary steps by which the Colt revolver developed from an inefficient noise maker to the world's most deadly weapon. It was, and still is, believed by many gun enthusiasts, to be by far the most successful type of one-hand, multi-shot weapon ever produced.

A History of the Colt Revolver, (Charles J. Haven & Frank A. Belden), 1940

The value of this book is shown by the provision of detail in terms of what was not a standard variant in the production of the Paterson Colt Revolver. These authors go on to identify the seven elements defining a Colt Paterson revolver, and, the most telling and significant bit of information, which will come up over and over again.

> "Perhaps the greatest single market for Colt arms during the Paterson period was the South and the Southwest, and especially the struggling Republic of Texas, engaged in its desire for freedom from Mexican and Comanche rule. Many of the Paterson revolvers went to this destination, that Colt, in later years, called the regular (No. 5) Paterson model, The Texas Arm." These weapons, particularly the Belt and Holster models, did

well in the hands of the hardy Texans,"[13] referring to the four models, the No.1 Pocket or Baby, No. 2 and No.3, Belt Models, and the No. 5, Holster or Texas Model.

Colt Firearms, 1836 to 1958, (James E. Serven) 1954

The book *Colt Firearms* is designed to provide facts and figures an arms collector or student of arms may wish to know and to have as an available reference. The book also provides some historical background, biographical reference and archive records with data.

The Story of Colt's Revolver, the Biography of Col. Samuel Colt (William B. Edwards) 1957

This book is known for its careful examination of previously published works, and cross checked with my own research in the field. He also examines the variations, experimental, prototype, and varieties of the regular factory machined or production models. Through a review of U.S. Patents with specific models, the development of the various revolvers is well described. An examination of the production tools, machines, and the effect of Colt's factory to the local area, along with developments of the metal working industry, show to some extent, the real value of the Colt revolver. The human side has not been forgotten, and if nothing else, the many somewhat shady tricks that Colt is alleged to have played, may in all fairness be blamed on his existence as a human being.

Paterson Colt Pistol Variations (Phillip R. Phillips & R. L. Wilson), 1979

The authors of the book, *Paterson Colt Pistol Variations*, Phillips and Wilson, are recognized as the authority on Colt Paterson Pistols. They provide the greatest detail in describing the differences between each of the four models of the original Colt Paterson Revolver, the No. 1 Pocket or Baby Model, the No. 2 Belt Model, the No. 3 Belt Model and the No. 5 Holster / Texas Model. However, the No. 4 Model has never been identified or discussed within this book, or in any other book, for that matter. This is a concern to me. (Issues regarding the Ehlers model revolvers are not included in this study).

Colt Firearms from 1836 (James Serven), 1979

The 4th book of importance is *Colt Firearms from 1836* by James Serven. This book provides a detailed history of the evolution of the Colt Paterson Pistols. In addition, to being a valuable resource, it goes into the life of young Samuel Colt.

---

13. *A History of the Colt Revolver*, C.J. Haven & Frank A. Belden, Page 24, Col 2, Par 3 L 1

The Colt Heritage (R. L. Wilson), 1984

The 5th book used in this evaluation is the *Colt Heritage* by R.L. Wilson. This book seems to pick up where others have left off in providing additional information in the life of Samuel Colt, his company, and his descendants.

The Paterson Colt Book (R.L. Wilson), 20ll

This book is a comprehensive technical history of the rarest of all Colt firearms, the Colt Paterson. It was made in Paterson, New Jersey from 1836 to 1842. *The Paterson Colt Book* presents text and illustrations of various experimental, prototypes and production models of Colt Paterson revolvers, but does not include the Colt537 design. Since there were the Nos. 1, 2, 3, and 5 models, this adds credence to Colt537 which some feel fits into the scheme of things. In depth research indicates it is definitely not the fabled or nonexistent No. 4 model. I believe that Colt537 is the experimental model from which all of the four production models took their internal and external design. Paterson Colt Pistol Variations, Wilson, Page 96 Col. 1, Par. 3.

Colt Brevete Revolvers (Roy Marcot & Ron Paxton), 20ll

For those of us who have heard the word, "Brevete" before but were not sure of its meaning, I provide the following definition. Brevete is the Belgian/French word for Patent. It can be observed marked on many Belgian model duplications of Samuel Colt's Hartford-made percussion revolvers. Brevete has taken on a secondary meaning in the Colt and general antique arms collecting community, to indicate not only Belgian-made Colt percussion revolvers but also those made in numerous other countries as well. Whether licensed or unlicensed, most foreign-made antique revolving arms fashioned identically to the Hartford made Colts, including revolvers from Germany, Austria, Turkey, Japan and Russia are all classified under the same heading, COLT BREVETE.[14] Roy Marcot and Roy Paxton have succeeded in filling the gap in the Colt anthology. An important trend developing among students of antique arms in recent years has been the notable advancement of knowledge in formerly unexplored fields of study. In almost every instance, following publications of such information and worthy studies, new fields of specialization have opened for collectors. In addition, these two authors have provided an image of Colt537, i.e., the Colt Paterson. They are not so sure that it is an actual Brevete, they state: “A variety of Colt Brevete Revolvers...Most are unmarked, and the makers are unknown.”[15] However, the pistol, in the lower right corner, is marked with the correct Colt address on the barrel, i.e., Patent Arms Mfg. Co. Paterson, NJ-Colt's Pt. It even has the correct finials associated with the Colt No. 5 Holster or Texas Model.

---

14. Colt Brevete Revolvers, Roy Marcot and Ron Paxton, Forward Page 2, par 4 & 5
15. Colt Brevete Revolvers, Roy Marcot and Ron Paxton, Page 63, Bottom, right corner

Image 14

Source: Roy Marcot

This is the Colt537

Most of these are unmarked and the makers are unknown

Marcot and Paxton reduce and even eliminate the stigma attached to some of the Brevetes produced in the early nineteenth century. But, for some reason, the above revolver has been continuously overlooked. **Image 14** is an image of the questionable revolver. It is, in-fact, the Colt537 in the bottom right corner.[16] The principal authors of the book, Colt Brevete Revolvers, Roy Marcot of Roy Marcot & Ron Paxton, indicated that they were not able to consider this revolver as a reproduction, it's an anomaly.

The following News Article appeared, as stated, in the New York, Spirit of the [illegible] **first time at the recent Fair of the American Institute. At this showing the revolver received high praise from the public and, *<u>the Colt Company was awarded a gold medal for its impact on the gun industry at that time.</u>***

It is strange that no other photos or information was found in any of the several documents or books reviewed during the seven years of research performed in writing this document. The fact that information about this particular revolver is non-existent adds a slight bit of credence to the story provided by Mr. Gunnerson, the previous owner of the revolver. His story on how he acquired the revolver borders validity. The sad part

16. Colt Brevete Revolvers, Marcot and Paxton, page 63

of it is that the gentleman was not able to provide any proof to completely validate his story. That story is found on **page 41,** and continues on when the subject is relevant.

IMAGE 15

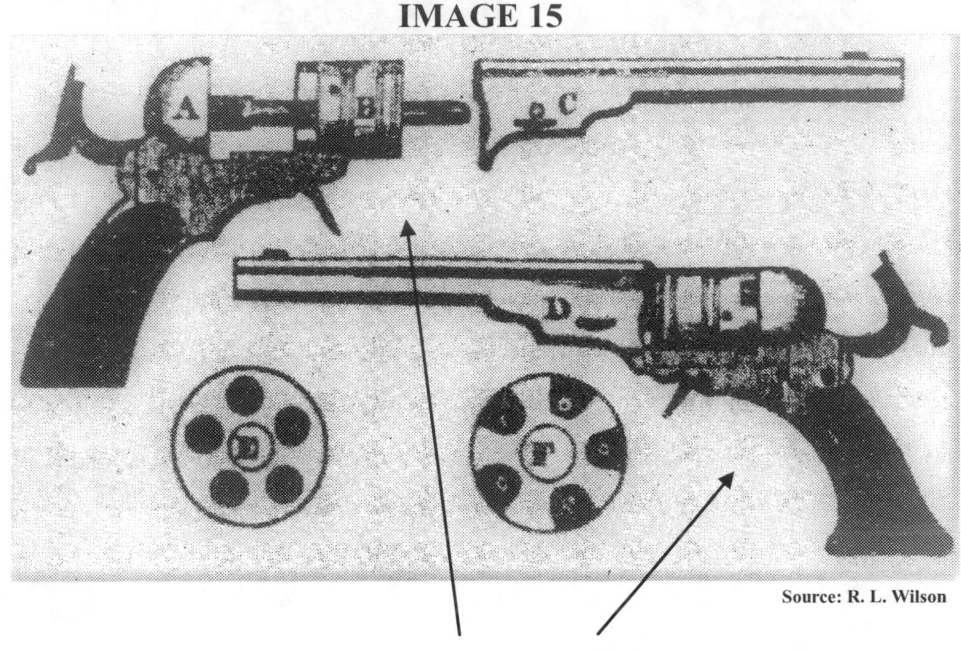

Source: R. L. Wilson

This is the Colt537

SPIRIT OF THE TIMES - NEWSPAPER

NEW YORK: SATURDAY MORNING, JULY 7, 1838.

I would ask that the reader compare the similarity of **Image 14 on page 31**, and **Image 15 above** each of these have a different version of handgrip. Pay particular attention to the revolver in the lower right hand corner. The image you are looking at is Colt537. It is the first hand made pre-production model of the No. 5 Colt Holster or Texas Model. **Refer to Image 7 on page 9;**[17] **see the Estimated Time Line of Development on page 17. The complete news article is found in Appendix 5 on page 152.**

Definitions

Experimental Revolver Webster's Dictionary, Designed to discover something yet unknown. There may be a mixture of serial numbers, normally in specific locations. This is due to using miscellaneous parts residing in scrap bins, or discards found to be yet usable in some fashion or another. Colt had been making versions of revolving pistols, according to U.S. military specifications. Nothing seemed to catch their interest until the

17. Colt Firearms, 1836 – 1958, Page 10, Col 1, Par 3, L 5.

development of Colt537 experiment and the Colt Paterson, .36 caliber Holster or Texas Model.

Prototype Revolver Webster's Dictionary, A revolver that serves as a model or pattern, i.e., perfect example, used as a template for production manufacturing. It may have serial numbers.

Manufactured Revolver Webster's Dictionary, The making of a revolver by hand or using machinery, often on a large-scale activity with a division of labor. Serial numbers may be present.

Three-piece Frame In this study, the three-piece frame refers to the left plate, middle plate and the right plate that together make up the composition of the three-piece frame of the Colt537. **See Image 51, 52 and 56 on pages 71, 72, and 73.**

Key Participants

Samuel Colt, as a young man, designed and produced the first successful multiple shot revolver. He hired John Pearson, who eventually became his principal gunsmith. Pearson built a series of sixteen experimental revolvers, based on Colt's designs. From three of those designs, experimental models were produced. From the Colt537 experimental model, machine ready prototypes were fabricated. From these approximately 4700 revolvers, over a six-year period, were manufactured. Being considered a man ahead of his time, the public, military, and government as a whole were slow to understand the significance of his invention. Hence, within six years, his enterprise slid into receivership.

John Pearson, a gunsmith/machinist acquaintance of Colt, was trained in England as a watchmaker. He also worked for another gun maker in the Boston area until Colt hired him full time. Pearson and Colt had a strained relationship. Most of the problems [illegible]
Pearson by providing him with a lump sum of $30,000 in 1861.

Dudley Seldon, Member of the Board of Directors, Treasurer, and cousin of Sam Colt, was one of the largest investors and provided a significant portion of the money used in building the Paterson, N.J., factory. Selden, seeking a quick return on his investment, grew impatient with his continuous experimentation, and he was also perturbed with his one hand washes the other business concepts. He was constantly urging Cousin Colt to get on with production."[18]

18. Paterson Colt Pistol Variations, R.L. Wilson, Page 151, Col 1, Para 31,

John Ehlers, second in the line of company treasurers, unscrupulously worked against Colt. He sent deficient guns to the military for testing, knowing they would fail. It was the outcome Ehlers had sought. In 1842 the company was forced into receivership with Ehlers acquiring the remaining inventory. He continued to sell Paterson revolvers as Colt's Repeating Pistols until the remaining inventory was exhausted in 1846.

Captain Jack Hayes and Samuel Walker, along with fifteen other Texas Rangers, using their Paterson revolvers, fought off approximately eighty Comanche Indians during the Battle at Bandera Pass. Their exploits gained the fame for the No. 5 Holster or Texas Model revolver, and since then has been called both the "Texas Arm, or the No. 5 Holster, or Texas Model."[19]

Harold B. Crosby, can be considered in the higher echelon of the company. He contributed significantly to the design of the Paterson revolver. When the Colt factory could no longer function,

> "H.B. Crosby (one of the workman) was a creditor of the company for back wages. The amount due him was considerable. The only way in which he could secure his own was to take about twenty-five sets of different portions of the arms. These he put together and realized a handsome sum."[20]

It may have been some of Harold B. Crosby's revolver parts that make up the composition of Colt537. Colt537 is an experimental version; it was assembled prior to the closing of the plant.

Pliny Lawton, Plant Superintendent, Pliny, along with Harold Crosby, designed and drafted the first experimental drawings and implemented several changes, including the rounding of the shoulders on the cylinders of the revolver. Previously they had been squared off and prone to cause jamming of the action if a split percussion cap became lodged. The rounded shoulders allowed easy removal of split caps. In August 1840, he designed the loading lever attachment which became standard on No. 5 Holster Models.

Robert Cummings, John Pearson's assistant, eventually became Sam's foreman at the cartridge loading shop. **Fred Brash or Brask** was another assistant. However, not much is said regarding their level of participation.

---

19. A History of the Colt Revolver, Haven & Beldin, Page 31, Title under picture
20. Paterson Colt Pistol Variations, R.L. Wilson, Col 1, Page 165, Col 1, Para 2, L 1

Chapter Five
The Puzzle

Colt537 Considered Early Copy of Colt Paterson Belt Model

Assessment Approach

In gathering facts as to how all this occurred, I began by accumulating various pieces of a puzzle, which in itself may not at first, make much sense. Like a pictorial puzzle, each piece has a different shape, color, and size. However, when one begins to organize these pieces, as in a puzzle or compiling a group of pieces, it forms a partial image. In doing so, the significance begins to take shape, and as more pieces are fitted together, the significance, picture, or idea becomes obvious. Throughout this book, a piece or two would come together. And without these pieces the end result may not make a complete picture to the reader. I ask to be patient and read the whole analysis.

There is a slight difference in the configuration of the frame of the Colt537 when compared to the frame configuration of the No. 1, No. 2, No. 3, and No. 5 Paterson production models. In the process of transferring the design of the handmade product to that of a production model, production machinery provides its own set of design restrictions. This is based on the machinery's capacity to follow the flow of the design. Other factors too difficult to describe have similar effects as well.

1. The frame of the Colt537 is composed of three pieces, a center piece flanked on both sides with containment plates, meaning that the side plates aid in keeping the interior parts of the revolver together. And this supports the thought that the three-piece frame was hand-made. Whereby, the frames of production models are composed of a single piece of metal.

2. The cylinder of the .31 caliber Colt537 is a ½ inch longer than the two .31 caliber Belt production models, i.e., the No. 2 and No. 3 Belt Models. When comparing the Colt537 cylinder to that of the .36 caliber Holster or Texas Model, the cylinder lengths were relatively equal. However, the diameter of the .36 caliber cylinder on the Holster or Texas Model was much larger.

3. When reviewing **Image 7 on page 9**, it becomes apparent that there is something special about Colt 537. The cylinder is extra-long, allowing an additional

amount of powder in each of the firing chambers. Why was this .31 caliber cylinder put on a larger frame? One obvious thought is that a larger frame is more than likely stronger and easier to handle the greater powder charge.

4. There are filing marks on most of the pieces, such as the inside of the frame and hand grips. Even some of the larger inner parts exhibit filing marks. This is an indication that the Colt537 was a handmade product.

5. The frame size of each of the production models are graduated in size, with the exception of the No. 2 and No. 3 Belt Models. The No. 1 is the smallest, just slightly longer than the length of a U.S. Dollar bill. The Nos. 2 and 3 are similar in size. The next largest is the No. 5, the Holster Model.

6. All production models have the Colt address stamped on the barrel. Lettering is from the breech to the muzzle. Each has a specific finial design before and after the address, designating its model type. Colt537 has the same finial design as the No. 5 production model. The Colt537 frame is relatively the same size as the No. 5, but is made of three pieces. If the frames are the same size, does that mean that Colt537 is a member of the Colt No. 5 Holster family or Texas Model family? It could be.

7. Coil springs were used in Colt537, whereby flat springs took their place in each of the four production models. Early coil springs broke easily and cost more to make.

Within the discussion of each observed set of facts, I will attempt to focus on the linkages of one fact or part of the revolver, as they relate to other parts. The fact is, the function of one part is entirely dependent upon its linkage to other functioning adjacent members or parts.

In the early months 1838, Colt and Pliny Lawton were working on the fourth and final production model design. This was the .36 caliber No. 5 Holster or what will be later known as the Holster or Texas Model aka, the Texas Arm. The size and function was extremely close to the handmade design of the Colt537. In comparing both the exterior and interior workings of the production models to the design of the Colt537, it became apparent that the only reason for differences was the ability of the gunsmith in transferring the handmade design of a specific part of Colt537 into a consistently similar machined product. During the 1800's product design had limited design capabilities.

By virtue of his successes with model Nos. 1, 2, and 3, Colt had proven the concept of a repeating pistol. These guns had five charges of ball and powder. They could fire each of the five charged chambers within seconds. The U.S. Military were impressed but not to the extent of acquiring this product as a weapon. The No. 3 Model, being only a .31 caliber, fell short of the needs of the military. It lacked sufficient stopping power to stop an attacker. An increased accuracy, reliability, size of the ball, and, amount of powder charge were factors requiring additional consideration by Colt, the military, and the common citizen. Colt's fourth production model, the No. 5 Holster or Texas Model, represents another step off into the unknown. As was mentioned numerous times before, this revolver was larger than the Belt Model. Being a .31 caliber, it had the larger frame, a longer cylinder, and five chambers, with an increased powder capacity. This enabled the revolver's five chambers to be loaded with a greater amount of gunpowder, providing additional punch, enough to take down an opposing force at a particular distance if the hit was in a vital part of the body.

In evaluating Colt537 Experiment, the sequence of the firing process needs to be broken down and discussed separately from the rest of the analysis. For that purpose, a certified Antique Arms Gunsmith participated in this pistol's evaluation. A description of his qualification begins on **page 19**. The discussion of the Colt Paterson components begins on **page 48**. His job was to analyze the internal parts design of Colt537. Many of the proving features of Colt537 as an official Colt product are found in comparing its interior workings with those of the four production models; recognizing parts found in the experiment model to improvements found in those used for the same purpose in the production models.

Colt had a number of gunsmiths working for him at different stages of each gun's development. They were Anson Chase, John Pearson, and his assistants, Robert Cummings and Frederick Brask. John Pearson and his assistants performed the major amount of work in the development of sixteen experimental models for Colt. In addition, there were two models that were produced by Pliny Lawton, and his in-house design specialist Henry B. Crosby. Pliny Lawton was the plant superintendent for Colt. The model numbers that were given to revolvers in the production were the No. 1 Pocket or Baby Model, Nos. 2, and No. 3 Belt Models, and the No. 5 Holster or Texas Model. This was to enable the Colt Company as well as the customer to discern one type of Colt model from another in the process of a determining which was best for their needs.

It is believed that there is a significant story to be told regarding Colt537's contribution to the development of the four of the production models. The interested lies in determining what made this experimental revolver so significant. Will the features found in the four models have a relationship with the Colt537 Experiment? What will the similarities or differences tell us about the authenticity and the genesis of the Colt537 Experiment? What was its ultimate effect on society during the mid-eighteen hundreds?

One can use the drawings found in the U.S. Patent No. 1304, **Image 16 on page 38** which includes a series of nine claims describing the functionality of the Colt Paterson revolver, and, also schematic drawings found in R.L. Wilson's Book on *Paterson Colt Pistol Variations*. Most of the terminology found in the aforementioned documents was used in discussing the individual parts of Colt537 Experiment and their relationship to each other in the four known production models. These nine claims are at the root of

Colt's Patent No. 1304, August 29, 1839. The drawings and photos are found throughout this manuscript. They include the following:

Image 16

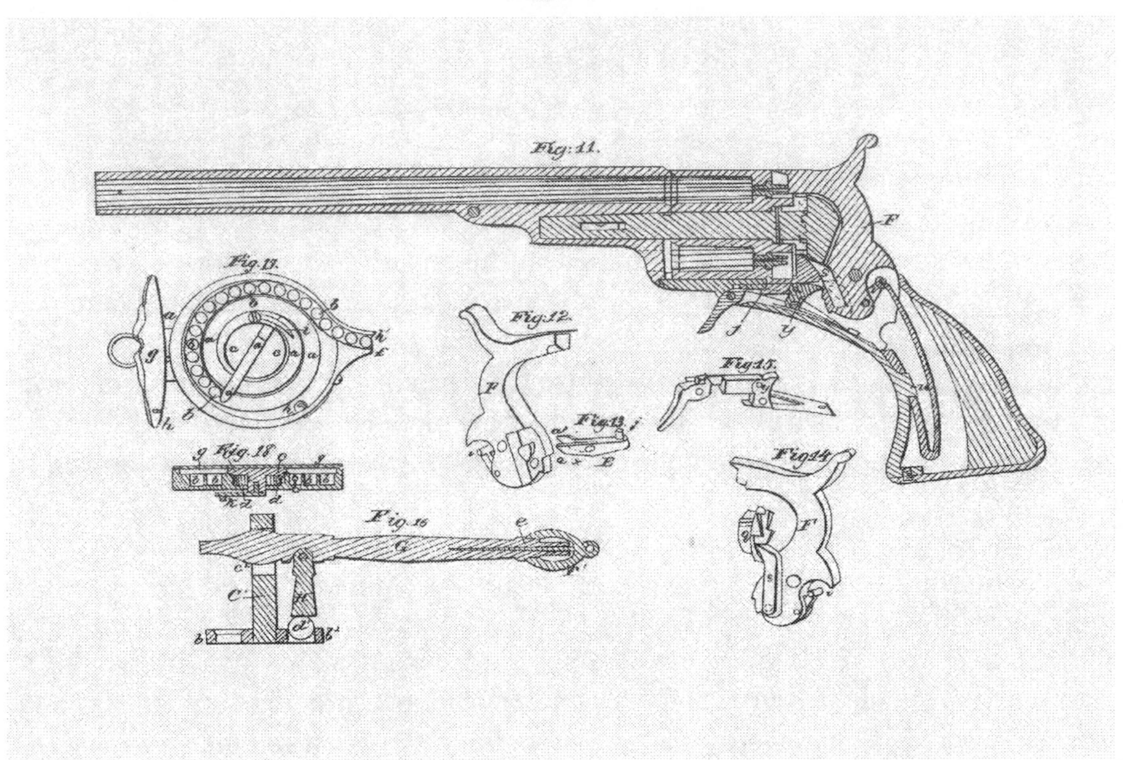

Source: Paterson Colt Pistol Variations, R. L. Wilson

August 29, 1839 Patent No. 1304 – The Second Patent

Patent Claims

1. Providing a way for the smoke generated from the burning powder during the firing process to escape.

2. The development of a wedge hole and fitting key or wedge on the barrel lug of the revolver. This keeps the barrel and the rest of the revolver together during firing.

3. Developing an aperture through the tubes or nipples, at the end of each of the five chambers, to carry the ignition/spark of the exploding cap to the powder chamber for the firing of the ball/round.

4. Developing a locking system which would allow the receiver/cylinder to rotate a specific distance and, perfectly line up with the breech of the barrel, enabling the ball/round to pass from the firing chamber into and through the bore of the barrel.

5. Creating the bolt system that would keep the cylinder locked in position during the firing until the revolver is cocked.

6. During the cocking of the hammer, the bolt drops out of the cylinder stop slot, and as the hammer continues to be pulled back, the hand is pushed upward. The spring loaded hand during this upward movement catches the one tooth of the ratchet, which rotates the ratchet in its upward push. The ratchet is connected to and rotates the cylinder. The hammer, bolt, hand, and the ratchet are working in concert with the cylinder during this rotation.

7. A lever device is used to hook itself onto the arbor of the revolver and enables the plunger to push the ball into the gunpowder loaded in that chamber. This plunger is not attached to the revolver and will not be discussed in this paper.

8. The capping device reduces the amount of digital dexterity needed to place a firing cap on each of the loaded chambers. This capping device is not connected to the revolvers, and will not be discussed in this paper.

9. The powder and ball magazine enables the shooter to automatically load five chambers with powder and ball in two easy steps. This magazine is not attached to the revolver and will not be discussed in this book.

It must be realized that the .31caliber No. 3 Belt Model has a smaller frame than both the Colt537 Experimental and the No. 5 Holster or Texas Model. The frame of the Colt537 and No. 5 are relatively the same size. In the process of making the Colt537 Experiment, the design of the internal firing mechanism of the Nos 1, 2, and 3 are roughly the same as that found in Colt537. These parts had to be slightly magnified and/or manipulated, in some way, to fit this larger frame. The real problem was that magnification and manipulation occurred with just about every part of the exterior and interior of each of these revolvers, while keeping in mind the characteristic Colt design of all of these pistols. They are similar in all respects to the Colt527 Experiment. Again Colt537 parts were handmade, exhibiting rough edges, here and there where, and rounded where need be. This finish certainly did not reflect a fine finished production model. Their goal in building this experiment was expediency and functionality. Get the thing to work, and then clean up the design. i.e., make it look good. Determine how much of the design can be manufactured using in-house machinery and how much would remain to be handmade and what was the cost benefit.

In making the Colt537 Experiment, there was evidence of expediency. The base of possibly a .31 caliber shop scrap hammer, i.e., the lower portion on the hammer, was spliced onto the neck of the upper half of another .31 caliber hammer. This, obviously, was done to correct the angle and/or increase the length of the neck of the hammer, which enables the hammer head to hit squarely on the percussion cap and assure the ignition of the charge. That hammer has a different configuration than that found in the No. 3 Belt Model, due to Colt537's larger frame, and being a .31 caliber revolver. It is different than that found on the No. 5 Holster or Texas model due to it having a similarly large frame but being a .36 caliber revolver. The expediency comes from splicing two hammers into one at the neck of each to provide the correct angle and length for the square hit on the percussion cap. To try to make a hammer from scratch would have taken a greater amount of time, yet arriving at the same final product, and involving less cost.

Chapter Six
History of Colt537 Prior to the Auction

Lineage of Colt537 Experiment: Information Received Prior to the Auction

> "The Barrel is five inches in length with a nickel silver front blade sight. It is called a copy of a .31 Caliber Belt Model," but it is not a Belt Model. It is fitted with Walnut grips. The revolver displays natural silver-gray, with a turning brown patina. The action is fairly tight for its age. The only known history is that it was purchased many years ago from an elderly couple attending a Baltimore gun show."[21] & [22]

However, new developments as to the location of the purchase recently surfaced that contradict the location of the above sale. The second previous owner indicated he purchased the revolver from an elderly couple in Sioux Falls, South Dakota in 1998. **Mr. Frederick's** stated that the revolver was purchased many years ago at a Baltimore Gun Show from an elderly couple. This contradicts the former owner **Mr. Gunnerson's** location of his purchase. See the above paragraph. **Note,** both **Mr. Gunneson's** and **Mr. Frederick's** names are fictitious on purpose.

There are more inconsistencies. The following is what is gleaned from eight years of research on this revolver. An elderly couple selling the gun claimed that the gun was kept in the family for several generations. They indicated to **Mr. Gunnerson** (the first purchaser from the elderly couple) that it was originally owned by an employee (a previous relative of the elderly couple) working in the Colt factory, during the time the company was going into receivership. The Colt Company could not pay the employee his final wages and indicated he could take some gun parts or a completed gun in lieu of his final pay. There is supportive evidence that this policy was ongoing at the time of closing. However, the name of the relative of the elderly couple remains somewhat a mystery.

---

21. Dakota Plains Auction Co, Appendix 1, Page 1
22. See Appendix 1, Page 5

The story goes that the person (a Colt worker) passed the revolver on to the next generation of his family. Realizing the significance of the ownership of this unique revolver, they then passed it on to the next generation of the family. This cycle occurred one or two more times, before the last elderly couple, now apparently desperate for funds, sold the revolver to **Mr. Gunnerson** of Sioux Falls, South Dakota.

Mr. Gunnerson's purchase occurred at a gun show in Sioux Falls in 1998. **Mr. Gunnerson** sold the revolver to a **Mr. Frederick**, of Montana, years later. Apparently, **Mr. Frederick** placed the revolver up for auction with the Dakota Plains Auction Company on November 16, 2011. I, the author, was the highest bidder.

Additional information leading to a possible resolution to the history of Colt537 is as follows:

> At the sale of all properties of the Patent Arms Mfg. Co, "most of the company's stock of arms and unfinished parts fell into the hands of Mr. Ehlers, the failed company's Treasurer, others also received some of the factory's parts and is the subject of an Interesting passage in the book of "The History of Industrial Paterson", by L.R. Trumbull (published in 1882, In Paterson)."[23]
>
> "When the crash came (failure of the firm), Henry B. Crosby (one of the workmen) was a creditor of the Company for wages due to a considerable amount, and the only way in which he could secure his own, was to take about twenty-five sets of the different portions of the available firearms. These he later put together and realized a handsome sum."[24]

In An Attempt to Straighten Out the Story

Henry B. Crosby was working at the plant (1837) when the economic crash occurred. He was due a considerable amount of back pay. It is not known if he was permitted to take the twenty-five sets of revolvers. Crosby was one of the most skilled workmen at the plant.[25] Based on this statement, he more than likely knew which revolvers were deemed most valuable. And, based on the fact that Colt537 had some issues relating to the last experimentation performed on it, that it may have been set aside, and almost forgotten. Crosby, knowing the full story behind Colt537, probably decided to pass Colt537 up for something that would bring an immediate profit. I am talking about the experimentation that went on, as found on page 78 of Wm B. Edwards' book – The Story of Colts Revolver.

---

23. Paterson Colt Pistol Variations, RL Wilson, Page 164, Col 2, par 7, L 1
24. Paterson Colt Pistol Variations, RL Wilson, Page165, Col 1, Par 2, L 1
25. Paterson Colt Pistol Variations, RL Wilson, Page 121, Col 1 Par 1, L16

Historical Significance of the Colt Paterson Experiment

That story is as follows. Sam Lawton and Sam Colt were trying their skill at shooting. They apparently were using the Colt537 at this time. This was prior to the 14th of December, 1837. They would be soon developing the .36 No. 5 Holster or Texas Model revolvers.

> "They discovered that, with the front sight on the barrel, and the rear sight on the hammer lip, five shots could be fired at a mark with the same point of aim, and all group as well as the ability of the shooter. Then, with the barrel removed, the cylinder reloaded, the barrel replaced, and another round fired, the shots would group as well, but in an entirely different part of the target. In the smaller pistols the No. 1, Nos. 2, and 3 Belt Models, the hand grip had not been large enough to hold the gun well for accurate shooting, and this inherent inability to hold a point of aim had gone unnoticed. Now it was evident in all its horrible reality – the Colts just wouldn't shoot! And this was the sort of thing with which they had been trying to revolutionize warfare. Why bother to even rifle the barrels, it was just a waste of labor. And then their cries stopped, as they discovered why. The remedy was simple! The hole bored to receive the fore part of the cylinder arbor was drilled with a straight drill, which bored a hole slightly oversize, but more or less cylindrical. The arbor, too, was basically cylindrical, and when the two mated, there was no fit at all. Had the barrel been part of the drill press and the arbor the tail of a drill holder, the veriest apprentice would have suspected that with this state of affairs their axes would never coincide. Therefore, each time the barrel was replaced on the arbor and the wedge tapped in to draw up the tight, the minute irregularities on both the arbor and the inner bored surface would cause them to match differently, and so the barrel naturally pointed in another direction. Observing the concentric wedging effect of two mating tapers led Lawton to change the arbor-barrel boring, and he wrote to Colt, after an afternoon of good shooting, "and I think we can make each (revolver) as accurate."[26]

That family kept Colt537 for three or four generations. That elderly couple, the last generation possessing the gun, may have been in need of additional financial resources decided to sell the family heirloom and in turn sold the Colt537 to **Mr. Gunnerson**."[27]

Gunnerson sold it to **John Frederick**. **John Frederick** sold it to me through the Dakota Auction Service.

Colt537, being in such good condition for its age adds some supportive credence to this story.

---

26. The Story of Colt's Revolver, Wm B. Edwards, Page 78, Col 1, Par 2, L 5
27. Mr. Gunnerson saved statement, Appendix 4

Part Two

Specific Model Features

Between the Four Production Models

Chapter Seven

Model Similarities and Differences

Also

Reference Schematic Drawings Needed for Interpretation of Model Features

Schematic Drawing

Image 17

Wilson Source: Paterson Colt Pistol Variations, R. L

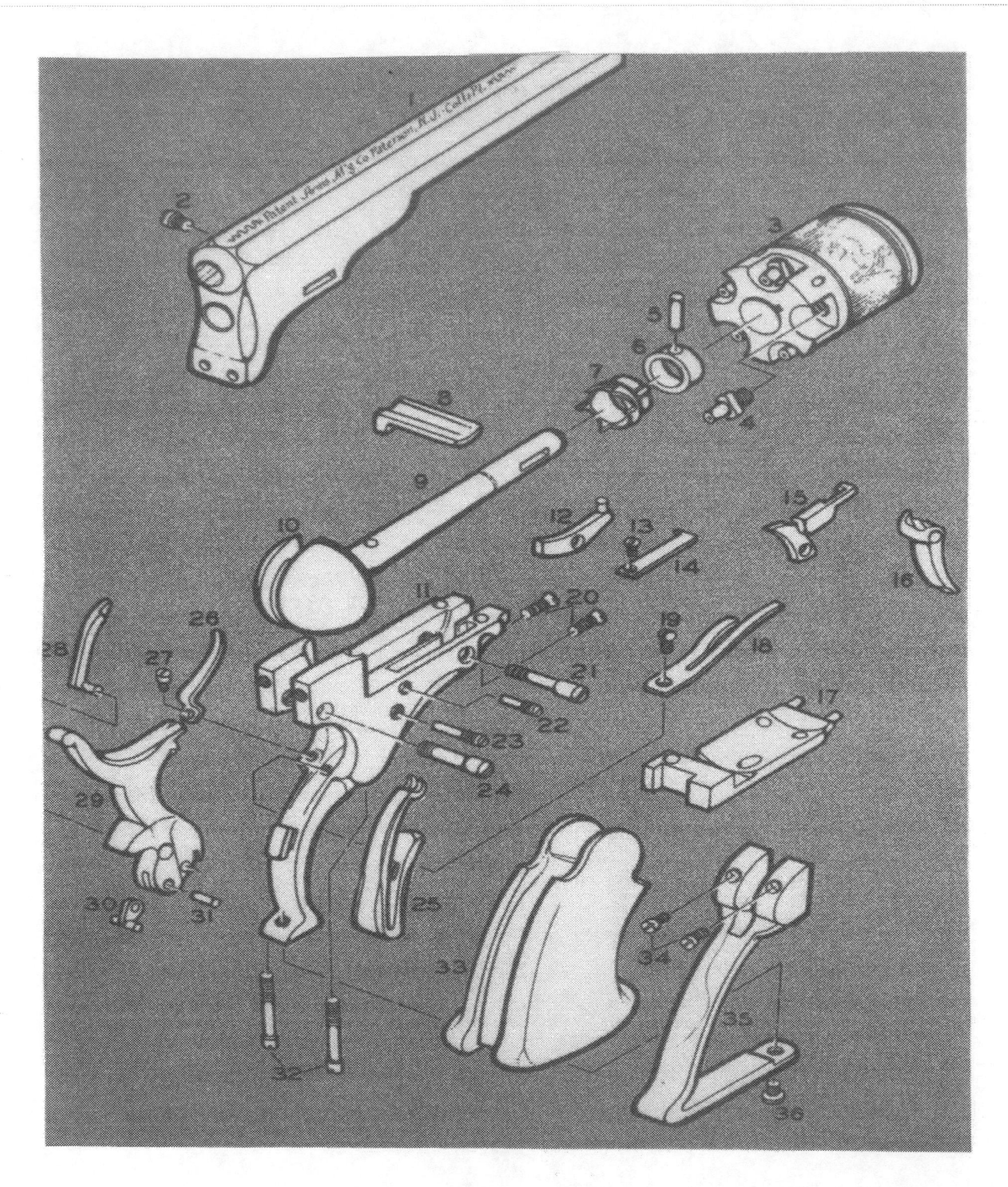

Image 18

1. Barrel
2. Wedge Screw
3. Cylinder
4. Nipple
5. Toothed Rack Link Pin
6. Toothed Rack Link
7. Toothed Rack
8. Wedge
9. Cylinder Arbor or Pin
10. Recoil Shield
11. Frame
12. Bolt
13. Trigger Screw

14 Trigger Spring

15 Sear Lever

16 Trigger

17 Frame Plate

18 Sear Spring

19. Sear Spring Screw
20. Frame Plate Screws
21. Trigger Screw
22. Bolt Screw
23. Actuating Bar Screw/Sear Lever Screw
24. Hammer Screw
25. Main Spring
26. Hand Spring
27. Hand Spring Screw
28. Hand
29. Hammer
30. Stirrup Assembly
31. Stirrup Plug
32. Recoil Shield Screws
33. Hand Grip
34. Backstrap Screw
35. Backstrap
36. Connecting Screw

Similarities and Differences of Colt537 and the Four Production Models

The Dis-Assembly

The dis-assembly of the revolver starts with the removal of the barrel**, Item 1, on page 48) and Image 19 below**, In order to remove the barrel from the revolver pull the hammer to the half-cocked position, the wedge **(Item 8)** must then be slid out. The wedge can be seen on the right side of the barrel in the area of the barrel lug. Usually a tap with a five-pound weight of some sort will loosen the wedge, and it should easily slide out. Once out, the barrel **(Item 1)** can be removed from the arbor by sliding the barrel away or forward from the rest of the revolver. Once the barrel is off of the arbor (**Item 9**), the cylinder (**Item 3**) will also easily slide off of the arbor, sometimes called the barrel spindle.

The barrel is 4 and 15/16" long. Some would round it off to a 5" barrel. The barrel lug retains a curve and reverse curve on its underside. The front sight is made of German silver. Both of the Belt Models and the Holster or Texas Models have this characteristic.

The size of the bore is .31 caliber and, at present, the bore is smooth. It is highly suspected that it had a five land and groove rifling. The present smooth bore also has one deep straight groove running the upper length of the bore. This is extremely uncommon to see such an alteration, the perceived purpose of which will be discussed further on in this writing.

Image 19

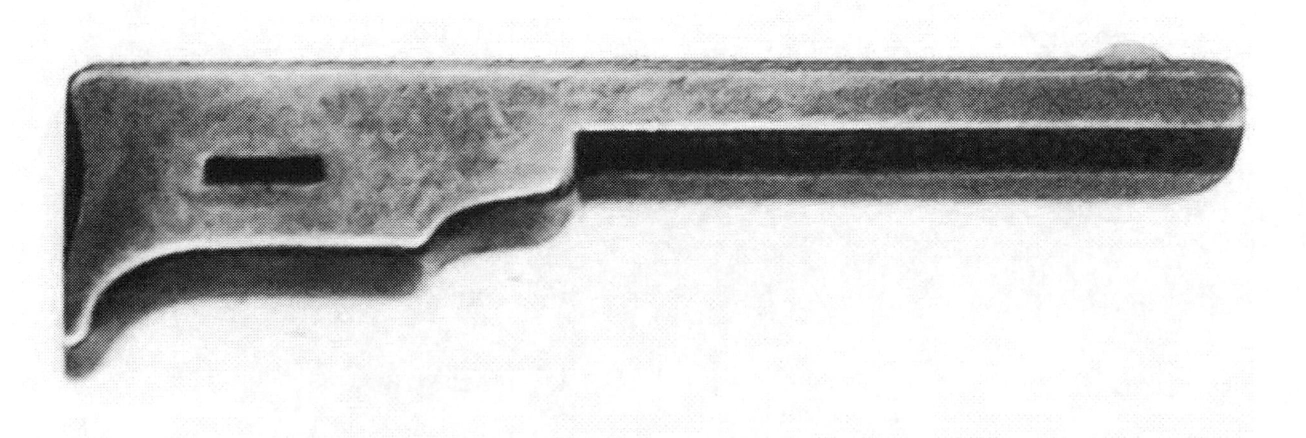

Source: M. Desparte

Barrel of Colt537

A .31 caliber bore, i.e., the land (of the lands and grooves in the rifling) will usually be designed to have a 0.300-inch diameter. The ball diameter would have a 0.310-inch diameter and a groove diameter of 0.314 inches. It is important to remember this alteration; it will be discussed later on in this manuscript, **See Image 81, page 97**

The Colt Address on the Colt537 Barrel

Behind the front sight, on the surface of the octagon barrel, can be found the factory address and finial markings, indicating that the revolver is part of the Holster or Texas Model family, **See Image 20.** This is the only visible marking, and is found on the top surface of the octagonal barrel, shown below. The address is difficult to read. Hence this printed copy comes close to what the photo depicts. It would be easier to read if a magnifying glass were used.

The space and angle of each letter must be carefully calculated for this lettering to end up so close to the breech end of the barrel. Lettering usually begins on the left margin or side of a page. And, for a novice to attempt to replicate the above for only one revolver is beyond comprehension. Consider all the unique parts required in the fabrication of this revolver. The interior parts for example, the Trigger Extension Arm, Sear, Hammer, Hand, and the Barrel. Not to mention the interior parts that can be identified. Recognizing that his is the first revolver being developed, the design of each part is original. And, for that matter, must interact with each of the other parts in order to function correctly. As mentioned above, it is beyond comprehension that this would or could be done when considering the ability, payback and amount of time it would consume.

Image 20

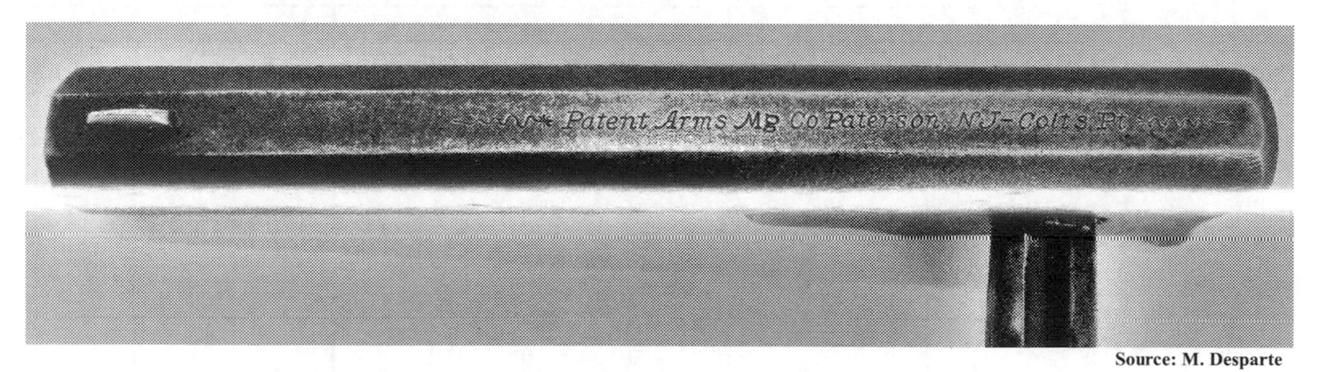

Source: M. Desparte

~~~~~~~* *Patent Arms Mg. Co Paterson, NJ-Colts Pt* *~~~~~~~

Address of Colt537

It must be noted that on page 155 of L.R. Wilson's book, *The Paterson Colt Book*, an image of the Colt address is shown on the top flat of a Holster or Texas Model No. 5 revolver having a serial number of 996. The snake's tail of the finial closest to the muzzle
~~~~~~~

(Left hand side) has a break in each of the last two valleys of its tail. This is due to wearing of the engraving device used on barrels longer than 5 inches. Notice that the serial number (996) is quite high. Therefore this anomaly may not be seen on models with earlier numbers. It also must be noted that the address on the longer than 5 inch barrel Holster or Texas Models have a larger and longer address than those with a 5 inch or shorter barrel. And, the address on the 9 inch No. 5 address will have a slightly greater slant to its lettering. Lastly, Colt537's address remains as crisp as the day it was stamped.

Colt537 is best portrayed as having some characteristics that are carried over from the No. 3 Belt and others to the No. 5 Holster or Texas Models. However, only the No. 5 Holster or Texas Model maintained the address and finial characteristics found on Colt537, indicating that Colt537 Experiment was a preliminary design. The one from which the four production models transitioned. It was used within the factory for experimentation, but never developed into a prototype or model for manufacturing or production. This supposition is reinforced later on in this manuscript.

As mentioned above, the address appears to be authentic. However, it is the reverse as to how it should read. It presently reads from muzzle to breech. All production models read from breech to muzzle.[28] Remember, Colt537 is in the experimental stage. This anomaly could be the result of a policy change. The flow of the address now is in the same direction as the flow of the bullet. It could be as simple as that.

The address slant is going the right way, i.e., the slant of the lettering is correct, and the final design appears to be correct as well. Anyone thinking Colt537 was a counterfeit has a significant amount to learn.

Evaluation of the Barrel and Address

	No			Possibly				Yes		
	1	2	3	4	5	6	7	8	9	10
Was the Barrel and Address made by the new factory?										X
Was the Barrel and Address made new for the Colt537?			Possibility of it being from a previous experiment						X	
Was the Barrel and Address taken from a scrap bin and reworked?					X					
Was the Barrel and Address made by a hobbyist?	X									

28. *The Paterson Colt Book*, R.L. Wilson, Page 132, Col 1, Par 4, L 1

The Reason for the Rating

It is thought that the barrel could have been used on a previous experiment, because it had more than two sets of extremely difficult numbers to read on the breech end of the lug, i.e., Nos. 58 and 714. The No. 58 was/is extremely large. The numbers are difficult to see. The barrel needs to be held and maneuvered under direct sunlight using a magnifying glass if one expects to see these numbers, and only if that person is lucky.

The Colt537 barrel has the finials imprinted on it, more than likely, as part of the experiment, since the address was printed in reverse, i.e., flowing from muzzle to breech, opposite to what is found on the production models. It may have been the first time this finial was engraved, and no policy as to direction of the lettering had yet been made. Also remember Colt537 is handmade, prior to the machine made production models.

The bewildering issue is that the Colt537 Experiment barrel address finials are similar to those found on the future .36 caliber no. 5, Holster or Texas production model. However, in spite of the fact that the address flow was reversed, this issue must have been noticed after the shop inventory or control numbers were stamped on the barrel. This also indicates that Colt537 was fabricated in the Paterson Factory, and that there may be some direct relationship between the experiment model and the manufactured Holster or Texas Model revolver. Also there are supporting in house comments made by Pliny Lawton and other members working on the Colt537 Experiment regarding this.

> "Soon after the signing of the August (1838) contract, Sam became anxious to go to Washington again. But first, he had to have something to sell. For the next three months, Colt aided Lawton in getting the largest size pistol, in this series of four (production models) ready in some quantity. This arm was the No. 5, and the most expensive size. Lawton called them the "belt" model. *(This last comment shows that Lawton was confused as to what to call it. Was it a Belt or Holster, i.e., relating back to the thought of it being a Belt Model due to its .31 caliber bore? Eventually the modern* [illegible]
>
> as a mechanical pattern, is identical in design with the other two sizes (Pocket/Baby and Belt) in production, "this largest pistol was a powerful and hard shooting gun, capable of really serious work. In all Colt revolving percussion pistols, the chambers were a little larger than the actual bore diameter, and the balls used are larger yet. There was a well understood and conscious reason for this, known as the avoidance of "windage." [29]

This last statement addresses itself to the condition of Colt537 prior to eliminating the rifling in the bore of the barrel. Also, notice the underlined and slanted

---

29. The Story of Colt's Revolver, William B Edwards, Page 77, Col 2, Par 3, L 1

verbiage used in the quote above. This refers to all of the parts used in each of the models similar in design but scaled down or up to the size of the model being worked on at that time. Colt537's parts are the original design, but the scale of the production parts is dissimilar. This is due to Colt537 being a .31 caliber and the production models of varying calibers, i.e., .28, .31, .34, and .36 calibers.

The Design and Structure of the Frame

At first thought, it didn't make sense to see this Colt537 Experiment having a .31 caliber barrel sitting on, what appears to be, a .36 caliber frame. Colt already had two types of .31 caliber models. They are the No. 2 Belt Models, having a straight hand-grip and the other, the No. 3 Belt Models with a flared hand-grip. Why would Colt have Pliny Lawton, his plant manager, design and build the Colt537 with a half inch longer than normal .31 caliber cylinder? **At first I didn't realize that Colt537 was first hand built, and was the original design, i.e., the genesis model.**

Here is Where the Issue Gets Interesting

Performing some measurements on the image of the prototype, experimental six-shot version of the (pre-production) No. 2 Belt model revolver, **Image 6 on page 8**, and that of the .31 caliber Colt537 Experiment, **Image 7 on page 9**, it was found that the length of their cylinders are similar. Both appear to be one half of an inch longer than what is needed for a normal gunpowder load, be it .29 or .31 caliber.[30] The length

Image 21

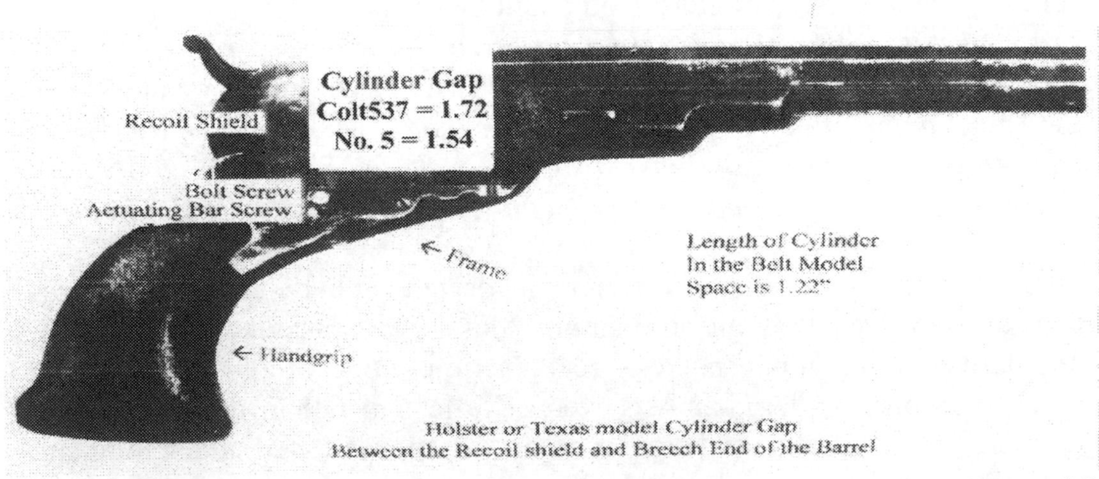

Source: M Desparte/L.R. Wilson

Structure of the Frame, Recoil Shield Enabled Extensive Flexibility

30. Paterson Colt Pistol Variations, R.L. Wilson, Page 80, in Plate 53

of the regular Belt Model cylinder is 1.22 inches, and the length of the Colt537 cylinder, is approximately 1.72 inches.[31] Why would Colt have Pliny Lawton make a longer .31 caliber cylinder? One could answer, without thinking, that he needed to fill the gap between the recoil shield and the breech of the barrel. Ok, but what was he going to do with a longer cylinder? It would require a considerable amount of work scaling down internal and some external parts to accommodate the .31 caliber cylinder on a .36 caliber frame. If everything fits snugly, and the revolver operates satisfactorily, one could shoot it. But now the gun can take on additional powder, and the ball can travel further, and leave the barrel at a higher velocity. In addition to all of this, the shooter experiences a greater recoil or shock. The question that should arise is; can the revolver handle the shock? Is the frame strong enough to handle the repeated shock? Can the cylinder withstand the greater shock to the side walls of each of the five chambers on the cylinder? Is the accuracy destroyed because of the shock? These questions will be addressed later on in this manuscript.

The Cylinder of Colt537 - Note: Lack of Shoulders on Firing Nipples

It is difficult to see, but **Images 22 and 23** are attempting to illustrate the lack of shoulders on each of the five percussion nipples. It isn't known as to whether nipples with shoulders were being made by the fall/winter of 1837. However, it stands to reason that additional improvements of the percussion nipples would continue and eventually would incorporate shoulders giving the owner an easier method for the removal of the nipple with the intent of periodically cleaning residue out of the cylinder.

The Cylinder of Colt 537

Image 22 Source: M. Desparte — **Image 23** Source: M. Desparte — **Image 24** Source: M. Desparte

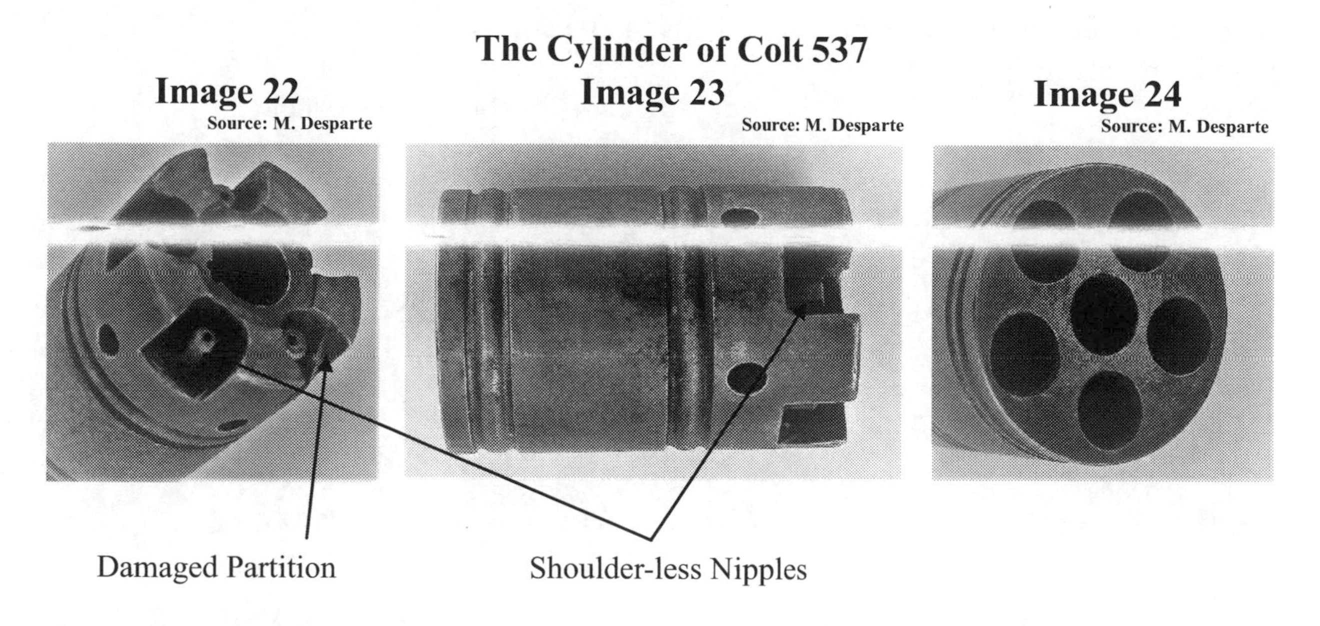

31. See Appendix 2, Page 3 and Page 4

Historical Significance of the Colt Paterson Experiment

Also found on the cylinder in **Image 22** is a rotary tool gouge out of the partition wall located at the four o' clock position (very difficult to see). In essence, this cylinder would not be allowed to be placed on a product destined for sale. It is too big of a flaw, but not a consideration when using the revolver for experimental purposes. The exterior of the revolver need not be a picture of perfection; it is the smoothness of operation and the strength of the weapon that are the primary factors in this experimentation. Stock or control numbers were present.

Image 23 illustrates the length of the Colt537 cylinder on a horizontal plane. The normal length of a .31 caliber cylinder is 1.22 inches. The length of the Colt537 is 1.72 inches. It is believed that Pliny Lawton chose this length to test out the strength and functioning of this revolver using the greater powder capacity in the longer than normal .31 caliber cylinder.

Image 24 exhibits the muzzle end of the elongated cylinder of the Colt537. The length of which is 1.72 inches. Its diameter is 1.22 inches. There is little difference in length between the Colt537 (1.72") and that of the No. 5 Holster or Texas Model (1.5425), a difference of 0.1775 inches. Measurements of the No. 5 were calculated from photos. The diameter of the cylinder of Colt537 is 1.22 inches, and the diameter of the cylinder of the No. 5 is approximately 1.322 inches, a difference of 0.10 inches (rounded).

The difference between the diameters of a revolver's cylinder creates a need for resizing almost all of its interior parts, including of those in the Colt537 Experiment. That is to say, in Colt537 a rescaling of the size of the hammer, the hand, and the distances between the teeth of the rotating ratchet attached to the breech end of the cylinder, etc. had to happen. This also had to be done for production models Nos. 1, 2, 3, and 5 revolvers.

Shouldered Nipple

Image 25

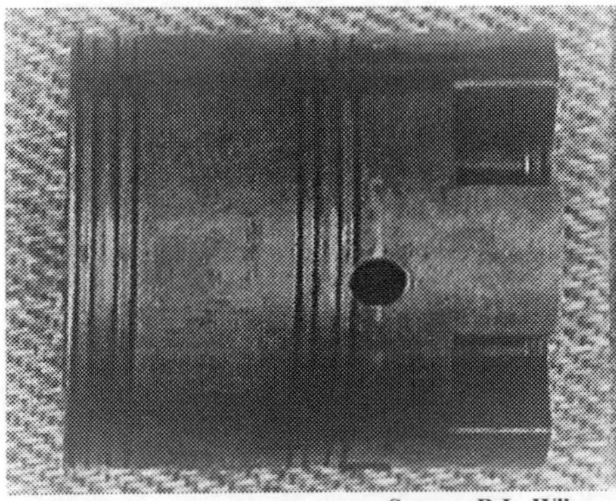

Source: R.L. Wilson

No. 3 Belt Model

Image 26

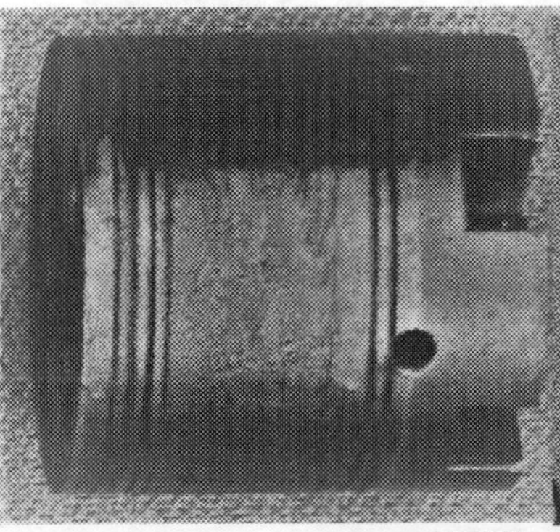

Source: R.L. Wilson

No. 5 Holster Model

Image 27

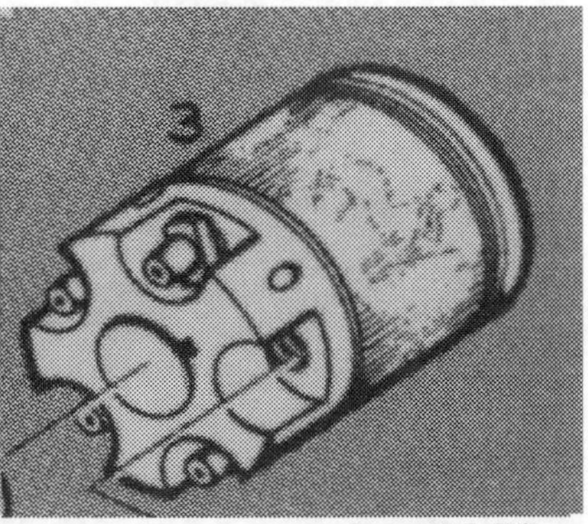

Source: R.L. Wilson

Revised Patent Drawing

Image 25 is that of a No. 3 Belt Model cylinder. Its dimension is 1.22 inches in length, and the diameter is also approximately 1.22 inches. It must be reemphasized that although the size of the cylinders in, **Image 25** and **Image 26 page 56,** appear to be similar, they are not. Attention must be given to the size defined in this paragraph. **Image 26** is that of a No. 5 IIolster Model cylinder. Its dimension is approximately 1.59 inches in length with a diameter approximately 1.322 inches. They appear to be the same, minus the dimensions. Calculations derived from photos of the No. 5 Holster or Texas Model.

Image 27, The U.S. Patent No.1304, is a three dimensional drawing, however, this drawing does not portray any specific one of the four Paterson production models. It is a schematic drawing and reflects what the patent drawing would look like if it were a photographic image. This drawing illustrates shoulders on the percussion cap nipple (the twelve noon position). As mentioned previously, the shoulders of the percussion nipple on the Colt537 are missing. It suggests that the shoulder less type of percussion nipple is an earlier product than those with shoulders found on the patent backup drawing; **Image 27**, illustrating the improvement in the invention. The shouldered percussion nipples may have been an improvement in transition at the time.

Colt537 Experiment Cylinder

At the end of each chamber, prior to firing the revolver, each nipple is covered with a percussion cap. When the hammer hits the cap, it ignites (fulminate of mercury) and sends a spark down the tube, igniting the powder and thus firing the gun. It was found that sparks would also spread in all directions when the cap was ignited. Imperfections in the chambers walls would ignite adjacent chambers as well.

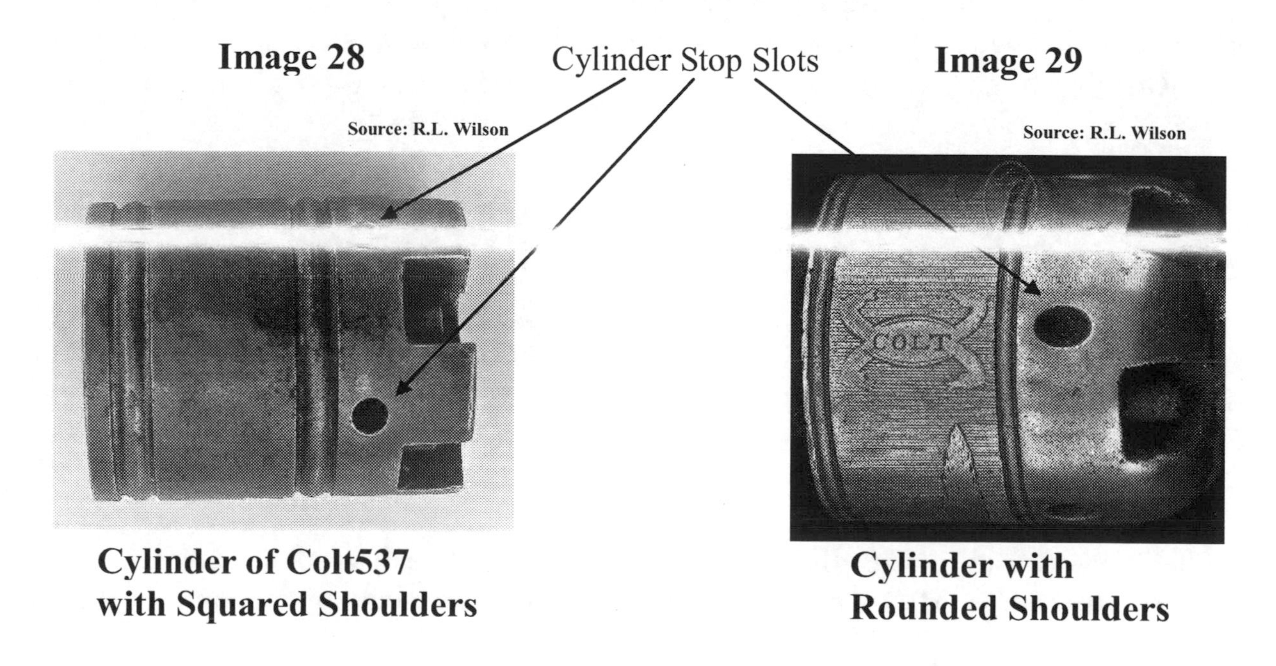

Image 28 — **Cylinder of Colt537 with Squared Shoulders**

Image 29 — **Cylinder with Rounded Shoulders**

The Inclusion of Partitions – Due to the ignition of adjacent loaded firing chambers, partitions between each of the five nipples were introduced. This alleviated the concern. However, a new problem arose. As the cylinder rotated in the firing sequence, the expended percussion cap, loosened by firing, many times would fall off. In doing so, it would have an opportunity to lodge in between the next set of rear cylinder partitions. The revolver would crumple the expended cap and jam it in between the cylinder partitions and the recoil shield, immobilizing the revolver and rendering it useless. Finally, in 1840 a solution was found. By rounding off the shoulders of the partitions, (**Image 29**) sufficient room was provided to allow a crumpled cap to fall away. The cylinder of Colt537 does not have the rounded shoulder as pictured below. Therefore indicating Colt537 was built prior to the 1840s.

Shoulder-Less Nipples

It has been noted that the nipples of Colt537 do not have shoulders, since the construction of Colt537 took place in late 1837 or early 1838. It was not much later that another problem was identified. As mentioned previously, nipple tubes were used to conduct the spark of the percussion cap into the powder chamber of the cylinder. After a short while the cylinder would require cleaning. As a part of the cleaning process, the nipple tubes were removed. The first type of nipple tubes used in the Colt Paterson was shoulder less and difficult to extract from the cylinder. **See Image 30.** In order to simplify the process of extraction, shoulders were placed in the nipple tubes which would allow the use of a small wrench to twist off the shouldered Nipple tube. **See image 31, below item 3.** The invention of the nipple tube to transmit spark was one of the ideas patented by Colt in the No. 1304 U.S. Patent. Apparently, shoulders on the nipples were not thought of during the construction of Colt537. Patent 1304 was not developed and submitted until August 29, 1839, which was after the revolver was completed and tested.

Image 30 Source: Michael Desparte

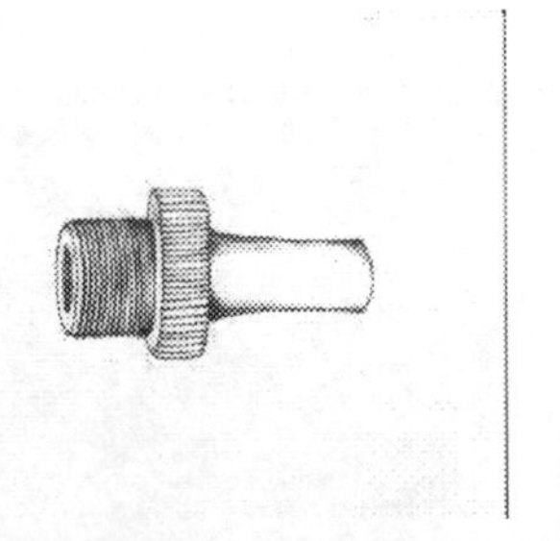

Ribbing to aid in thumb twisting off the Nipple

First Percussion Nipples
Nipple without Shoulders[32]

Image 31 Source: L. R. Wilson

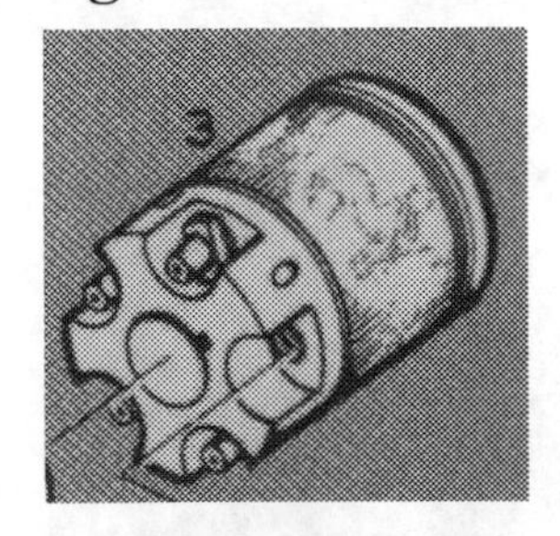

A wrinch is used to twist off the Nipple

Later Model Percussion Nipples
with Square Shoulders

Another patent feature was the installation of five bolt stops on the surface of the cylinder. **See Image 31, to right of Item 3.** During the cocking process, the bolt is

32. Note, this illustration is not an exact representation of shoulder-less nipples.

energized and releases itself from the Bolt Stop on the cylinder, enabling the cylinder to rotate a specific distance, and then, perfectly aligning the next firing chamber with the bore of the barrel. The bolt again locks the cylinder and its loaded chamber in position for firing.

The Reason for the Erroneous Description Colt537

So, putting all of the above together, we have a .31 caliber barrel with a longer cylinder backed up by a .31 caliber Belt Model recoil shield, all sitting on an experimental .36 caliber three piece frame, **see appendix 2, page 4**.

On the exterior, the gun appears to be similar to a Belt Model, but it is larger, and therefore the reason for the original mistake in the identity by the selling owners and the auctioneer. These frame adjustments were principally made to test this new enlarged frame's ability to withstand the repeated shock from continuous firing at greater charge levels. No other reason comes to mind. Colt, in collaboration with Pliny Lawton, the plant manager, again employed his policy of incremental advances in developing Colt's revolvers, this time, built on a frame larger than that of the No. 2 and No. 3 Belt Models. The product ended up being a .31 caliber Colt537 Experiment with an elongated cylinder. By virtue of its additional length, the cylinder now has deeper firing chambers, and therefore is now a more powerful revolver. With this greater powder capacity, given that each chamber has an extra half inch in length, each would now be capable of firing powder loads ranging from what is needed for a .31 caliber, all the way up to that of a .44 caliber moderate powder charge. See the loading chart, **Image 32 on page 60**. In other words, Colt could experiment with different loads and different sets of lands and grooves to determine what combination would best support the final version of the .36 caliber revolver.

The Redesign and Scale of the Four Production Models

With the knowledge gained from the construction of this experiment (Colt537), Colt and Pliny Lawton used Colt537 as the basis for a scaled down design of the No. 1 Baby or Pocket Model revolver. Lawton's thinking at the time was to start production on the smallest of the proposed revolvers. It would appear, based on positive letters from Colonel of Ordnance George Bumford, U. S. Army, and members from the Navy Commissioner's office, to be providing high praise on the concept of his invention. It would also appear that the P.A. Mfg. Co. (Colt's Company) felt the diminutive arm, the No. 1 Pocket/Baby Model, would have a good market, and that the relatively small size meant a relatively small investment when breaking in the workmen on the almost miniature arm. It also allowed Pliny Lawton and Colt to improve the manufacturing process and possibly develop details which would lead to more imposing larger-sized pistols.[33] The concept was to train his gunsmiths on the manufacturing of something small, and therefore, minimizing the loss of material through mistakes to a negligible amount. The production of the Pocket or Baby Model would be followed by the slightly larger No. 2 straight grip Belt Model, and so on, **See page 17 (Estimated Time Line for Development).** Around this time, Dudley Seldon, the Treasurer of Patent Arms Mfg., admonished Colt for spending too much time on experimentation. One can only imagine the tone of his voice (Seldon's) if he were speaking to Colt face to face. It is believed that the Board of Directors were constantly pushing Seldon to get something on the market. Being investors in the Company, they were looking for a quick return on their investment, the sooner the return the better.

> "Dudley Seldon complained that too much time and effort had been devoted to samples and experiments, delaying the attention necessary to begin manufacture. As late as April 18, 1837, Seldon complained to Colt, had you developed (disclosed) to the company all the defects in the original plans the state of its affairs would have been different from what they are."[34]

Image 32

Colt Blackpowder Pistol Loading Data

Model	Caliber (Ball diameter)	Minimum Charge	Recommended Charge	Maximum Charge
1849 Pocket	.31 (.319-.323 inch dia.)	10 grains	14 grains	15 grains
1851 Navy	.36 (.372-.378 inch dia.)	15 grains	18 grains	20 grains
1860 Army	.44 (.451-.457 inch dia.)	25 grains	25 grains	30 grains

- The data in the above table was taken from the **Colt Black Powder Instruction Manual.**

It would appear that the factory had been completed somewhere in mid-1836, but sections of the structure, production wise were already in use before then, and now it was the fall of 1837. Can one imagine the number of miscellaneous barrels, frames etc. that were made, prior to the development of Colt537, experimented with, and then discarded to a corner of the shop or placed in a non-descript parts bin, parts that may have been utilized in the construction of Colt537, parts that had all kinds of numbers on them, representing something, but not serial numbers. With this additional pressure placed on Colt, ongoing production on the Belt models, and experimentation virtually ceased. From this point on, i.e., April of 1838, the repeated use of the Colt537 Experiment design as a template centered on the development of the .36 caliber No. 5 Holster or Texas Model. All that Colt and Pliny Lawton had learned through experimentation with Colt537 was put into the development of this model. For instance, the additional length of its .31

33. Paterson Colt Pistol Variations, R.L. Wilson, Page 96, Par 3, L 8
34. Paterson Colt Pistol Variations, R.L. Wilson, Page 151, Par 2, L 1

caliber firing chamber, in a way, was performing as an economic substitute for a .36 caliber cylinder. Time and money were saved by not having to remake the appropriate size hammer, recoil shield and cylinder for the .36 caliber revolver. Colt had determined the strength of the Colt537 frame, in spite of the fact that Colt537 had a three piece frame, was strong enough for the job. In addition, the above described powder loads, seen in the chart above or something similar to it would have been used to test the reliability of the cylinder and, the altered firing system. This was a historic moment in time for Colt. Developmental issues and circumstance came into focus. As the factory came closer to completion, the effort given to experimentation increased. This gave way to improved direction and confidence by management, and in turn, initiated the final steps for the development of the No. 5 Holster or Texas Model.

Evaluation of the Cylinder/Receiver

	No			Possibly				Yes		
	1	2	3	4	5	6	7	8	9	10
Was the Cylinder made new at the Colt factory?										X
Was the Cylinder made new for Colt537?										X
Was the Cylinder off another Colt Paterson Experiment?				X		It had a flaw...				
Was the Cylinder taken from a scrap bin & reworked?			X							
Was the Cylinder made by a hobbyist?	X									

The reason for the 10 rating – A 10 was given due to the fact that the cylinder was a half inch longer than the normal .31 caliber cylinder, No. 2 or No. 3, Belt Models. The Prototype, experimental, six-shot version of a proposed No.2 Belt Model pistol had a cylinder similar in length, however, the diameter may have been slightly larger due to it being a six-shot.[35] The first revolver made by Colt and Lawton, identified as a No.2 model was far from the No. 2 version production model, it lacked a frame plate. The absence of the frame plate is an indication that there may have been an alteration in the makeup of internal parts. This model, more than likely had a three piece frame.

The Recoil Shield, Hand, and Ratchet

The recoil shield is semi-hollow which provides room for the ratchet and hand to function. The hand is attached to the base of the hammer and moves up against the ratchet (which is connected to the cylinder) with the cocking of the hammer. **See Image 40, page**

35. Paterson Colt Pistol Variations, R. L. Wilson, page 80 Plate No. 53

63. As the hand (**Item "s"**) moves up through the face of the recoil shield, it connects with one of the teeth on the ratchet (**Item "q"**), causing the cylinder to rotate a precise distance, to end up with one of its chambers being perfectly aligned with the bore of the barrel. The recoil shield has an arbor/spindle which is attached to the center of the face of the shield. Encircling this arbor/spindle is the ratchet ring with an extension. A cam, (visible just below the face of the recoil shield in **Image 33**) is attached to the extension. Therefore, when the hammer (**Item "f"** in **Image 40, page 63**) is cocked, the attached hand moves upward, causing the ratchet to rotate. The attached cam, which fits into a groove in the cylinder, also rotates, causing the cylinder to rotate. That rotation stops as the chamber becomes perfectly aligned with the bore of the barrel. A composite of parts described above are found in the **Schematic Drawing on page 48**. Recoil Shields are removable from the frame and can be replaced by one of three different sizes. The Belt Model frame can support a .28, .31 or .34 caliber recoil shield, and the Holster or Texas Model frame can support a .36 caliber set up. Colt537 has a Belt Model recoil shield size backing up a .31 caliber cylinder. The reason for the Colt537 mismatch is because this revolver is an experiment. It was apparently put together to eventually check out the larger sized frame during the process of designing and building the .36 caliber No. 5 Holster or Texas Model.

Colt537 Recoil Shield Screw Size

Location	Screw Number	AOL Thickness	Head Diameter	Head Diameter	Shaft
Top Frame, breach end	No. 5	.939	.086	.187	.128
Bottom Frame	No. 5	1.105	.090	.185	.128

Image 33
Source: M. Desparte

Colt537 Experiment

Image 34
Source: R.L. Wilson

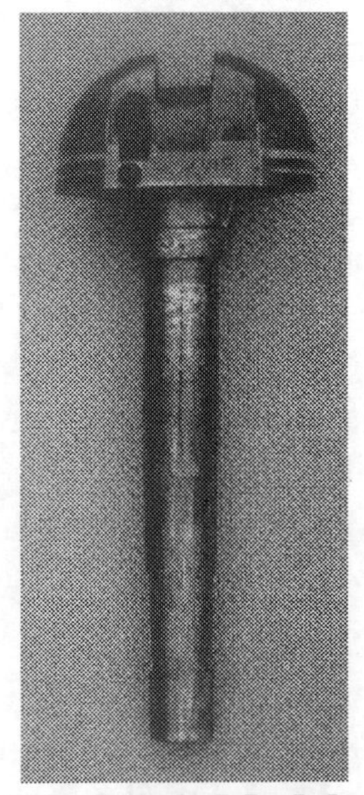

No. 3 Belt Model

Image 35
Source: R.L. Wilson

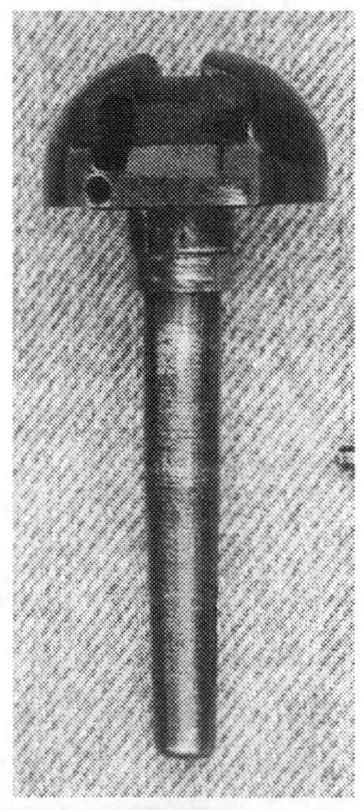

No. 5 Holster or Texas Model

Image 36
Source: R.L. Wilson

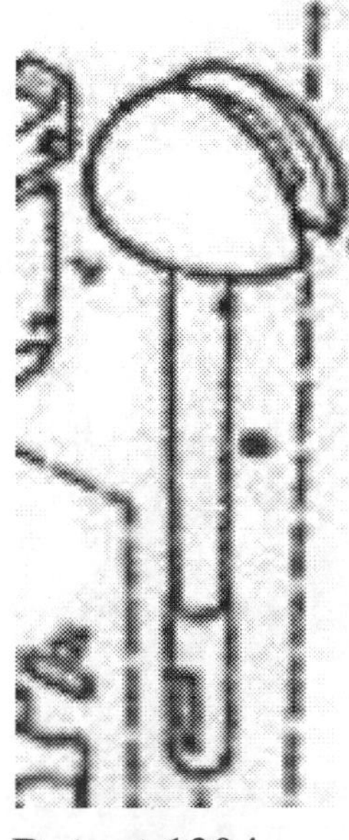

Patent 1304 Schematic

Evaluation of the Recoil Shield

	No			Possibly				Yes		
	1	2	3	4	5	6	7	8	9	10
Was the Recoil Shield made new for Colt537?								X		
Was the Recoil Shield taken off another Colt Paterson?			X							
Was the Recoil Shield taken from a scrap bin & reworked?		X	Improbable							
Was the Recoil Shield made by a hobbyist?	X	Would require vast experience								

. **The reason for the 8 rating** – The recoil shield, more than likely, was fabricated anew. This is based on the fact that it is a revised version of the prototype, experimental in Plate 53,[36] said to be a No. 2 Belt Model found, in *Paterson Colt Pistol Variations,* page 80, **also Image 6 page 8**. That image appears to be a direct predecessor to Colt537. It is a predecessor because this particular model does not exhibit a frame plate.

The recoil shield may have been developed in some previous experimentation. It was the arbor or spindle on which the cylinder rotates, that is new, i.e., an extended length to facilitate the longer Colt537 cylinder.

The Hand and Hand-Spring

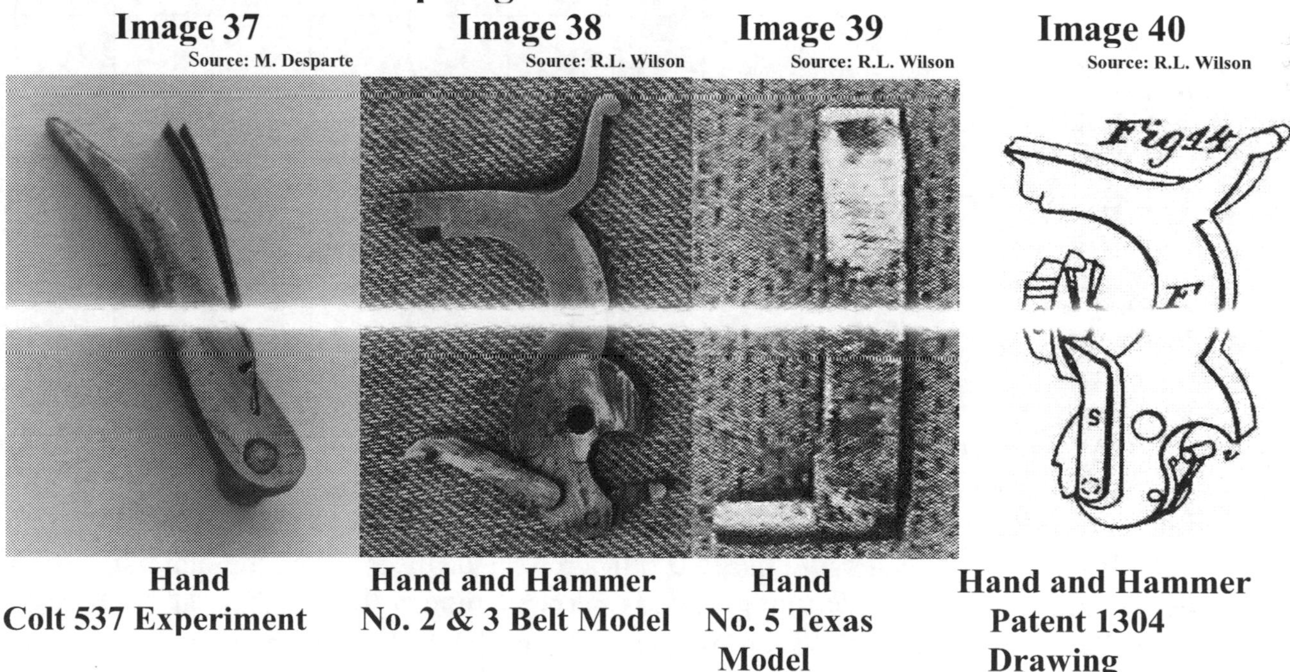

Image 37 Source: M. Desparte — **Hand Colt 537 Experiment**

Image 38 Source: R.L. Wilson — **Hand and Hammer No. 2 & 3 Belt Model**

Image 39 Source: R.L. Wilson — **Hand No. 5 Texas Model**

Image 40 Source: R.L. Wilson — **Hand and Hammer Patent 1304 Drawing**

36. Paterson Colt Pistol Variations, R.L. Wilson, Page 80, Plate No. 53

According to the Schematic Drawing, **Image 40**, the off-set hand and spring should be a visible attachment on the left side of the hammer. No similar spring is found in that location on the Colt537.

However, in **Image 37,** two extremely fine leaf springs are attached to the base of the hand by a diagonal notch, making a groove and sliding the end of the leaf spring into the groove. There also was another small notch, perpendicular to the surface of the hand just above the diagonal notch location. At this location, a remnant of a broken spring was found. Observing that there was a change in the way the spring was attached and the fact that an alternate type of groove was finally installed indicates that this was a troublesome location within the revolver. More than likely the diagonal groove resolved the problem. There is less tension on the spring at that angle, rather than a spring with a 90-degree angle caused by the perpendicular groove. No springs are shown in **Images 38 and 39 on page 63.** The broken spring in **image 37** is additional proof that Colt537 is not a counterfeit.

However, in the **Schematic Drawing, Item 26 on page 48**, there is a hand spring that is a separate item attached to the rear, left side of the frame, above the hand grip. This would apply to all the production models and Patent 1304. Obviously an improvement from the spring arrangement found on Colt537 Experiment as seen in **Image 37 on page 63**. This Colt537 type handspring does not reoccur until the 1851 Navy.

Evaluation of the Colt537 Hand and Hand-Spring

	No			Possibly				Yes		
	1	2	3	4	5	6	7	8	9	10
Was the Hand and Hand-Spring made as a new factory part?				Handmade		X				
Was the Hand and Hand-Spring off another Colt Paterson?					X	but doubtful				
Was the Hand and Hand-Spring from scrap and reworked?					X	but doubtful				
Was the Hand and Hand-Spring made by a novice?	X									

The reason for the "6" rating – Due to the fact that the hand had repairs made to it is an indication that the part was not new, more than likely was repaired by the Lawton team before production of some parts began. Therefore lack of a 10 rating. The 5's are self-explanatory. Observe the two thin grooves at the base of the hand shown in **Image 37, page 63**. One very thin groove is perpendicular to the surface, at the base of the hand. The second groove is more tangential from the surface of the hand, at its base. The groove perpendicular to the surface has two small pieces of broken leaf spring in it. The tangential groove retains the two very fine springs that are performing their job quite adequately. The tangential groove with its two very fine leaf springs appears to be the result of a repair after the original spring or springs in the perpendicular groove broke. It is believed the breakage was due to the tension on the spring's right angle making it extremely frail. File markings on the hand indicate that the hand was handmade by a Colt factory gunsmith. It was an obvious mistake by the original fabricator.

The Back-strap Comparisons

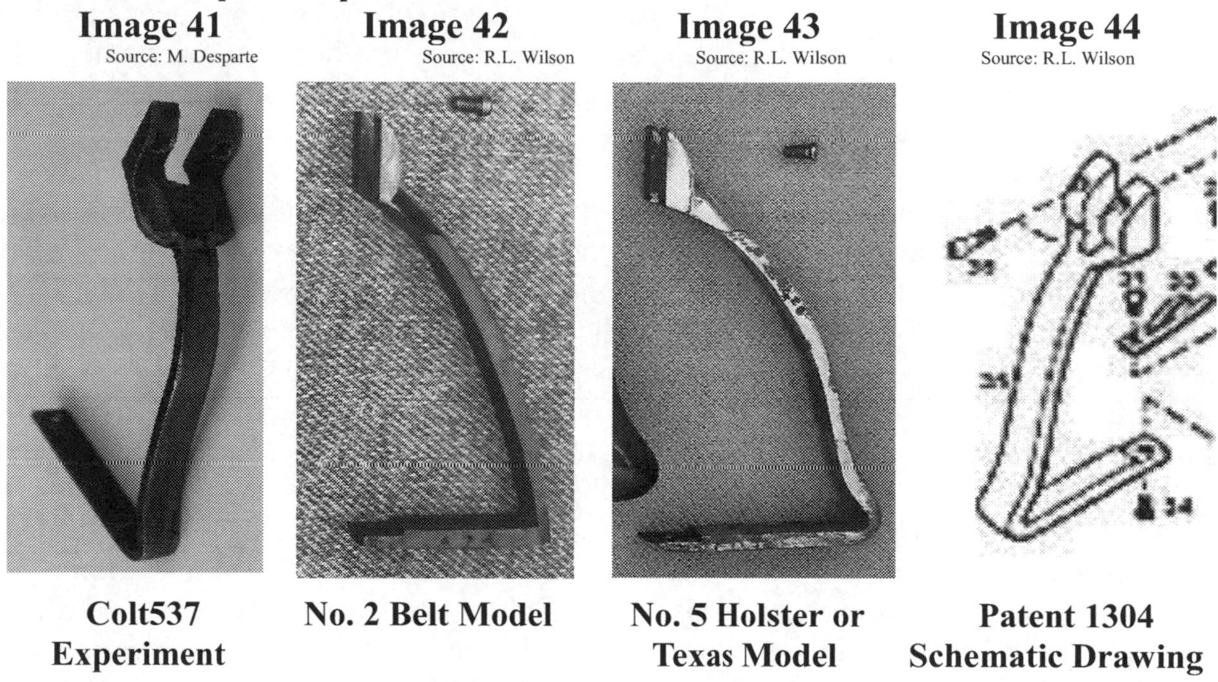

Image 41 Source: M. Desparte — **Colt537 Experiment**

Image 42 Source: R.L. Wilson — **No. 2 Belt Model**

Image 43 Source: R.L. Wilson — **No. 5 Holster or Texas Model**

Image 44 Source: R.L. Wilson — **Patent 1304 Schematic Drawing**

The schematic patent drawing, **Image 44,** does not represent any particular size or caliber**. Image 41** is of the Colt537 Experiment. **Image 42** is a straight back-strap of the Colt No. 2 Belt Model. The No. 3 Belt Model is a flared back-strap (not shown) is similar to that found on Colt537 and No. 5 Holster or Texas Model and is shown as **Image 43.**

Also important is the amount of filing found on Colt537. Coarse file markings are on rear of the frame grip. Not having a polished or refined appearance indicates that it more than likely had been handmade. It also is a fair indication that the pistol was made prior to the completion or installation of machinery for mass production. There is a fine coating of rust which had been more or less neutralized with a light amount of gun oil.

Colt537 Back-Strap Screw Sizes

Location	Screw Number	AOL	Head Thickness	TPI	Shaft
Left side - Worn	No. 4	.388	.086	.36	Short
Right side - Worn	No. 4	.388	.090	.36	Short
Bottom Grip Screw	No. 4	.268	.052	.36	Short

Historical Significance of the Colt Paterson Experiment

The screws, plus the screw at the bottom of the back-strap, **Items 34 and 35 in the schematic drawing, on page 48,** can be unscrewed. This will enable the detachment of the back-strap, including the wooden portion of the hand-grip, **Item 33**. The back-strap and hand-grip of Colt537 come off as a unit. The wooden hand-grip is then able to be separated from the back-strap without running the risk of damage. Many times, markings were written in pencil in the groove of the wooden hand-grip. The screws holding the back-strap to the frame were significantly worn from excessive use, as if it were taken apart numerous times in the past. The exterior of the revolver, however, does not display that same amount of wear. The comparative amount of use between the frame and the back-strap created more questions than answers. The back-strap may be made of a lesser quality of metal than would be expected.

I will repeat this over and over, that the continuous dismantling of the revolver, as evidenced, by the worn and scarred appearance of the screws, may be due to the need of previous prospective buyers, to inspect the internal firing system and compare the findings with that of the No. 3 Belt or the No. 5 Holster or Texas Model. For some reason, those inspectors missed the significance of what they were seeing. The problem is that Colt537 Experiment is just that, an experiment. From this experiment, the parts for any of the production models, and especially the No. 5, may not have the exact same configuration as those fabricated in the Colt537 Experiment. This is due to the fact that Colt537 is the fore-runner (mostly handmade) of the first .28 caliber No. 1 Pocket or Baby Model, the .28 and .31 caliber of the No. 2 Model, and .31 and .34 caliber No. 3 Belt Model, and finally, the .36 caliber No. 5 Holster or Texas Model. This last revolver was more than likely completed in early 1838. The parts of the Colt537 Experiment are larger than those used in the No. 3 and possibly slightly smaller than those fabricated for the No. 5, since Colt537 is a .31 caliber. For example, in all cases, the hammer has a slightly different angle of attack when rotating onto the percussion cap, when released in the firing process. Another part under serious scrutiny is the sear, and Trigger extension arm. It may be longer, or shorter, depending on which of the four production revolvers one is discussing, at any particular time.

Evaluation of the Back-Strap

	No			Possibly				Yes		
	1	2	3	4	5	6	7	8	9	10
Was the Back-Strap made as a new part at the factory?								Hand-made		X
Was the Back-Strap taken from a used or faulty parts bin?				Possibly		X				
Was the Back-Strap off another Colt Paterson Experiment?				Possibly		X				
Was the Back-Strap reworked for Colt537 Experiment?								X		
Was the Back-Strap made by a hobbyist?	X									

The reason for the "10" ratings – The back-strap is thinner than the normal Colt back-strap. It is the same thickness as the fore-grip extension of Colt537's frame, i.e., both are the same thickness. There is a sufficient amount of file markings on this strap to believe it was hand made by factory personnel. And, therefore, this is not a part regularly made by machinery that may have been in the Colt factory at that time. The back-strap also had the following markings or numbers on the butt end of the strap, "AH" or "71". Because of the amount of filing found on the back-strap, and the numbering on the butt of the back-strap, it could be a recycled part found in the Colt factory scrap bin.

The Wooden Hand-Grip

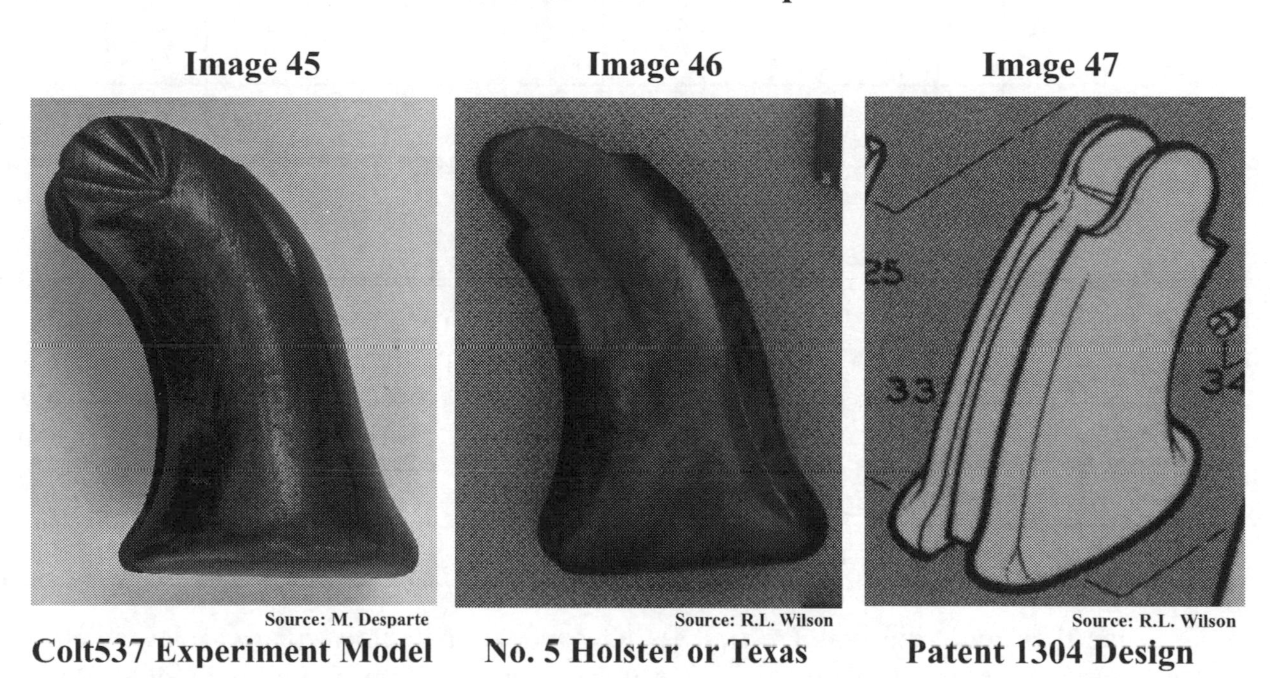

Image 45 — Source: M. Desparte — **Colt537 Experiment Model**

Image 46 — Source: R.L. Wilson — **No. 5 Holster or Texas**

Image 47 — Source: R.L. Wilson — **Patent 1304 Design**

Notice the neck of the hand-grip of Colt537, it appears to be thicker than that of the No. 5 Holster Model and that of the profile image found in the August 29, 1839, Patent drawings. Colt537 was powered by a flat or leaf mainspring rather than the "V" type mainsprings found in the production models. The curvature of the flat mainspring may have been such that it required additional freedom in this area of the hand-grip. **One must remember that this is the first full flared grip, the beginning of a new concept in handgrips.** The wooden hand-grip had a groove that enabled the mainspring and back-strap to fit neatly within it, **see Image 47,** if the groove was part of the manufacturing process, the groove would have been neatly done. It would have had sharp corners and flat surfaces. This one was made by using a crude file and chisel. Little time was wasted on making this grip; therefore, its expediency was employed to obtain a working experiment within the shortest amount of time. Colt was continuously under pressure to make a salable product. Therefore, the most expedient way to proceed in the development of Colt537 experiment was to take available existing parts and fit them to the situation

Evaluation of the Wooden Hand-Grip										
	No			Possibly				Yes		
	1	2	3	4	5	6	7	8	9	10
Was the Wooden Hand-Grip made as a new part at the factory?							Grip had an odd shaped neck...			X
Was the Wooden Hand-Grip taken off another Colt Paterson?	X									
Was the Wooden Hand-Grip taken from a scrap bin & reworked?	X									
Was the Wooden Hand-Grip made by a novice?				Poor quality		X				

The reason for the, "10" rating - This flared hand-grip is not shaped exactly like other flared hand-grips. The neck of the grip is thicker than those grips on the production models. It also doesn't have the quality of workmanship it should have. Its crudeness dictates that this flared grip is the first hand made grip ever produced by the Colt mfg. Later, others picked up on the shape of the design. The mainspring within the grip, because of it being a flat or leaf mainspring, may have required more room to operate correctly, thus the thicker neck of the grip. The power of a mainspring is determined by the location and thickness of the curve when activated.

Since the hand grip was the first flared hand grip, it shows that Colt was having thoughts about increasing accuracy even before he made the production models. Recall that the first and second production models, i.e., the Pocket/Baby and No. 2 Belt did not address any serious concern in this area because the design of the first two models had straight handgrips, i.e., void of any concern regarding accuracy.

The Mainspring

The mainspring and screw attachment to the lower end of the front strap is shown in **Images 48** and **49, next page,** illustrates a "V" type mainspring attachment. This is the mainspring found in all of the Colt Paterson production models, and represents a shift away from the use of leaf/straight mainsprings found in the last two experimental revolvers[37]&[38] and futuristic drawings of what was to be the production model[39].

37. Paterson Colt Pistol Variations, L.R. Wilson, page 80, plate 53, and Colt537, Image 7 page 14 of this manuscript
38. The Story of Colt's Revolver, Wm Edwards, page 54, Engineering drawings of pre-production Lawton-Colt at Paterson
39. Paterson Colt Pistol Variations, L.R. Wilson, page 77, figure 11

Image 48

Leaf Mainspring
Source: L. R. Wilson

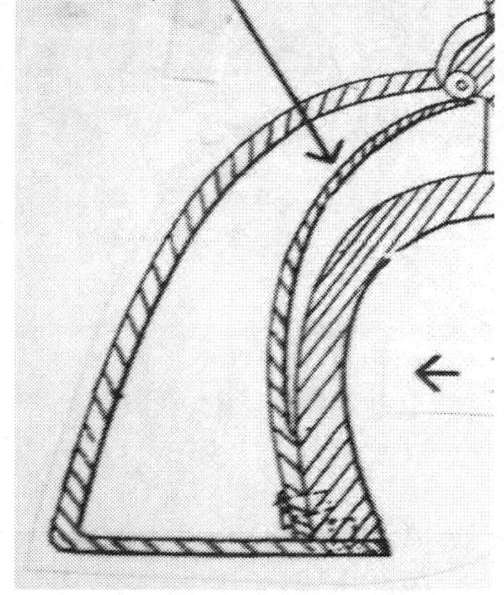

Colt537 Experiment

Image 49

"V" Type Mainspring
Source: L. R. Wilson

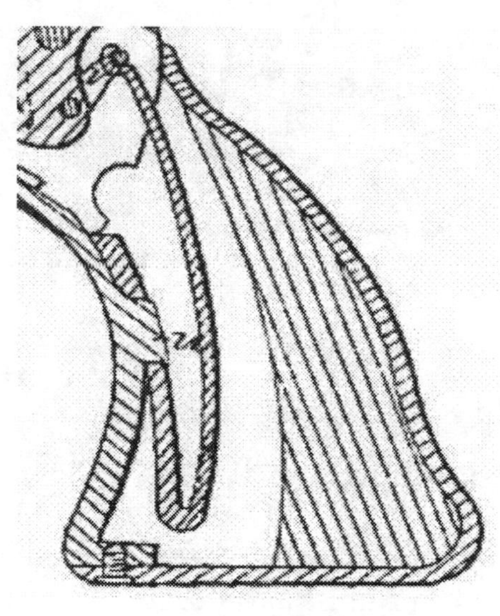

U.S. Patent 1304
Production Model

The leaf type or flat mainspring is found in the first Colt-Lawton experiment, what was then called the No. 2 Colt Belt Model, **Image 6 on page 8**. Another image of this No. 2 Belt Model experimental is shown on **page 54** of The Story of Colt's Revolver by Wm Edwards. There may have been others, but **what I am trying to bring out is that flat mainsprings were used in many of the Colt experimental revolvers. The shift to "V" type mainsprings occurred with the four production models.**

The Difference between the Colt537 Experiment and the Production Models

The articulation point on the two Lawton-Colt Experimental Models is between the hammer and the upper end of the mainspring. In the patent design the mainspring articulates with a cam or stirrup. This is not the case with Colt537 Experiment. Here a roller is attached to the hammer and rides the leaf spring during the activation of the hammer. The other end is screwed to the end of the fore-strap. The Colt537 leaf mainspring is a crudely constructed, rough cut piece of metal showing file markings in all directions. The screw hole, enabling it to be attached to the bottom of the fore-strap, was noticeably off center, obviously a rush job. It is evident that the individual assigned to making this part was not concerned with aesthetics. An image of the Colt537 leaf mainspring is shown in **Image 50.** Functionality was his principle objective. This single

Image 50

Single Leaf Mainspring of Colt537

Source: M. Despaarte

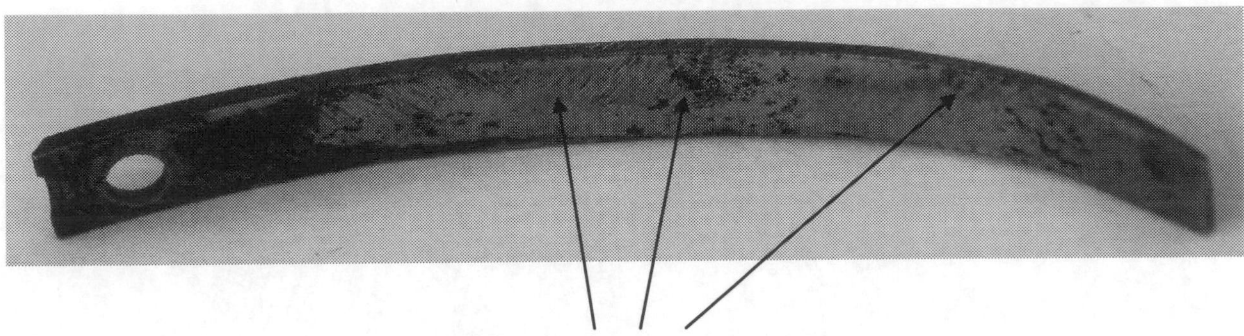

Notice the File Markings

leaf mainspring is similar to that found in the single action handguns such as, the Paterson prototype Belt experimental,[40] the Lawton - Colt pre-production pistol engineering drawings,[41] the Colt 1851 Navy, Colt 1860 Army, and others. The mainspring screw on Colt537 had a partially filed off screw head, not an original Colt product. The screw, bottom right-hand corner of the grip, **Image 48, on the previous page** is found to have a thinner head and be completely flat. The screw used to attach the flat mainspring to the fore-strap may have been the work of a novice. This does not imply that the other parts of the gun were also made by the hands of a novice.

Evaluation of the Leaf or Flat Mainspring

	No			Possibly				Yes		
	1	2	3	4	5	6	7	8	9	10
Was the Flat Mainspring made as a new part at the factory?										X
Was the Flat Mainspring taken off another Colt Paterson?	X									
Was the Flat Mainspring taken from a scrap bin and reworked?				X						
Was the Flat Mainspring made by a shoe maker?					Looks as if it was...			X		

The reason for the, "10" rating – the rough filing marks indicate that this leaf-spring was not made for show, but for expediency, and built by a low-level employee, possibly learning gunsmith craftsmanship within the Colt factory.

40. Paterson Colt Pistol Variations, R.L. Wilson, Page 80, Plate No. 53
41. The Story of Colt's Revolver, Wm Edwards, Page 54

The Three Piece to Single Piece Frames of Production Models

The Colt537 Experiment is a .31 caliber revolver. The production models varied in caliber and size. The Colt537 Experiment, although originally described as a copy of a Belt Model, isn't a copy, and isn't a Belt Model, nor is it a Holster or Texas Model. The size of the Colt537 Experiment frame is that of a .36 caliber. It was the last experimental design. It was used as a reproducible model. Once the first production models were proven safe and operational, replications of the images were shown in the August 29, 1839 Patent 1304. However, since Colt537 is a .31 caliber, on a frame sized to carry a .36 caliber cylinder, I designated Colt537 as a Colt537 Experimental Model; **see Appendix 2, pages 1 through 5**. A simple analogy would be the advancement in design of an experimental car worked up in clay form. The design was used in making four different cars of similar design, but each a different size, and use.

The Frame of Colt537 Experiment Was Made From Scratch

Colt537 was made from three plates, roughly 5/16 thick. These three-pieces, **view Image 51**, were cut and shaped into what was to become the frame of the Colt537 Experiment. The left and right side were odd, triangular, mirror images of each other. The center housed the internal workings, but also had an extension which was to become the beginning of the front hand-grip. Notice the irregularities in milling and filing out the pockets and recesses needed for the placement of the internal firing system. Before this description goes too far, the size of this frame depended on the size of the cylinder which was governed by the volume of the chambers, which, in turn, would contain a sufficient amount of powder to propel the bullet or ball at a menacing velocity and impact. Colt, realizing he was stepping off into the unknown, took what appear to be some short, cautious steps in planning this experiment.

Image 51

Source: Michael Desparte

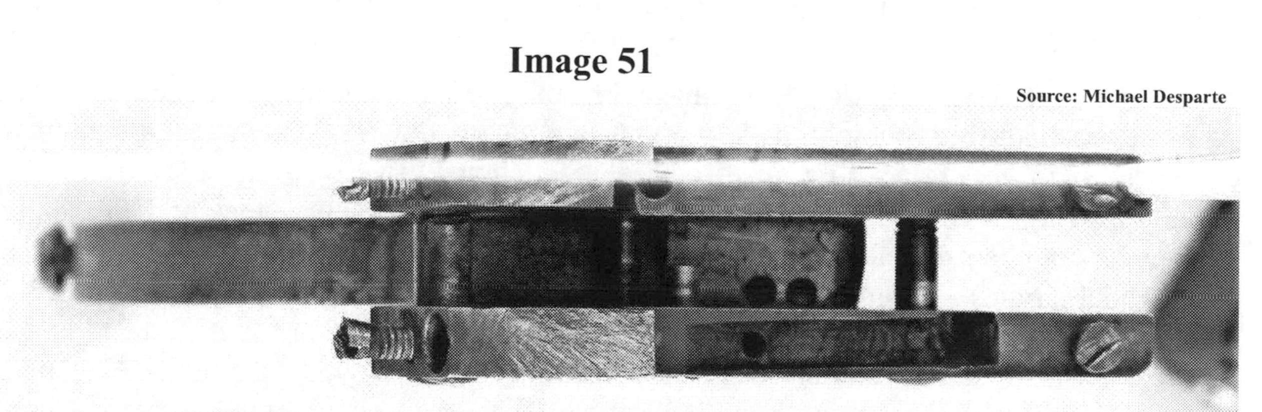

Three-Piece Frame of Colt537 Experiment

In making the .36 caliber model, the frame was going to be slightly larger, and capable of incorporating a cylinder with five .36 caliber chambers. He realized he would be making a shortcut if this frame would be strong enough to sustain the shock of firing a .36 caliber ball. The recoil shield, the barrel coupled with an elongated .31 caliber cylinder would form the needed large pieces. The three frame pieces would then be brazed together and become the enlarged frame of the Colt537 Experiment.

Colt Paterson Frames

Image 52 **Image 53** **Image 54** **Image 55**

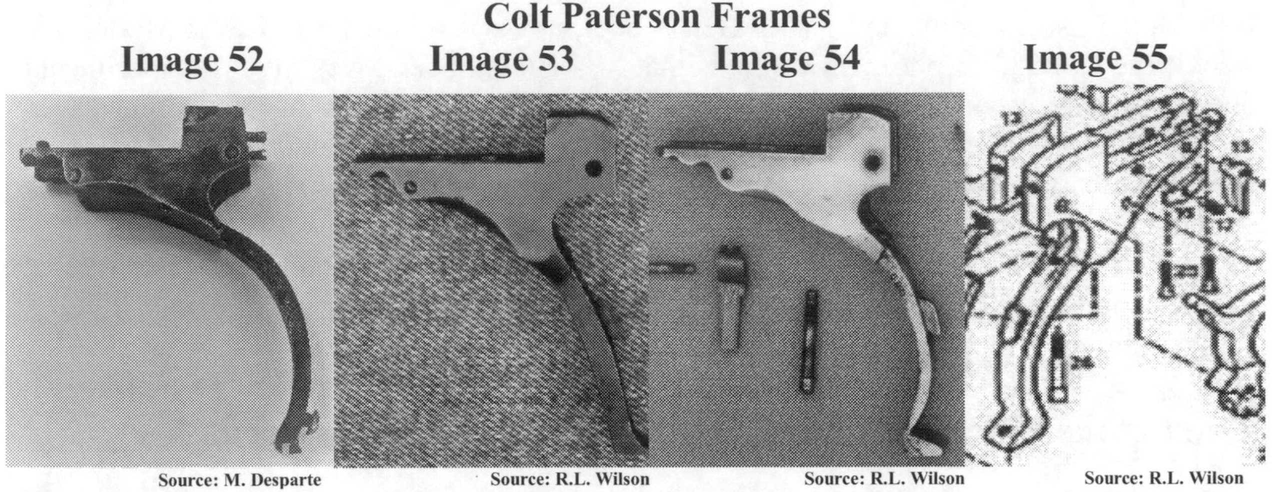

Source: M. Desparte Source: R.L. Wilson Source: R.L. Wilson Source: R.L. Wilson

Image 52	Image 53	Image 54	Image 55
Colt537 Experiment	**No. 2 & 3 Belt**	**No. 5 Holster/Texas**	**U.S. Patent 1034**
Three Piece Frame	**Single Piece Frame**	**Single Piece Frame**	**Single Piece Frame**
Hand-Made 1837-38	**Machined Late 1837**	**Machined 1838-42**	**Pat. Aug 29,1839**

The internal firing mechanism would also have to be scaled down or up to completely accommodate the size of the cylinder. That size could be a .28, .31, .34, or .36 caliber cylinder. The four internal firing systems (associated with the four different calibers) would need to be fabricated, and then attempt to install all of these pieces into the estimated size of the cavity within the frame. Repeated adjustments to the frame and internal parts would be made and eventually an operational frame would be composed. The activity would be similar to that of constructing a pocket watch. Good luck. The tolerances need to be within 1,000th of an inch.

Compare **Images 52 and 54 to image 55, Image 52** and **54** are almost exact images of each other and of the schematic drawing similar to the U.S. Patent 1304 schematic design seen in **Image 55** submitted to the U.S. Patent Office on August 29, 1839. The patent drawing was completed after the frame in **Image 55** was machine fabricated. **Image 53** does not appear to be similar. This is due to this Image being that of a No. 2 Belt Model having a straight hand grip. The only difference between **Image 52** and **53** or **54**, is that **Image 52** is of the Colt537 Experiment, acknowledging the difference in size of the internal firing mechanism and other parts associated with it being a .31 caliber, with parts having the same configuration. Of course there are slight exceptions; including **Image 52** (Colt537) is a three-piece frame. **Images 53, 54** and **55** are depicting single piece frames. The internal irregularities and cavities could not have been designed without it, initially being pieced together for correct internal part location and operation

Image 56

Source: M. Desparte

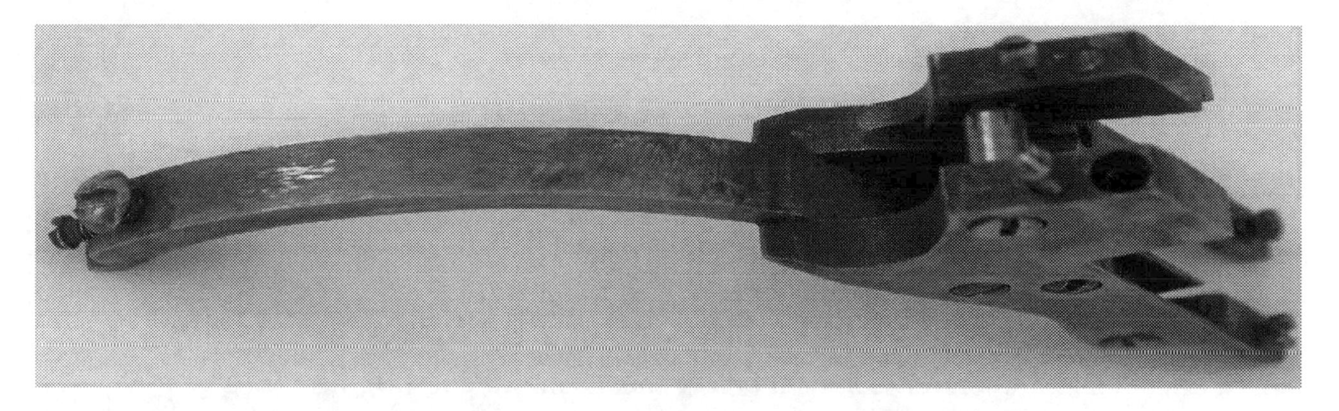

Additional Image of the Frame of Colt537 Experiment

The forward part of grip strap pieced together with the left and right frame plates.

The design of the frame was shaped so as to take on a particular cylinder size. The amount of gunpowder needed for the weapon to be effective had to be determined prior to the cylinder's development. If one were to determine a particular revolver was to be a .36 caliber, then the volume of gunpowder for each chamber must be known. If the revolver were to be a five-shot revolver then one begins to understand the size by volume of each chamber within the cylinder. Hence, the length and diameter of the cylinder can be determined. Once the diameter and length of the receiver/cylinder are determined, the dimensions of the recoil shield can be found. Then the length of the arbor holding the receiver/cylinder in place can be estimated and finally, after all this has been completed, the needed size of the frame to support the barrel is determined. The arbor length is calculated and the first blush frame can be fabricated. The three plates are cut and shaped to resemble the silhouette of any one of the production models.

The frame found in **Image 55 on page 72**, i.e., U.S. Patent No. 1304, August 29, 1839, resembles the design of any one of the production model frames found in either one of **Images 53** and **54.** They are exact products of patent 1304. Colt537 is not an exact replica of any one of the production models, due to its three-piece composition and adjustments in design made for machine manufacturing.

Additional images of Colt537's three-piece frame are **Images 53,** and **54,** except they have one-piece frames. The exact location of screws, and platforms, are now needed to be identified, for the mounting of the internal firing system. Identifying the precise location of cavities and ledges within the frame, which will afford a location for specific internal parts, is necessary. It is assumed that this will be a difficult task. The internal mechanisms, although being similar to those in the earlier models, will require their own exact location, size, and configuration. It is understood that every fabricated piece of the revolver must be a perfect fit with each member piece. It is suspected the miscellaneous parts bin was filled with mistakes.

.

In developing the first frame, it is not known exactly where those cavities, drill holes and part locations might be, since the internal firing system had not yet been developed. Each piece or element is roughly made and tested. During the refinement stage, many of the functioning parts must have a tolerance of, equal to or less than, one thousandth of an inch. The frame, more than likely, would have had to be disassembled and reassembled several times before a satisfactory, finely tuned revolver is accomplished. It is not known as to how many times these three plates needed to be taken apart, adjusted, and then reassembled before the gunsmith got it right.

Evaluation of the Three-Piece Frame

	No			Possibly				Yes		
	1	2	3	4	5	6	7	8	9	10
Was the Three-piece Frame a new factory handmade part?							Handmade		X	
Was the Three-piece Frame taken off another Colt Paterson?	X									
Was the Three-piece Frame made for a specific revolver?									X	
Was the Three-piece Frame made as an experiment for production models?									X	
Was the Three-piece Frame taken from scrap and reworked?	X	Depends if it was a large scrap piece...								
Was the Three-piece Frame made by a novice?	X									

The reason for the "10" ratings – A three-piece frame more than likely was made as a model for all four production models. This was due to the size of each model. The gunsmith, more than likely, had to make his own three-piece frame.

Paterson Production Model Revolvers Were Not Entirely Machine Manufactured

Machinery had to be designed and made in order to manufacture the Colt Paterson parts. Some parts were too complex to be fabricated with the primitive machinery existing in the 1836 era. Workers were relegated to perform many finishing tasks by hand. The significance is, working parts of other Paterson revolvers of similar caliber, were not interchangeable."[42] Colt537, being an experimental model, is composed of almost all manually finished parts.

A perfect example of complex handmade parts is the Sear, and the Trigger Extension Arm.

Image 57

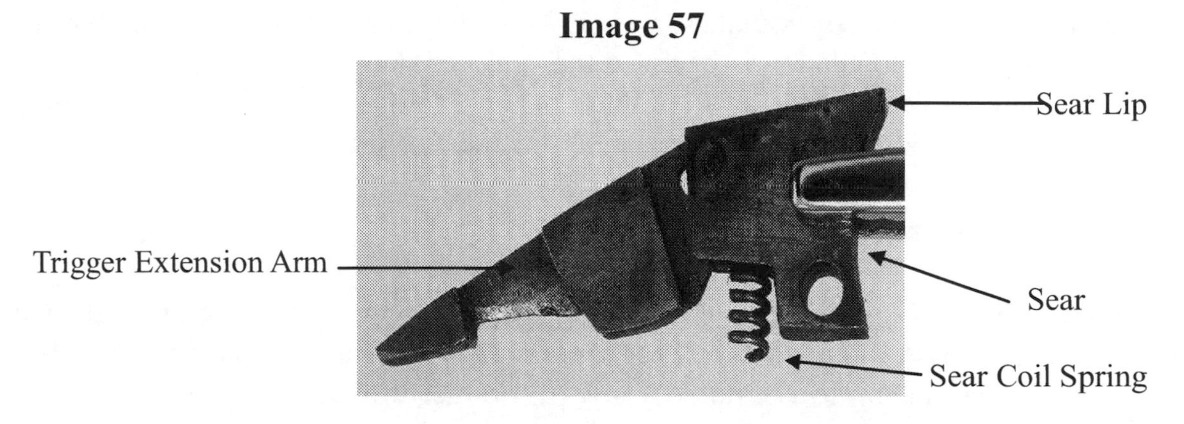

Source: M. Desparte

Trigger Extension Arm and Sear of Colt 537

The sear assembly has two coil springs. One of these coil springs is visible here in **Image 57**; This visible coil spring is extending downward from the bottom of the sear; the other can be seen in **Image 58.**When the hammer is pulled back into a firing position, the lower portion of the hammer face forces the sear to move forward, left, against the trigger extension arm which then forces the trigger to flip downward, readying the revolver for firing, **see Image 79 on page 91**. At the same time, the upper right corner, the lip, of the sear catches the full cock/firing ledge on the hammer preventing the hammer from slamming forward and hitting the percussion cap. The revolver is now ready for firing. When the trigger is squeezed the trigger extension arm/bar is then being pulled forward, left, placing stress on the coil spring by stretching it between the trigger extension bar and the sear. As the stress increases to its ultimate limit, the sear detaches itself from the hammer notch. The hammer then slams forward igniting the percussion cap and fires the revolver. While all this is happening, the lower coil spring forces the sear upward and back into a position to catch the hammer in its next cocking recycle with the hammer. There will be greater detail later on in this paper.

The sear and trigger extension arm/bar shown in **Image 57** and **58** appear to be slightly different from that shown in **Images 59** and **60**. That is because Colt537 was the experiment, actually the last revision for this experimental revolver. The model previous to Colt537 was that found in **Image 6 on page 8,** of this manuscript, and **page 80** in **Paterson Colt Pistol Variations**, Plate No. 53. This revolver looks quite similar to Colt537 with some exceptions. The hand grip is straight rather than flared, as the

42. Paterson Colt Pistol Variations, R.L. Wilson, Page 6, Par 2, L 1

Colt537. Its cylinder length is the same. Being a .29 caliber, it also had a smooth bore, a flat leaf mainspring, and lacked a frame plate. It was labeled as a No. 2 Belt Model. In summary, there is a significant difference when compared to the No. 2 Belt production model.

What is most important is that the Colt537 sear assembly has two points of articulation. The upper point of articulation is between the trigger extension arm and the sear. The other point of articulation is between the sear and the hammer, pivoting around the sear screw. This is the second most complex part within the revolver, the first being the hammer which will be addressed further on in this manuscript.

Colt537 was Meeting All Expectations

The trigger extension arm of Colt537 was doing its job by acting as a link between the sear and the trigger. It extended it, but not completely. That was a minor problem. The production trigger extension arm required a slightly longer trigger extension arm. Also, Colt537 was powered by two coil springs attached to the sear. The upper coil spring was fitted in between the trigger extension arm and the sear, as seen in **Image 58 page 77.** Take a close look at this piece. It is obvious that it was hand made. The slot was difficult to make in such a small part. If it were to break it would render the revolver useless. The lower coil spring had greater accessibility. Here the difficulty would hinge on not losing this coil spring when cleaning the revolver. Breakage was another factor. Hence, Pliny Lawton and Colt agreed to eliminate coil springs in favor of leaf/flat springs. They are less costly, easier to install, with less labor required in making the sear as well as the springs. What is seen in **Image 61 on page 78** is that the patent drawing of the trigger, trigger extension arm, and the sear are powered by one split sear spring. The same points of articulation are retained. The functions are similar to those found in Colt537. All production models had this adjustment, as seen in **Images 59** and **60 on page 78**. After Colt537 was completed and tested, Pliny Lawton and Colt concentrated on the production of models for sale. The first production model was the No.1 Ring Lever rifle, followed by the No. 1 Pocket or Baby Model. **See Time Line, Page 17**. The original Colt537 Experiment was used as the prototype. Each part of the revolver was studied so as to determine the type of machinery that would be needed to duplicate (as close as possible) one or more of the Colt537 parts. Once the machinery was acquired, pieces of Colt537 Experiment were copied or revised, and placed into production with the obvious.

”importance of sales to the government. The No. 1 rifle was an understandable product, but why the pocket Revolver”?[43]

“It would appear that the P.A. Mfg. Co felt the diminutive arm would have a good market, and that the relatively small size meant a small

43. Paterson Colt Pistol Variations, R.L. Wilson, Page 96, par 3, L 2

investment. Breaking in the workmen on this arm also allowed for Pliny Lawton and Colt to improve the manufacturing process and develop details leading to more imposing larger sized pistols."[44] **See Time Line, Page 17.**

Consequently, the No. 5 Holster or Texas Model was the last to be manufactured. And it is the revolver that created the greatest demand. In addition it enabled the greatest effect to occur on the growth and prosperity of the Southwest.

Image 58

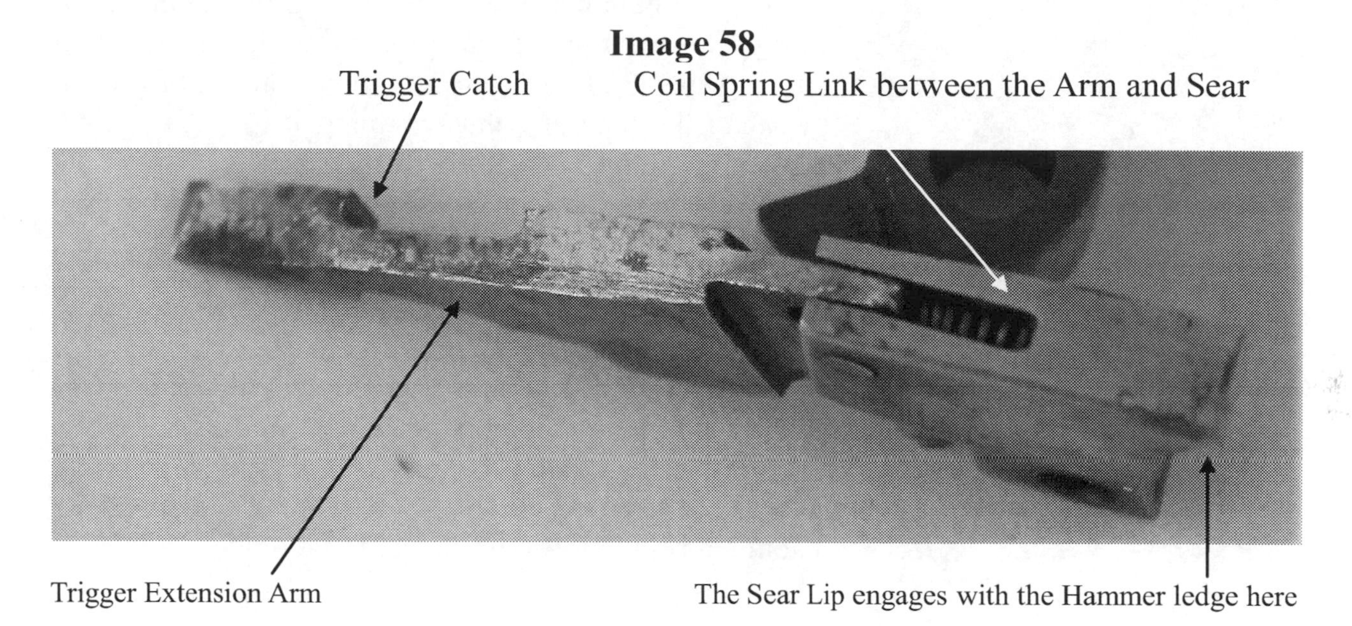

Top View of the Trigger and Sear Assembly, Unique to Colt537

Important in the above image are the file markings, the lack of squared corners and the fact that the assembly is powered by coil springs. The file markings and rough cuts indicate that this key piece in the Colt537 was hand made. Take a close look at all of the corners and angles in **Images 57** and **Image 58.** Coil springs powered the Colt537 sear and trigger assembly, however, in the production model, coil springs were set aside and leaf or flat-springs were employed. It is obvious that the leaf or flat-springs are less expensive and more serviceable than the coil spring. All of the four Paterson models were powered by leaf/flat-springs. Colt537 was made as the last experiment. It eventually satisfied all the requirements that Pliny Lawton and Colt wanted in the performance of this revolver. Most of the Colt537's parts were then machine produced, having the same points of articulation, and as close as possible to that of Colt537. Production of these revolvers was made during the late months of 1838. It took over a year to produce the patent drawings. These drawings reflect each of final machined parts of the basic design. These drawings, because they lack any scale, represent all four of the production models. It is amazing as to how close they came to the original handmade product.

44. Paterson Colt Pistol Variations, R.L. Wilson, Page 96, par 3, L 8

"Fall, 1837, first production rifles (were) completed, the No. 1 Ring Lever model, followed shortly by the first production handguns, the Pocket or Baby Paterson."[45]

Image 59 - Nos 2 and 3 Belt Model

Source: R.L. Wilson

A concave curve on the back of the sear (the lip) fits against the lower round of the hammer. The hammer is cocked; a flat spring situated under the sear forces this lip into the hammer/sear catch, setting the hammer for firing. This rotation will also force the trigger extension arm forward. Pulling the trigger forces the sear forward, releasing the hammer, thus enabling it to slam against the percussion cap and firing the revolver.

Image 60 - No 5 Holster or Texas Model

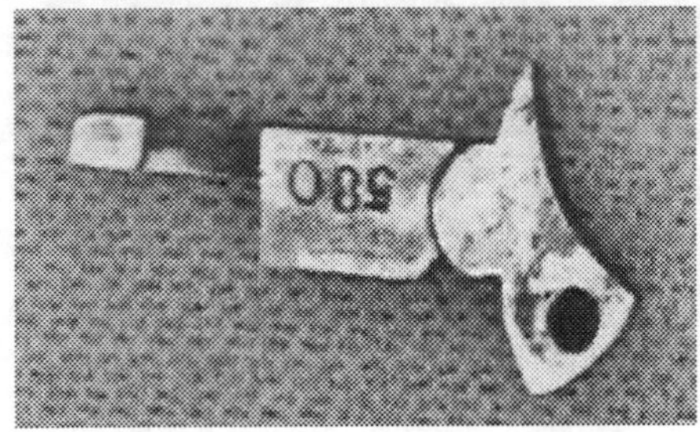

Source: R.L. Wilson

This sear assembly is similar to that of the Colt537 as well. The only significant difference between the No. 1 Pocket or Baby (not shown) and this No. 5 Holster or Texas Model sear assembly is the scale of the assembly. The No. 5 is significantly larger than the Pocket Model, and also larger than the No. 2 and 3 Belt Models. The machined right angle cuts appear to be obvious.

Image 61 - Sear Assembly with Trigger (1839 Patent 1304 Drawing)

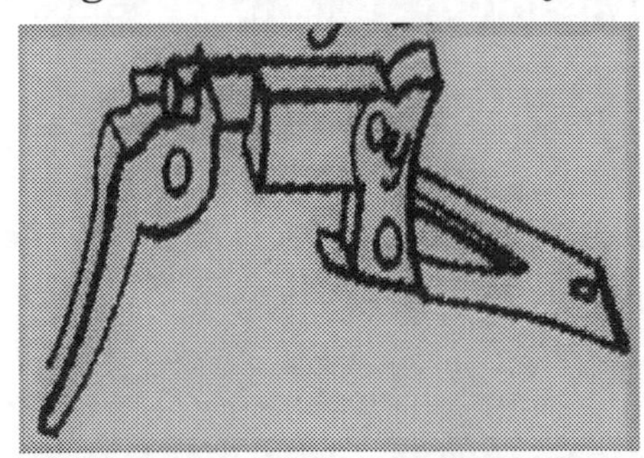

Source: R.L. Wilson

The patent drawing of the sear and the trigger arrangement are drawings of the patent and are not of any particular scale. That is to say that the image of the sear is a general drawing. The same conceptual drawing can be used in describing any of the four production revolvers. The sear of each of the revolver models are of a different scale. Except the No. 2 and 3 Belt Models which have the same size frame and all of its parts are relative to the scale of the frame. The No. 1 Pocket or Baby Model is the largest scale, meaning it is the smallest of the four production models, and the No. 5 being the smallest scale, meaning the largest size of the four production models.

The above statement is key to understanding the appearance of a particular part used in any one of the Colt revolvers. The principal thought should be, when looking at an individual part; does its function meet the claim in the patent? If the function does not meet any of the claims, it more than likely would not be a product made by Colt. If there

45. Paterson Colt Pistol Variations, RL Wilson, Page 67 Col 2, Par 3, L 1

are functions of a part that meet one or more claims, that part more than likely is a Colt product. Many times the function of a claim is proven, but the part does not appear to be exactly shaped as a corresponding specific drawing found in the U.S. Patent No. 1304.

A good example would be the difference in design, between the sear and trigger extension arm found in Colt537 Experiment **Image 57 on page 75** (which is minus the trigger and one flat spring) and the design drawing found in the U.S. Patent No. 1304, in **Image 61 on page 78,**. Also, observe how closely the production pieces of **Image 59**, i.e., Nos. 2 and 3 Belt Model and **Image 60** compare to No. 5 Holster or Texas Model, and that of Colt537.

It is worth noting, the trigger extension arm is composed of almost all 90 degree cuts and grinds. It was obviously machine made. Also, there are no coil springs powering this assembly. The sear labeled "Y" above is powered by a dual purpose flat spring extending under the sear shown in **Image 72 on page 86.** The other prong of the forked spring powers the bolt.

Colt537 was the experiment; it also the design guide for all four of the production models. Only the size of each of the revolvers is different. All were made by newly acquired Colt factory machinery. Each workman fabricated an individual part, be it barrels, cylinders, or frames, using specific jigs or patterns which the parts were to resemble. As the jumble of parts was collected at the end of the processing line, one or several individuals would assemble the revolver. Parts requiring additional attention were filed or touched up as they came together, and eventually were made to operate smoothly. Sometimes, it only took a one thousandth of an inch to cause and/or rectify the problem. At this point, each assembly may have appeared similar to the next, but not close enough for parts to be interchangeable with others of the same model. Here again, it must be reiterated that since Colt537 was a .31 caliber sitting on a .36 caliber frame, the internal working parts would not be interchangeable with a .31 caliber model, nor would they from a .36 caliber model. They had to be made individually for that specific revolver. Therefore, again it speaks to the fact that it is experimental. Without the experience gained working at the Colt Patent Arms factory, it is hardly imaginable a private gunsmith would spend the time to make several parts of, say, the hammer, before it was able to fit within the frame, and have it operate in conjunction with other internal pieces of Colt537 or any one of the four production models, for that matter.

Getting back to the lack of interchangeable parts, guns manufactured in Paterson, New Jersey, often ended up in the southern states or on the southwestern frontier. If a hand-grip were damaged and needed to be replaced, more than likely, that individual part would be nowhere to be found, in say, Texas. Consequently, a closely fitting piece of discarded metal, found in some scrap bin, would be filed or ground down and adjusted to fit in its place. Many a Colt has been denied authenticity because of foreign parts added in a repair. Speaking to that issue,

"Paterson pistols were not entirely machine manufactured; therefore, various parts of the pistol may or may not be interchangeable with another of the same size."[46]

And, before completion of each revolver, hand fitting was required.

"Colt had a production line similar to those of present-day automobile assembly lines where workers fabricated or machined some parts of the automobile and then passed it on along the line to the next worker. But, at the Paterson Plant, a certain amount of hand fitting was required by each, with the result that small differences were evident."[47]

This could explain the rough surfaces found on the barrel, frame, and hammer of Colt537.

The Colt537 Hammer

The Colt537 Experiment, **Image 62, next page,** is made from two hammers. The hammer is composed of a lower section, the base, i.e., the forward face of the lower part of the hammer. The other end of the hammer is called the thumb spur. One uses the thumb spur on this section of the hammer to cock the revolver, i.e., pulling the hammer back by the thumb spur until the cocking ledge of the hammer engages with the lip of the sear, **see Image 63,** making the gun ready for firing. The final section of the hammer is the hammer's striking face. When firing, the trigger is squeezed, the sear disengages the hammer, and the hammer head swings forward and strikes the percussion cap. This ignites the cap, causing a spark which travels the length of the nipple or tube and ignites the powder charge. The explosion sends the bullet on its way.

The Construction of the Hammer

As mentioned previously the Colt537 Experiment's hammer is made of two pieces, **see Image 62.** Obviously, there was no existing hammer with the correct length or strike to hit any one of the five percussion caps loaded on the nipple of each of the firing chambers. A splice was done by using a tongue and groove technique. Apparently, one of the Colt factory gunsmiths took two hammers, cut off the striker, just ahead of the thumb spur, and then cut the second hammer roughly in the same place to elongate the stem of the striker

46. Paterson Colt Pistol Variations, R.L. Wilson, Page 6, Par 2, L 1
47. Paterson Colt Pistol Variations, R.L. Wilson, Page 6, Par 2, L 4

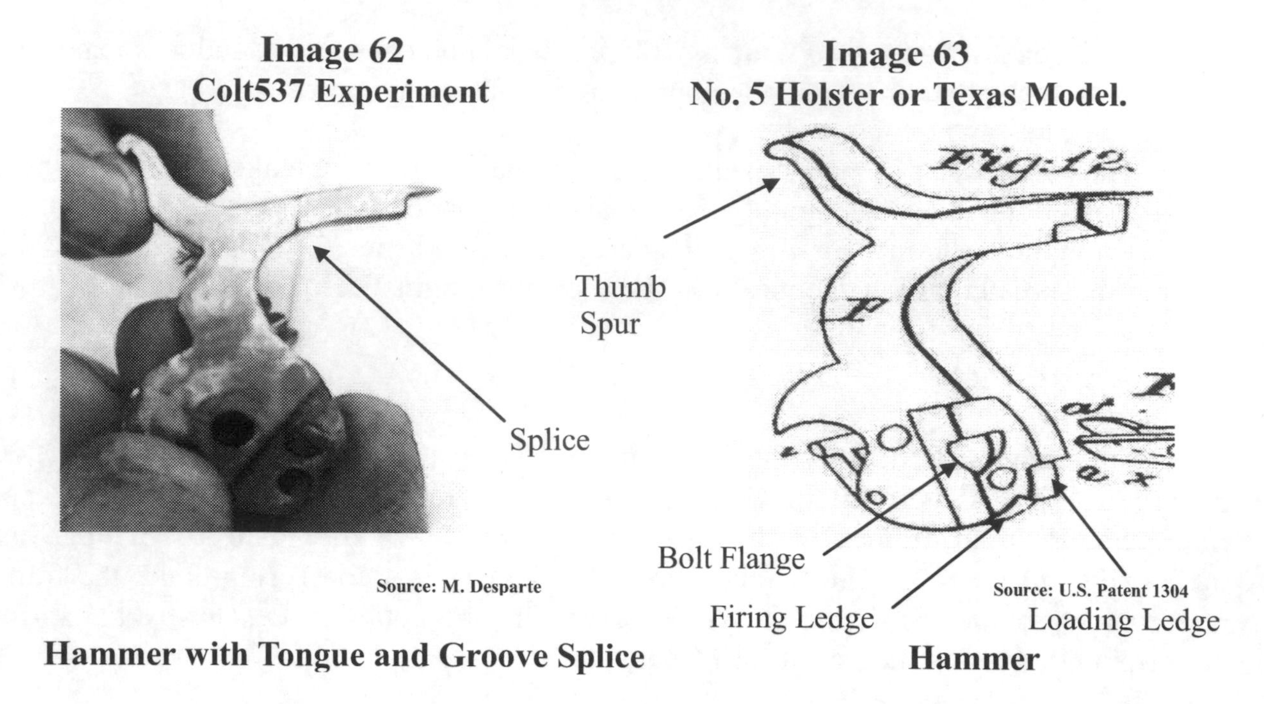

Image 62
Colt537 Experiment

Source: M. Desparte

Hammer with Tongue and Groove Splice

Image 63
No. 5 Holster or Texas Model.

Source: U.S. Patent 1304

Hammer

The number of operations the hammer performs during the cocking process is phenomenal. As the hammer is drawn back for firing, the bolt drops out of the cylinder stop slot. At the same time the hammer is also forcing the hand upward, catching one of the teeth of the circular ratchet. **See Item 7 on page 48**. This forces the rotation of the cylinder to the next firing position. The bolt then reestablishes itself in the next bolt stop slot assuring that a cylinder remains aligned with the bore of the barrel.

Once this is accomplished, the shooter's thumb is released from the hammer spur. This then enables the shooter to aim the revolver by utilizing the rear sight, on the tip of the spur, and align it with the front sight, thusly lining up the barrel with the target. The tongue and groove splice is visible in **Image 62.** The quality of workmanship is marginal at best, however, the accuracy of the splice was phenomenally superb.

Evaluation of the Hammer

	[illegible]			[illegible]				[illegible]		
	1	2	3	4	5	6	7	8	9	10
Was the Hammer made as a new factory part?					X					
Was the Hammer off another Colt Paterson?	X	Needed two hammers								
Was the Hammer taken from scrap and reworked?								Taken from bin		X
Was the Hammer made by a novice?	X	Too masterfully crafted								

The reason for a "10" rating – It was less time consuming, and less expensive to splice two scrap hammers and together than make a new hammer.

The splice was also performed to assure the hammer would make complete contact with the percussion cap. The ignition chemical (fulminate of mercury) may not be equally spread throughout the interior cup of the percussion cap, hence, if not a flat surface, that of a poorly spread ignition chemical may be a setup for a misfire.

The Frame Plate

This plate, **image 64** straddles the frame of Colt537, just above the trigger assembly. On the production models it straddles the one piece frame, residing between the cylinder and frame. **See Page 48. Item 17 rests on top of the two forward parts of the frame, just to the right of Item 11 (the frame).** On Colt537 there is a coil spring under the frame plate which provides tension to the trigger lever. The production models have a flat spring performing the same function, **Item 14 page 48.**

Image 64

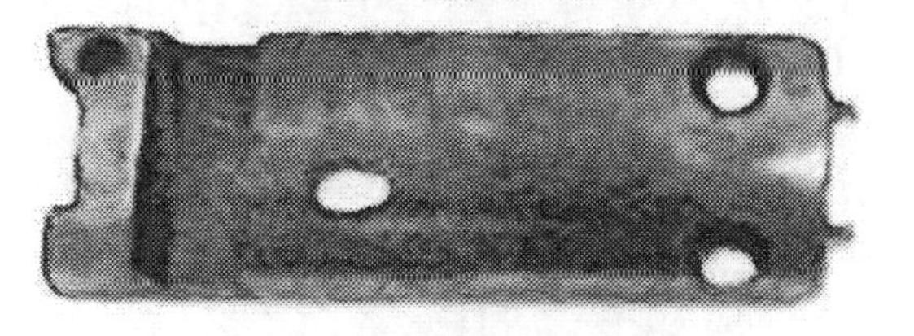

Source: M. Desparte

Colt537 Frame Plate
The purpose of the frame plate is to cover the internal workings of the firing mechanism. Scaled slightly larger than the No. 2 or No. 3 Belt Model .36 caliber frame

Image 65

Source: R. L. Wilson

Colt No. 2 and No. 3 Belt Model
Scaled slightly smaller than Colt537 Experiment .31 caliber frame.

Image 66

Source: R. L. Wilson

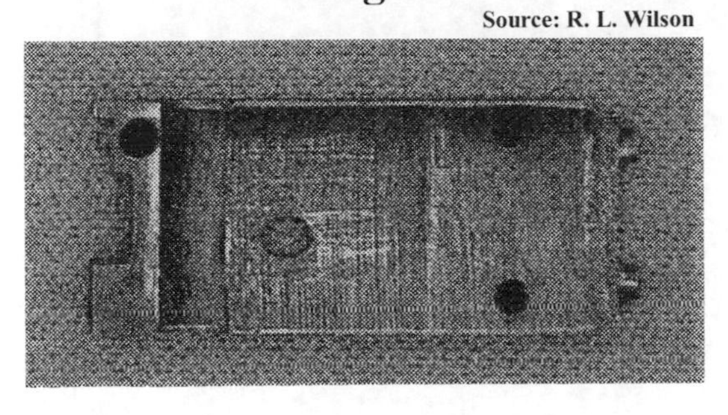

Colt No. 5 Holster or Texas Model
Similar in scale to Colt537, both Frame Plates are .36 caliber in size.

Image 67

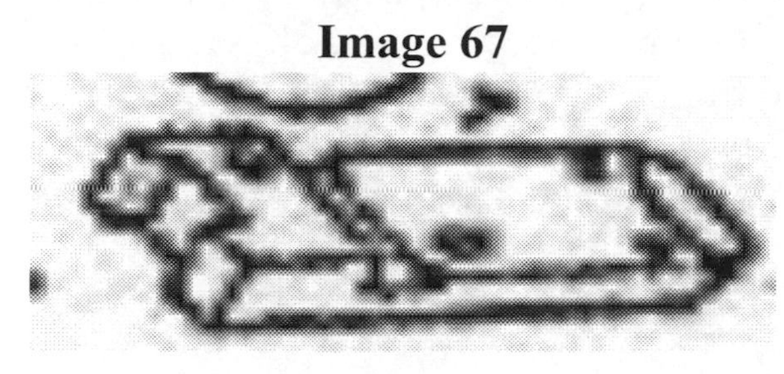

Source: R. L. Wilson

Colt Patent No. 1304
No scale associated with patent drawing
Drawing is conceptual but controlling.

There are four holes in the frame plate. Two opposite each other are screw holes that allow the frame plate to be fastened to the forward part of the revolver's frame. The single hole, to the rear of the frame plate, is another screw hole to fasten the rear of the frame plate to the frame. The hole to the right of center, in the frame plate, is to allow the stem of the bolt to come up through the frame plate and lock the cylinder prior to firing the revolver. It is interesting to note that although all the frame plates are of various sizes, the proportional relationship of the hole is in the same exact location on the plate. This indicates that the hole location of Colt537's frame plate was copied onto the four production models. Again, verifying Colt537 as the prototype for the four production models. A clarification is needed here. The bolt of the production models is powered by a forked flat spring. Colt537's bolt is powered by a coiled spring. **For the production model flat spring see Image 72 on page 86, and for Colt537 see Image 70 on page 86.**

All plates are exactly similar, save for the scale of each. As mentioned above, the chief reason for the frame plate is to provide cover as well as give access to the area without having to completely dismantle the revolver to access a malfunction in this area of the frame.

Evaluation of the Frame Plate

	No			Possibly				Yes		
	1	2	3	4	5	6	7	8	9	10
Was the Frame Plate made as a new factory part?										X
Was the Frame Plate made specifically for Colt537?										X
Was the Frame Plate taken off another Colt Paterson?	X									
Was the Frame Plate taken from scrap and reworked?	X									
Was the Frame Plate made by a hobbyist?	X									

The reason for 10 rating the Frame Plate - This frame plate appears to be machine-made since there has been no change in its design from Colt537 to the Colt No. 5 which was the last of the four production models copied from Colt537, each of the four different sizes, the No. 1 Pocket, the smallest, and the No. 5 being the largest. Colt537's frame plate had a shop number on it. It is believed that many of the parts may have been taken from other experiments that, in some way failed to accomplish a specific purpose.

The Colt537 Experiment Firing System

Regarding the Coil537 Flat Springs and Production Model Flat Springs

The coil spring was patented in 1763, before Colt's time. There are numerous references to springs breaking throughout R. L. Wilson's book, *Paterson Colt Pistol Variations*. It was suspected that the quality of the internal coil spring wasn't dependable. This was due to the age of the spring industry. Coil springs were not yet perfected. The quality of the spring never seemed to be constant. Corrosion and different winding processes caused variations in quality, as well as variances in metal content. These factors caused gun makers to shift from coil to flat springs. Flat springs are found in all the four production models of the Paterson, and unfortunately, not all are visible in the drawings of the U.S. Patent 1304, August 29, 1839.

Milled out for the Trigger Lever and Trigger Lever coil spring   Source: M. Desparte

Colt537 Bare Three-Piece Experiment Frame

Starting with the spring arrangement on the Colt537, the same firing system parts are found within the frame of the Paterson Colt537 Experiment and all four Paterson production models. However, there is a difference in the type of springs found in the Colt537 Experiment than those of the production model. Colt537 utilizes four coil springs. Each of the four production models function with four flat springs. They are other examples of improvements through simplification. These four are the Trigger Spring, **Item 14, page 48**, the Split Sear Spring, **Item 18, page 48** also **Image 72 on page 86**, the Main Spring, **Item 25, page 48, and Image 49, page 69,** and the Hand Spring, **Item 26, page 48**. Also **Images 37 on page 63**. All **Items** are found on the **Schematic Drawing on page 48.** The four production models utilize a "V" type mainspring, **Image 49 on page 69.**

The Coil Springs of the Trigger Lever and Split Leg Bolt of Colt537

After the removal of two screws in the forward part of the frame plate, **Image 69**, the frame plate jumped up, releasing the tension on the first of four coil springs. This spring is the trigger lever spring. It is located on the right side of the frame, nested in a milled out depression. This coil spring is attached to the trigger lever. In the four production models, i.e., Nos. 1, 2, 3 and 5, the trigger lever is called the trigger lever spring. This trigger lever places pressure on the trigger which enables the trigger to snap down into a ready-to-fire position. The complete sequence is as follows: The hammer is drawn back for firing. It squeezes against the sear. The sear rotates slightly and forces the trigger extension arm forward. This arm pushes against the trigger, forcing the lower portion of the trigger to rotate downward. The trigger lever assures the trigger is fully deployed.

Image 69

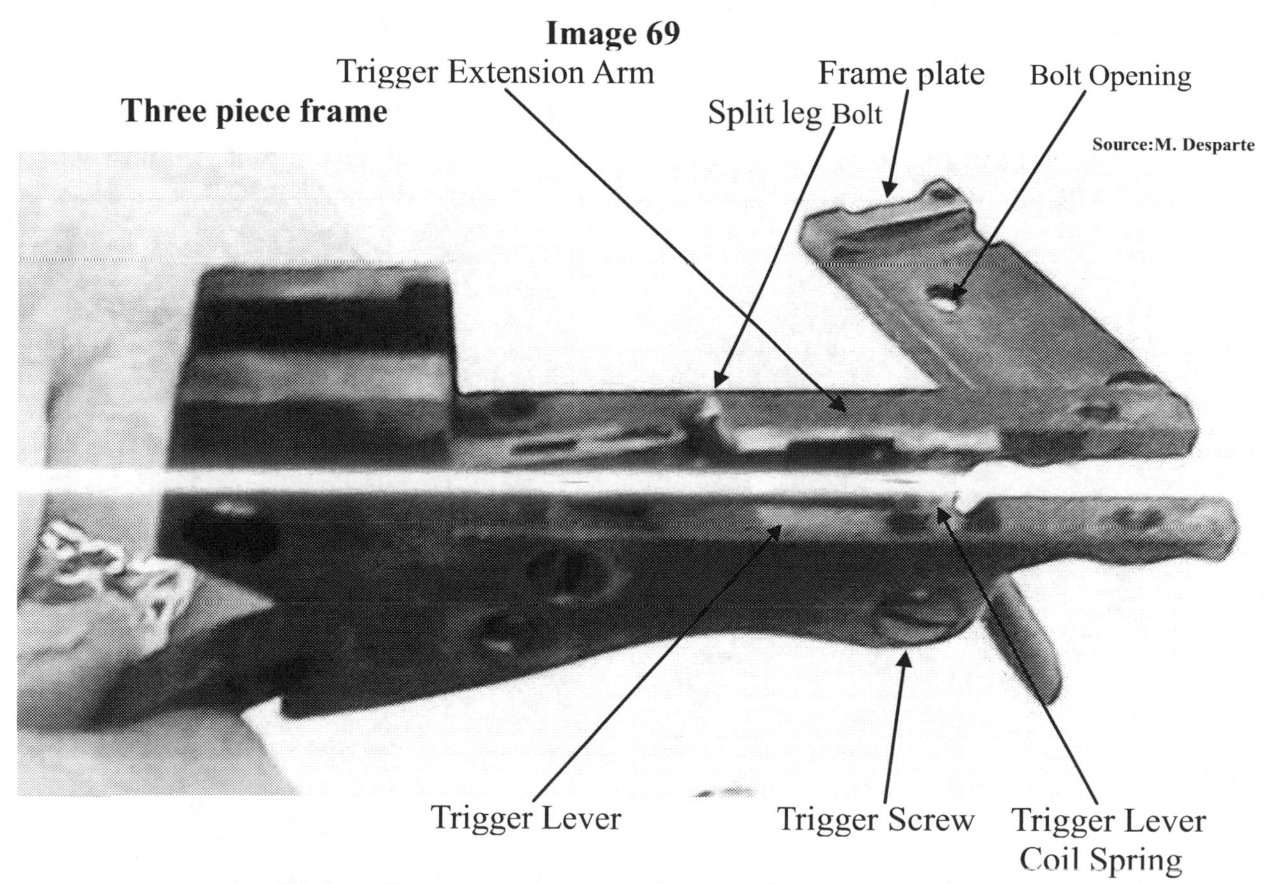

Firing System with the Frame Plate Removed

The Split Leg Bolt, in **Image 69**, **on the previous page,** and the attached bolt coil spring, the second spring of four is attached to the bottom of the bolt head or stem side of the bolt. If one were to replace it in its original position, one would see how that bolt would protrude up through the hole in the center of the frame plate. Its protrusion would be sufficient to interact with one of the five cylinder stops slots located on the periphery of the revolver's cylinder. This piece is activated when the hammer is pulled back into a firing position. During this action, the bolt, being connected to the hammer, rotates and recedes from the cylinder stop slot, **Images 28 and 29 on page 57** and allows the cylinder to rotate into the next firing position. This concurrently resets the bolt stem into the next stop slot, and prevents the cylinder from rotating out of the firing position, i.e., maintaining alignment with the bore of the barrel. The trigger lever coil spring, **Image 69 on page 85**, has two spring pockets in the milled out area in the middle of the frame. This is where the unattached end of the coil spring, **Image 70**, resides. There is a slight curve in the coil spring, indicating it may have rested in the rear spring hole. These pockets, formed within the middle part of the frame, illustrate an error in the location of one of the drilled out pockets. Perhaps the forward pocket did not enable the bolt to seat satisfactorily in the stop slot of the cylinder, so the spring may have been re-fitted into the rear hole for proper seating. One can see that there is a curve in the spring, indicating that the pocket may not have been positioned correctly in the frame. This supports the fact that errors were being made in drilling the pocket for the coil spring, proving it was the last authentic experiment revolver prior to the production models.

The Split Leg Bolt

Image 70

Forked End

Source: L.R. Wilson

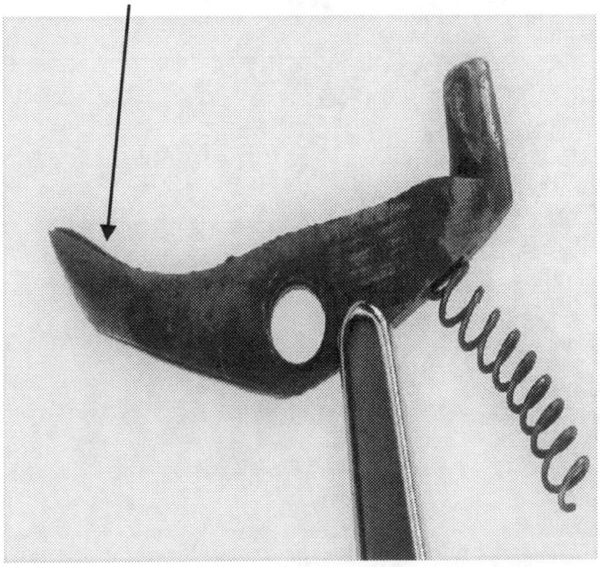

Source: Michael Desparte

Colt537 Experiment
Bolt powered by Coil Spring

Image 71

Forked End

Source: L.R. Wilson

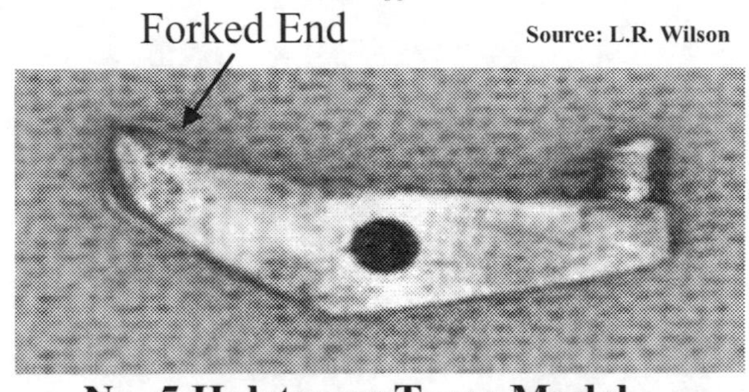

No. 5 Holster or Texas Model

Image 72 **Source: L.R. Wilson**

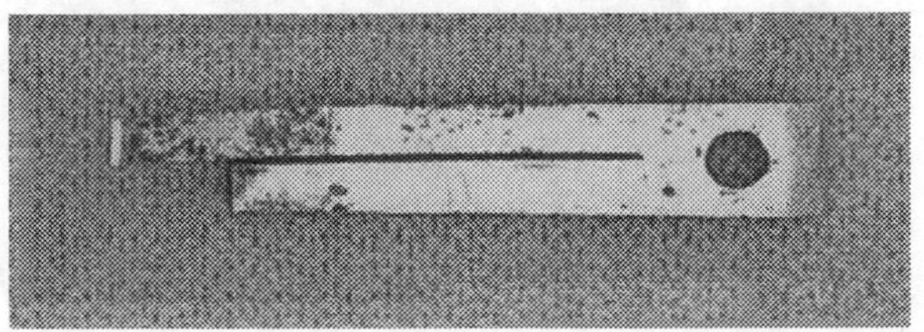

Source: L. R. Wilson

No. 5 Holster or Texas Prod. Model
Bolt & Sear Flat-spring

Historical Significance of the Colt Paterson Experiment

One is able to imagine the tip of the bolt projecting itself up from the firing system nest. The tip is in the exact center of **Image 64 on page 82**. The leaf or flat spring is used in the No. 5 Holster or Texas Model. **See Image 72**. It is obvious that there is less time spent in manufacturing this spring for the No. 5 split leg bolt. The coil spring may have been more difficult to make and required slightly more machining for the platforms used to position coil springs. This demanded time which converted to man hours, which led to needless expenditures. Compare **Image 70 to Image 71**. **Image 70** was hand made.

Evaluation of the Split Leg Bolt

	No			Possibly				Yes		
	1	2	3	4	5	6	7	8	9	10
Was the Split Leg Bolt made as a new factory part?								This was an experiment		X
Was the Split Leg Bolt made in the factory for Colt537?								In-house expertise required		X
Was the Split Leg Bolt taken off another Colt Paterson?	X	Too large or too small								
Was the Split Leg Bolt taken from scrap and reworked?	X	Too large or too small								
Was the Split Leg Bolt made by a novice?	X	Too detailed for a novice to craft								

Reasoning behind the Evaluation – For the No. 2 and No. 3 Belt Models, a slightly larger bolt was needed than that found in the No. 1 Pocket or Baby Model. Utilizing the same concepts in building the Colt No. 5, the bolt would have to be similar or slightly larger than that found in the Colt537 Experiment. The transition from the coil spring to flat spring, assured a significant reduction in failures. The bolt found in Colt537, **Image 70**, has exactly the same design as those found in the four production models.

Colt537 Firing System Regarding the Colt Bolt Comparisons

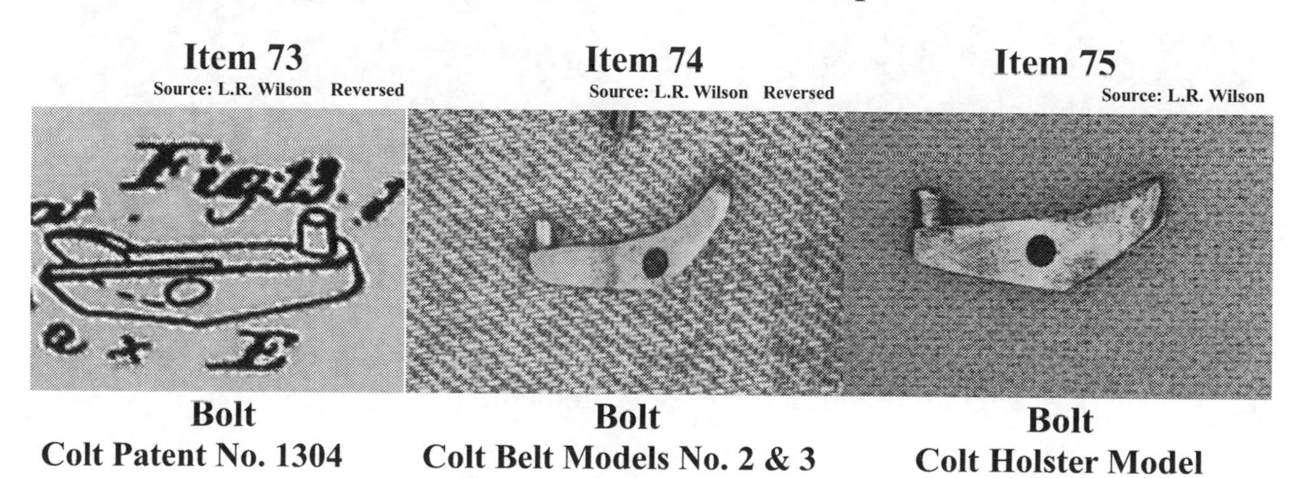

Item 73 Source: L.R. Wilson Reversed — **Bolt** **Colt Patent No. 1304**

Item 74 Source: L.R. Wilson Reversed — **Bolt** **Colt Belt Models No. 2 & 3**

Item 75 Source: L.R. Wilson — **Bolt** **Colt Holster Model**

Note! Throughout this section, the reader may wish to refer back to **the Schematic Drawing, Colt Paterson Parts on Page 48**. The No. 5 trigger spring in the Colt537 is called the trigger lever, and the No. 5 sear lever is the sear and the trigger extension arm.

In Image 76 Source: M. Desparte

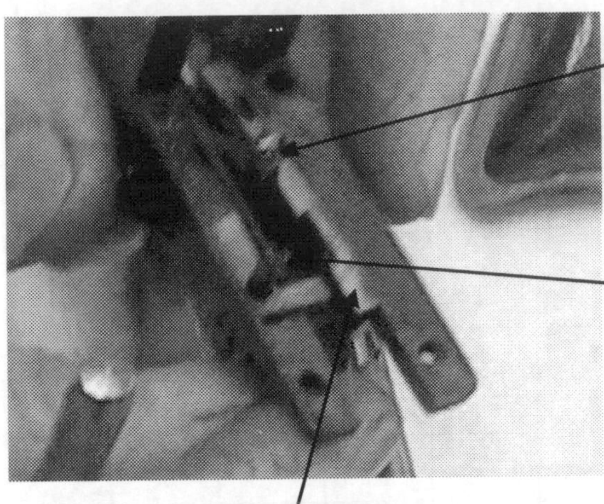

One can see the tip of the gg Bolt head extending upward, from the center of the frame. Remember, this is a Three-piece Frame.

One can also observe the Coil Spring extending upward from the Trigger Lever, nested in the milled out area in the right side of the Frame

Sear, Bolt and Trigger Ext. Arm between frame plates of Colt537

Sear and Trigger Extension Arm Assembly

Image 77

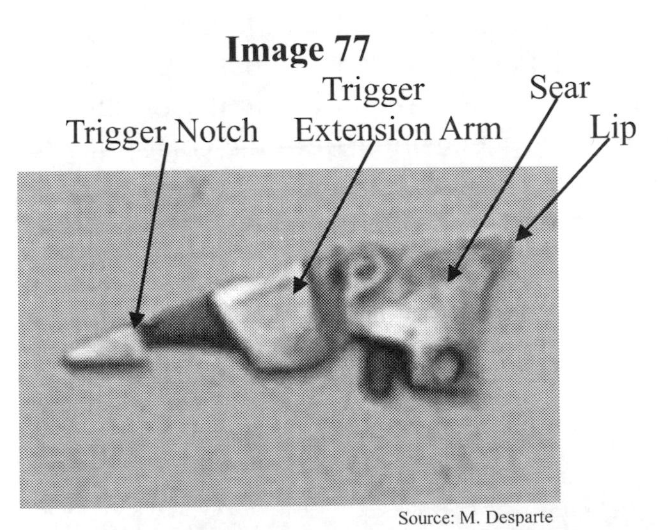

Source: M. Desparte

Handmade Sear Extension Found in Colt537. Not shown is the Trigger Sear Coil Spring replaced by Flat Spring in production models

Image 78

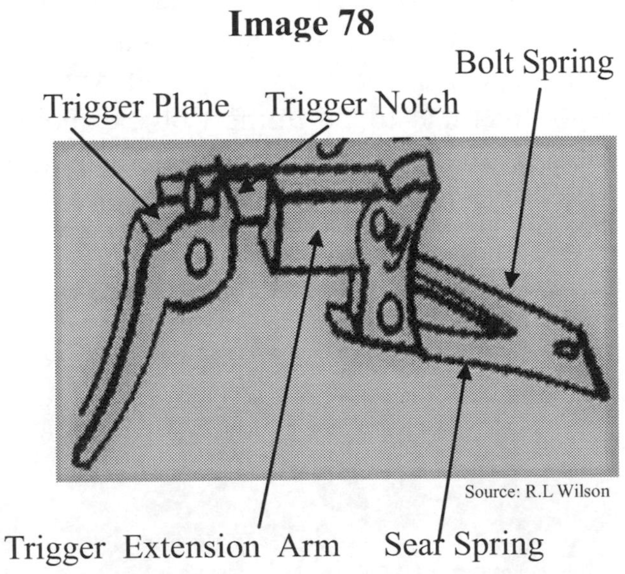

Source: R.L Wilson

Patent 1304 Schematic, with Trigger and Flat Spring in all four production models

Activation of the Firing System When Firing the Revolver

With the thumb on the spur of the hammer, pull back the hammer to the load position (the first click). The following occurs.

1. The hammer interacts with the bolt. This is a rocking device designed to rock back and forth locking and unlocking the cylinder from rotating. The bolt has a forked end that interfaces with the lower end of the hammer and the other end had a bolt head that inserts and extracts itself from any one of the five cylinder stop slots. As the hammer is pulled back a click is heard indicating that the hammer has reached the load position. By pulling back on the hammer to this position, the forked end of the bolt interfaces with the convex face of the lower part of the hammer, pushing the forked end upward and therefore pushing the bolt head downward, thereby extracting the bolt head from the cylinder stop slot, freeing the cylinder to rotate by the touch of the hand, **see Images 70 and 71 on page 86,** and **Images 73 to 75 page 87**. The cylinder stop slots are seen in **Images 28 and 29 on page 57.**

2. Now that the cylinder is free to rotate, it is in a position to load the five firing chambers.

3. Simultaneously, with the rotating motion of the hammer: the convex face of the lower part of the hammer, due to its shape, begins to push up against the concave portion of the sear. The sear in turn, pushes against trigger extension arm. The trigger extension arm pushes up against the trigger, **see Image 77 on page 88.** The forward part of the trigger extension arm narrows down to a point, **see image** 77. As the trigger extension arm is being pushed forward the point begins to ride up on the upper portion of the trigger. There is a trigger screw on which the trigger rotates. The portion of the trigger above the trigger screw has two different surfaces, on the right side is a small inclined plane, and on the left side is a notch. The point of the trigger arm is pushed onto the inclined plane. In doing so the [illegible]

tip of the trigger extension arm in an interlocking arrangement assisted by the trigger lever, with help of the trigger lever coil spring. A click is heard indicating that the trigger is in the safety position.

4. As the hammer continues its downward cocking, it is bypassing the load position, the shooter hears the click. That click also tells the shooter that the barrel has stopped rotating and the bolt head has now injected itself into the next arriving cylinder stop slot indicating that the cylinder is in perfect alignment with the bore of the barrel. The bolt has reset itself in the cylinder stop slot preventing the cylinder's misalignment.

5. The hammer is in the full stop position, the sear lip is extended into the hammer firing ledge, and the coil spring between the sear and the trigger extension arm is in a resting state. The trigger extension arm's trigger notch connected with the trigger, also in a resting state. The revolver is ready to be fired.

6. Firing the revolver. When the trigger is gradually squeezed, it pulls the trigger extension arm forward. The trigger extension arm is connected to the sear by coil spring link between the trigger extension arm and the sear. At this point the sear lip is still retaining the hammer from firing. The sear lip is still wedged into the hammer firing ledge.

7. As the trigger continues to be pulled, the trigger extension arm transfers that pull to the sear spring (between the trigger extension arm and the sear), the tension increases, the spring eventually pulls the sear out of the firing ledge on the face of the lower part of the hammer. It is being powered by the revolver's main spring. It is set free to rotate forward onto the percussion cap. Due to the force of the hammer the percussion cap is ignited and sparks shoot down the nipple tube to the firing chamber, causing the gun powder to explode, sending the ball down the bore and on its way to the target.

The most interesting segment of the firing system is the sear and trigger extension arm, working together as an assembly. It is by far, the most sophisticated set of parts in the revolver. There are eight interacting pieces in total, and by far the finest polished and fitted unit in the Colt537 Experiment revolver. **See Images 79 and 80, on the next page**. The parts consist of: 1. the hammer, 2. the sear, 3. a top sear coil spring, 4. a bottom sear coil spring, 5. a trigger extension arm, 6. a trigger, 7. rigger lever, and 8. the trigger lever spring. This is indicative of the great deal of genius; time and care put into its creation, fitting, and design by Pliny Lawton and Henry Crosby.

Surprisingly, the flat sear spring found on the four machined production models perform the exact same function as described above. **See Item 18, page 48**. The short side of the spring works the sear and the long side of the spring works with the bolt.

Based on the above scenario, it is felt that the firing system of Colt537 Experiment was not put together from parts and pieces of other guns. The parts in this pistol are exhibiting unique features; most appear to be handmade. Another interesting fact is that the bolt screw is forward of the sear screw, running through the lower portion of the sear. This is not the case in the No. 2, or 3 Belt Model. The bolt screw is behind the sear screw. This means that the Colt537 Experiment was the original interior arrangement. It is the same concept, only an alteration in design. This design, of the interior of Colt537, must have taken a significant amount of time to develop; causing Pliny Lawton great consternation in scaling down to the No. 1 Pocket Model and back up to a perfected No. 5 Holster or Texas Model.

The Remaining Two Coil Springs and Their Interaction with the Hammer, Sear, Trigger Extension Arm, Trigger Lever, and Trigger

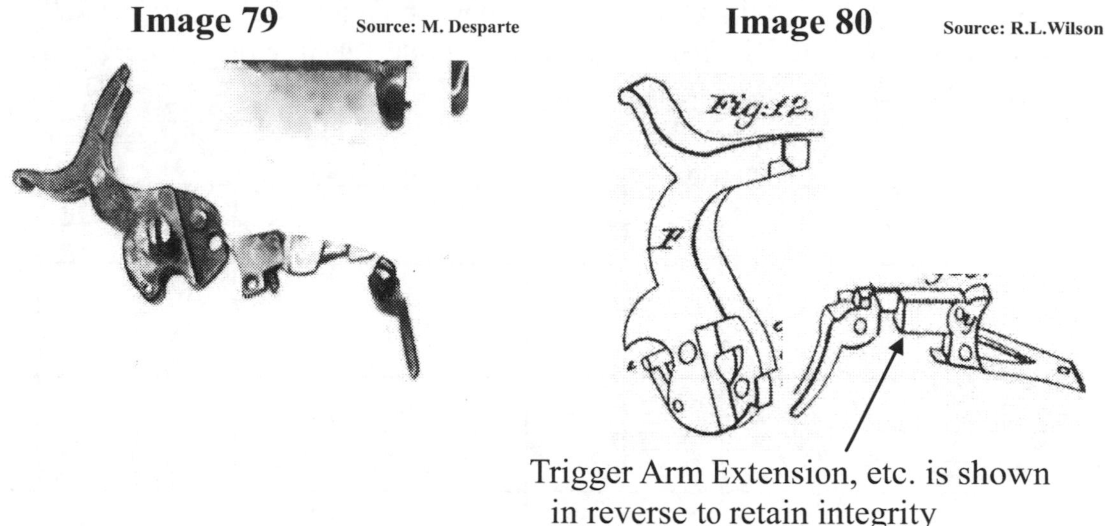

Colt537 Experiment **U.S. Patent 1304 Drawing**

The question remains as to why Colt537 isn't or wasn't called the No. 4, model? It could have neatly fit in between the No. 3 and the No. 5. The only logical answer is that it never was moved forward to the prototype level. Could it have been Seldon's insistence that Colt get on with a salable product? It had all the potential, but time and money may have had a lot to do with it. Colt537 is a .31 caliber. Its design already produced a .28 caliber Pocket Model and two Belt Models that were of .31 and .34 caliber. Colt537 having a large frame, suitable for a .36 Holster or Texas Model. And Colt 537 having the holster model address on the barrel, see **Image 20 on page 51**. Therefore indicating Colt537 was also in the same family as the No. 5 model.

Colt537, the .31 caliber, and the future No. 5 Holster or Texas Model being a .36 caliber, both were filling niche. Seldon's pressure on Colt to get on with producing a salable item, for all intents and purposes, caused Colt to limit Colt537 from becoming a prototype for a .31 caliber, .34 caliber or a .36 caliber No, 4 production model. There went the magnum concept as well, a loss for approximately another one hundred years. It had served its highest purpose, being the template for the No. 1 Pocket or Baby Model, the No. 2 and 3 Belt Models, and the No. 5 Holster or Texas Model. What an honor for this revolver, yet it never was placed on its most deserving pedestal**.** Time and pressure from Dudley Selden, the Company Treasurer, negated Colt537 from becoming the .31 caliber magnum, and receiving any other high honor.

The definition of a model is, any of a series of different styles or designs of a particular product, such as a two-door model car, vs. a four-door model car, or pickup model truck, vs, a pickup extended cab model truck.

Historical Significance of the Colt Paterson Experiment

In this case the No.1 Pocket Model and No. 2 or 3 Belt Models cannot really be called experimental models. What is called the experiment really isn't a model. The intent seems to have been to design the Colt537 for experimentation. Again, time and money, i.e., circumstances, prevented it from obtaining a model designation. There may have been No. 4 models, but none have surfaced.

Evaluation of the Trigger/Sear Assembly

	No			Possibly				Yes		
	1	2	3	4	5	6	7	8	9	10
Was the Trigger/Sear Assembly a new factory part?										X
Was the Trigger/Sear Assembly made for Colt537?										X
Was the Trigger/Sear Assembly off another Colt Paterson?	X									
Was the Trigger/Sear Assembly reworked from scrap?	X									

The reason for the determination – The thought and workmanship put into this assemblage of parts requires a particular type of person. Prior to John Pearson's leaving the Colt Company Pliny Lawton in working closely with John Pearson, picked up some of Pearson's ideas and may have worked them into the final design, but it is believed that Colt537 was hand made in the Colt factory circa 1837 and most of the credit is due Mr. Colt, Mr. Lawton, and possibly Mr. Crosby.

The revolver is, as of this writing one hundred and eighty years old. It is still as tight, and as smooth in operation as the day it was made.

Chapter Eight
The Other Differences

Physical Differences and Features between Colt537 and the Paterson Production Models

Part Numbers, Shop Control Numbers, or Serial Numbers and Their Locations

Colt537 Experiment had many different numbers stamped on many pieces, all were almost completely obliterated. All were identified in defined factory locations. This statement in itself speaks to the gun's authenticity. However, there are so many different numbers on any particular piece. It is suspected that many parts of the Colt537 Experiment were taken from a damaged or flawed parts bin, or the shop where experimental design and development took place; they certainly were control numbers. I would suspect the smaller the piece the more difficult it was to maintain its whereabouts. And once found, how definite, that it was the correct piece. This could be true for just about any part, such as those found in the internal firing system, which more than likely were very small, being made by hand.

Almost all the numbers are extremely difficult to see. I had to use a magnifying glass in bright sunlight. And by maneuvering the revolver to different angles in direct sunlight, faint numbers became slightly visible. It was then extremely difficult to find that same number in that specific location again, amazingly difficult. There are also one or two numbers on the grip that are readable but may not be a complete set. Mulling over these numbers, I begin to believe that within the Colt factory, there may have been several men working on different approaches to finding the right combination of designed parts that would make a completely operational revolver. Therefore, these numbers, more than likely, represented a specific part, for a specific experiment, being made by a specific gun maker, within the factory's shop. Can you imagine the amount of parts that would be floating around in that particular room or shop if say two or three workmen were in the same room, working on experimental pieces of revolvers? There had to be a way of identifying who had what, or who was working on what. Imagine if one part was accidentally misplaced on a long workbench with parts belonging to other experiments. There had to be a parts ledger to reduce the number of miscellaneous *"don't know where it came from"* parts.

Standard Locations for These Numbers

On the breech end of the barrel, below the cylinder sleeve, the number, No. 710 was found. The No. 58 was farthest to the left, in the same area, in extremely large numbers. No. 6 was found to the left of the cylinder sleeve, just below the arbor or cylinder pin hole. On the breech end of the barrel lug, there is a buildup of hardened black powder or other substances preventing the identification of complete number sets. All numbers found where in predictable locations. The barrel of Colt537 in all respects appears to be a .31 Belt Model barrel slid on the enlarged frame of Colt537. The confusing thing about this is that it has the address that is normally found on the Colt No. 5 Holster Model.

Bottom of the Wedge, Number 7?4 the wedge is kept in place by a screw. The screw may be of recent manufacture. The question mark indicates that the specific number was not discernible.

Hammer, no number was visible. The two-spliced hammer appears to be authentic, with the corrected amount of curl, the spur is also checkered. It also has the appropriate sight groove.

Trigger Actuating Bar, no visible number.

Hand, no visible number.

Cylinder, The Number 521 was located on one nipple partition. The amount of wear on the cylinder is also an indication of authenticity.

Toothed Rack/Toothed Rack Ring, had no visible number. Wear is present on the ring, and is consistent with the wear on other parts of the revolver.

Cylinder Pin/Arbor, no visible number.

Recoil Shield, no visible number.

Back Strap, the Number 71 was found on exterior heel or bottom of hand-grip, and on the inside of the back strap.

Frame Plate, the Number 5?0 was found, the middle digit is questionable. Found between assembly pins on frame plate. The question mark indicates that the specific number was not discernible.

The Barrel Address and Authenticity

The Colt537 Experiment has a barrel address that is similar to the (i.e., 1837/38) .36 caliber No. 5 Holster or Texas Model. This illustrates that Colt537 Experiment was fabricated in the Paterson Factory, and has a valid mother offspring relationship between the experimental model and the manufactured No. 5 Holster or Texas Model revolver.

1. This revolver does have the correct address on the barrel. No counterfeit has ever been found having the star with snake tail finials on the barrel address. The address was placed on the barrel using a rolled engraving process. Most counterfeits employ engraving address not rolled.

2. If the revolver was a Pre-Paterson product of John Pearson's making, the Colt537 Experiment would not have had the address on the barrel. The Colt address stamp was and is a product of the Colt factory.

3. The address runs from muzzle to breech. This is the reverse of what it is on all the production Paterson models, i.e., address flowing from breech to muzzle. This may give an indication that a policy on which way the address was to flow may not have been determined, or the barrel could have been a reject product, and thrown into the reject bin, or further; proof parts from the reject bin were reused, and the multiplicity of numbers found on many of the parts of revolver support this belief. These numbers are extremely faint. But, they are there, and they are in the right locations, according to what may have been Colt practice at that time. Additional proof the revolver is not counterfeit.

When it is indicated that a part may have come from a reject bin, or the design shop, all that really means is that there may have been as little as a blemish on the surface of the part, like the slip of a grinding tool, which left a deep or ugly scratch on the surface of the part. But, in all other respects, it was perfectly safe to operate. For example, [illegible]

On the next page are the characteristic addresses of each of the models produced at the Paterson factory during the period of 1837 to 1842. Colt537 has the same size, but not the exact same frame as that of the .36 caliber, No. 5, Holster or Texas Model. The only significant difference between the two is that the Colt537 has a three-piece frame, which indicates it was a first make or experiment leading to the No. 5 model. This difference separates Colt537 from all the production Paterson models. The reader will notice that the following model address finials are grouped by model. Each model's finial design is located before and after the company's address. Particularly interesting are the No. 2 and No. 3 models. They have the same finial characteristics, and the same model name, i.e., the “Belt Models”, yet they are separated by model numbers, i.e., model No. 2 and model No. 3. The only significant difference between these two is the shape of their hand-grip. The No. 2 has a straight hand-grip and the No. 3 has a flared hand-grip.

The Finial Chart or Code:

This handmade model was produced first, very early in 1837

Company	Finial Design	Model	Model Number	Caliber
Colt	~~~~* Patent etc.*~~~~	Experiment	Colt537	.31

These models were partially mass produced from mid-1837 to 1842

Company	Finial Design	Model	Model Number	Caliber
Colt	--------Patent etc.--------	Pocket	No. 1	.28
Colt	-<><>-Patent etc.-<><>-	Belt	No. 2	.31
Colt	-<><>-Patent etc.-<><>-	Belt	No. 3	.31 - .34

This model was produced in late early 1838

Company	Finial Design	Model	Model Number	Caliber
Colt	~~~~* Patent etc.*~~~~	Holster/Texas	No.	.36

Cylinder and Bore Considerations

Measurements of the cylinder chambers of Colt537 are presumed to be .300ths of an inch in diameter (.30 caliber). The measurements of the bore of Colt537 are presumed to be .310ths of an inch in diameter (.31 caliber). The presumption is based on possible inaccuracies of the measuring device and the fact that the bore of Colt537 has been altered significantly. The lands have been removed. The above coupled with the following quote from the Colt factory.

> "Careful measurements taken from specimen Paterson revolvers, including chamber, bore and groove diameters, bullet mold cavities, actual bullet and ball diameters and correlated with research done by Larry Wilson in the Colt Archives at the Connecticut Historical Society and the Connecticut State Library. Bear in mind that machinery during that period, between 1830s and early 1840s was not all that precise; therefore, it's not surprising to find variations from one gun (of the same model) to another."[48]

[48] Paterson Colt Pistol Variations, R. L. Wilson, Page 218, In part letter from the Colt factory regarding calibers, R.E. Domain, Sr. Product Designer

	Cylinder Chamber Diameter	Bullet Mold Diameter	Bore Diameter
Belt Models	.320 - .325"	.325"	.350 - .360"
Holster Models	.370 - .373"	.375 - .378"	.390 - .410"

In keeping with Colt's Hartford arms identification and accepted practice by today's collectors, these calibers are best called:

Pocket and Fourth Model Ehlers:	.28 caliber
Belt and Fifth Model Ehlers:	.31 and .34 caliber
Holster or Texas Model:	.36 caliber

Image 81

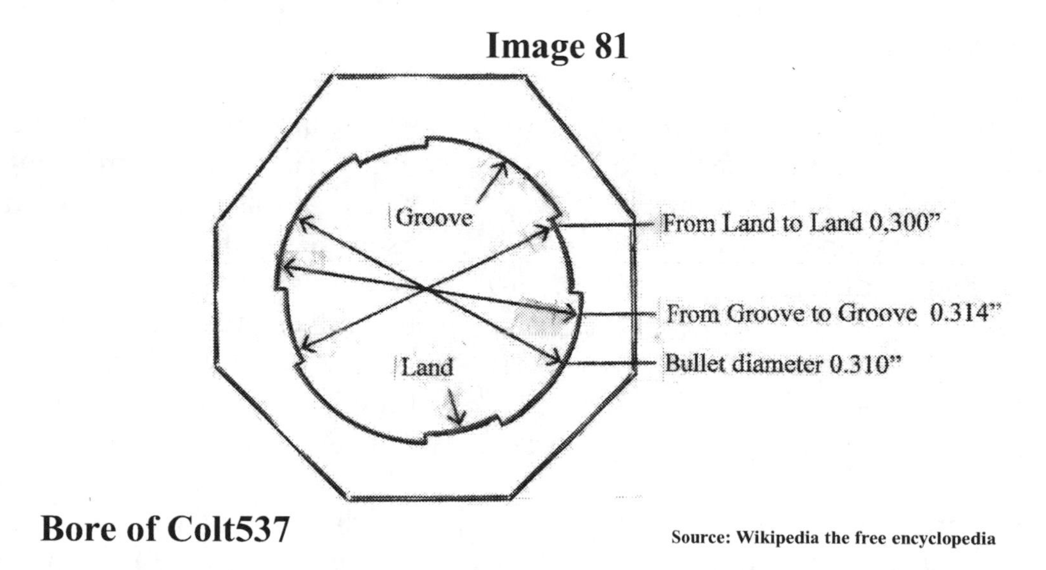

Bore of Colt537

Source: Wikipedia the free encyclopedia

The reason why the barrel bore diameter measures larger than the diameter of any one of the cylinder's firing chambers:

> "Black powder leaves a notable amount of residue in the barrel on firing. It is likely that a significant reason for the barrel bore diameter being larger than the chamber was to allow for the building of fouling. Tests [illegible] rounds have been fired, by virtue of the bullct or ball passing through the bore along with the burning powder, gasses, etc. Note that such would be particularly important with the Paterson handguns, due to their deep rifling grooves, and their greater number (eleven grooves as opposed to the (1851) .36 caliber Colt Navy (with) seven (lands and grooves)."[49]

The bore of Colt537 Experiment, at present is by definition a smooth bore, i.e., no lands present, and is presently between 310" and .314" in diameter. The bore with its lands would have been between .300" plus, but no greater than .310."

49. Paterson Colt Pistol Variations, R.L. Wilson, Page 218, A letter from the Colt factory regarding calibers.

According to Colt Industries:

The Holster model rifled bore diameter is between	.350 - 360"	Colt537 is .310"
The Belt Model cylinder chamber diameter ranges from	.320 -.325"	Colt537 is .310"
The difference between the two	.030 -.035"	.005"

At present the Colt537 is a smooth bore having a diameter of .310". Therefore, according to the conceptual sample found in **Image 81 on the previous page**, the smooth bore of Colt537 should be somewhere between .310" and .314". The previously rifled bore of Colt537 may have been extremely close to a .300" in diameter. There is no accurate way we can determine what the previously rifled bore on Colt537 measured. A rough guess would be .310 caliber.

As the Paterson arms were designed for round balls/bullets, the rifling in the pistols has so slight a twist that it looks nearly straight. The grooves are semicircular rather than straight sided, and appear to be about half again as wide as the lands. As uniformity was not one of the virtues of the Paterson plant, the number of grooves probably differs in different arms, but some of them at least had eleven grooves, R.E. Domain, of the Colt Company, indicates that Paterson revolvers had deep rifling grooves, whereby, Haven and Belden, Authors of, "A History of The Colt Revolver," state that the grooves were semi-circular rather than straight. Hmmmmm."[50] Deep grooves would increase the revolver's ability to manage variances in powder charge.

If it were not for the difference in shading of the bore of Colt537; one could possibly say that it may have been a smooth bore revolver, with a .310" in diameter, but that was not the case. **See Images 86, 87, and 88 on pages 109 and 110.** Assuming the firing chamber measured .300" in diameter. This would require a lead ball to be slightly larger than .300, but no more than .310 caliber. This slightly larger ball would have had some skimming or shaving off of a slight amount of lead as it was shoved into place within the firing chamber. This would assure (hopefully) that there were no leaks of gun powder due to this trimming off of the lead. This was considered the normal practice associated with loading the cylinder. However, this activity of trimming could cause the ball to be less than perfectly round, and therefore affect the accuracy of the shot.

Colt537 Lands and Grooves in terms of Accuracy and Explosive Gas Pressure

Accept the fact that rifling in the bore of a gun barrel improves the accuracy, in terms of hitting an intended target. Regarding the lack of rifling; if the lead ball is not a perfect fit, it may only have a fair amount of accuracy, for a limited distance. The spin of

50. A History of the Colt Revolver, Charles T. Haven and Frank A. Belden, Page 24, Col 1, L 3

the lead ball would be similar to throwing a football; the spinning improves accuracy and distance it can be thrown.

There are limitations to the number of lands and grooves the bore of any barrel may have. The lands are parallel ridges running the length of the bore; these ridges may have a slight twist to them, causing the ball to slowly spin, as it passes through the bore.

If the lead ball or bullet is slightly larger in caliber than the bore having lands and grooves, the motion of the ball will cause an increase in friction between the surface of the ball and the lands of the bore. The ball, as it moves through the bore, begins to slightly reshape itself as it comes in contact with the lands, producing slight grooves on the surface of the ball as it rides down the bore of the barrel. There normally is a twist in the lands of the bore. The ball having been imbedded with by the lands performs a gripping effect on the ball, causing it to rotate along with the twist of the lands.

The explosive pressure of the gunpowder forces the ball to ride through the bore with a slight rotation caused by the twisting lands. The speed/velocity of the ball corresponds to the amount of pressure/expanding gas caused by the exploding gunpowder. Hence the greater amount of gunpowder the greater the speed of the bullet.

Due to the friction of the bullet with the lands of the bore, the ball is slowed. If there is too much gunpowder, the bullet may not be able to exit the bore of the barrel in time (nanoseconds) and this would cause a rupture of the firing chamber, or the bore of the barrel. The problem may have been created by the number of lands and grooves in the barrel of the gun. Too many lands reduce the amount of space in the grooves of the bore. The grooves actually can be considered safety valves, in that excessive pressure from the explosive gas can bypass the bullet as the gas rides down any one, or all of the grooves in the bore. Once this pressure or exploding gas (or whatever one might call it) gets in front (through the grooves) of the bullet, due to the space in front of the bullet, the gas expands in all directions. Some of this expanding gas would actually push back against the bullet and slow the bullet down. Again, If the pressure of the gas is too great, the bore can rupture, i.e., explode. If too little, the bullet can become lodged in the barrel. The volume of gunpowder in the firing chamber would be the controlling factor. It continues to amaze me as to the various ways a gun can explode or rupture.

The following is an interesting happening. "On June 19th, (assuming it is 1838) a musket was fired with a maximum charge of 134 grains of "U.S. Rifle Powder" at a target 10 inches distant, penetrating 2.64 inches of oak boards. Reducing the charge to 110 grains increased the penetration to 2.75 inches, while later it was shot with 100 grains, giving a penetration of 3.0 inches. (These were the) mean averages of the several shots at each test (level), indicated to the Board Members that here was proof of a phenomenon long suspected: that guns shoot less well, with less force and penetration, when overcharged, and that there is one charge which may prove best all around."[51]

Now how does this apply to the bore of Colt537? The size of the bore of Colt537 is .31 caliber. There is a designated amount of gunpowder for a .31 caliber pistol. That is, according to the loading data chart in **Image 32 on page 60**, using 10 to 15 grains of gunpowder. However, the cylinder of Colt537 is longer than the normal length of cylinder required for a normal load of gunpowder. After analyzing the volume of the Colt537's firing chambers, they are capable of containing a gunpowder load up to 25 grains. That is a charge sufficient to fire the normal load of a .44 caliber pistol. By adjusting the charge used in the elongated cylinder one would eventually be able to find the optimum charge.

On analyzing the lands and grooves of Colt537, one can see that the chosen number of lands and grooves in the four production models is eleven lands and grooves. In Colt537 prior to removal of its lands and grooves there were five of each.

Image 82
Production Model

Eleven Lands
& Grooves

Image 83
Colt 537

Five Lands
& Grooves

Source: M. Desparte

it becomes evident that the reduction of what would be considered eleven lands to that of five lands was a conscious acknowledgment that the greater volume of charge/gunpowder in the firing chambers of Colt537 would require more groove space for escaping explosive gasses.[52]

Reducing the Number of Lands, reduces Explosive Pressure

There is a considerable amount of groove space between each land as shown in **Image 83.** This enables excessive gasses to exit through the grooves without damaging the cylinder or any one of the five chambers, or for that matter, the barrel of Colt537. It would appear that eleven lands and grooves, through testing, was considered safe for all four of the production models, using a specific amount of gunpowder, the amount is controlled by the volume of the firing chamber for a specific caliber. Colt537's five lands and grooves were due to the fact that this revolver had a one half inch extension to the cylinder, and therefore an additional half inch in each of the five firing chambers. These

51. The Story of Colt Revolvers, Wm Edwards, Page 55, Col 1, L9
52. See Image 27, page 54 for a comparison of Pyrodex Gun Powder loading recommendations

five lands and grooves, because of their limited number enabled, during the firing of the revolver, a way to quickly reduce the pressure buildup. The escaping explosive gases would by pass the ball and yet there would be a sufficient force to propel a .28, .31 or .36 caliber lead ball at a deadly velocity

Image 84

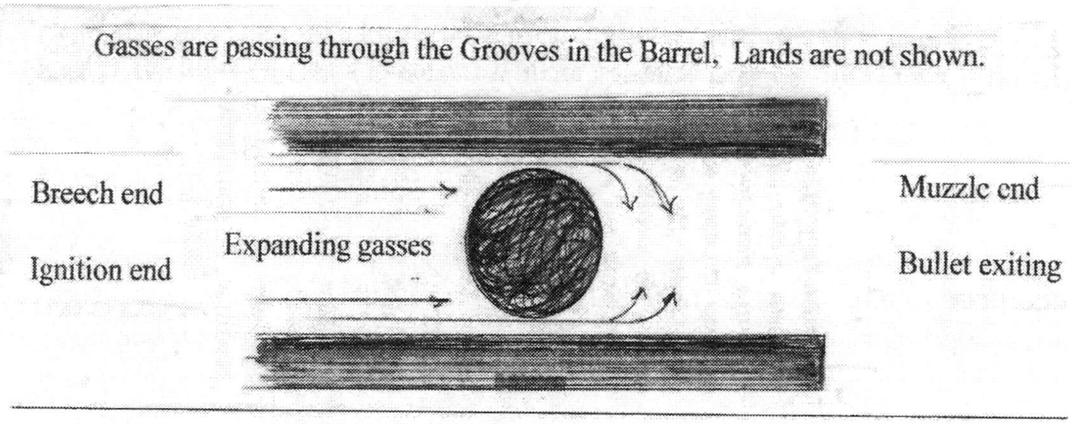

Gasses are passing through the Grooves in the Barrel, Lands are not shown.

Breech end

Ignition end

Expanding gasses

Muzzle end

Bullet exiting

Source: M. Desparte

Expanding gasses passing around the ball through the grooves in the bore

The fact that Colt537 had the lands removed from the barrel, making the bore smooth (relatively speaking), with the exception of a deep groove now running the upper length of its bore, makes one wonder what was going on in the minds of Sam Colt and Pliny Lawton. This is the beginning of the transition in thinking about accuracy, as it relates to the effect of lands and grooves, and even hand-grip configurations. Was it that Colt wasn't too concerned with the level of accuracy he was getting from any of his production models? How is it that Colt determined the first two models, the Pocket and Belt were to have rifling. It is hard to understand. **All of the Pre-Paterson experimental models were smooth bore**. That included the first Lawton-Colt experiment spoken of back on **Image 6 on page 8**. Colt's original focus must have been on the operation of their internal parts. **Colt537, Image 7 on page 9, originally had five lands and grooves. Pocket Pistol (One of the first production models, No. 1) Serial Number .31, Image 8 on page 13 had ten lands and grooves. Most of all production models had eleven. The pistols with serial numbers (SN) lower than SN. 31 may have been a mix of various smaller or larger sized revolvers having lands and grooves. In my opinion, Colt537 was the initial model with rifling, having five lands and grooves. The mother gun, so to speak.** From this revolver all production models took their design. No significant amount of research can be found dealing with lands and grooves of varying calibers of revolvers. The Pocket Pistol SN 31 apparently was not the first attempt at a production model, based on the serial number of 31. The first production model may not have had a complete step down to the final design size from Colt537. But, it was a step down in size from Colt537. Apparently, No. 1 Pocket Model with the SN 1 wasn't small enough; and therefore, Lawton-Colt could have determined that the next pocket needed to be smaller, to be called a pocket or Baby Model. It probably had to depend upon the average size of pant pockets at that time, and its ability to extract the revolver from a pant pocket in seconds. Since Pocket Model No. 1 was a .28 caliber, the size of the bore may have something to do with the number of lands and grooves that can be squeezed into this dimension, therefore; really limiting the volume of escaping gas that was able to pass through these grooves.[53]

Reviewing a select few samples for each of the four models, one can observe the change in thinking when it comes to the improvements made to the revolvers over time.

> Pocket pistol (No. 1 model); SN 31, had .28 caliber, and ten lands and grooves..[54]

> Pocket pistol (No. 1 model); SN 258, had .28 caliber and eleven lands and grooves, supporting the theory that ten lands and grooves may have been, not tight enough [55]

> Pocket pistol (No. 1 model); SN 340, had .28 caliber and eleven lands and grooves[56].

What has become apparent is that the caliber stabilized at .28 caliber and the number of lands and grooves stabilized at eleven. All No. 2 Belt Models, Plate Nos. 8 through 11, had .31 caliber with eleven lands and grooves. They also had straight walnut grips. However, the angle of the grip from the horizontal line of the barrel varied. Possibly these revolvers were not made by the same plant worker. Or the design team was searching for the right fit. There was some experimentation going on as to which angle of grip was most comfortable or practical. The subject of accuracy was beginning to enter the picture.[57]

All No. 3 Belt Models, i.e., Nos. 2 and 3, Plate Nos. 12 through 16, are .31 and .34 caliber with eleven lands and grooves. All had a flared walnut grips with a similar angle to the horizontal line of the barrel.

All No. 5 Holster models, Plate Nos. 18 through 21, are .36 caliber with eleven lands and grooves. All had flared grips with a greater angle from the horizontal line of the barrel. It seems that the angle of the grip had stabilized at a greater angle than those of the No. 3 model.[58] One realization recently surfaced, the Colt537 was hand made prior to the

---

53. Paterson Colt Pistol Variations, R.L. Wilson, Page 21, Plate Nos. 4, 4A
54. Paterson Colt Pistol Variations, R.L. Wilson, Page 21, Plate Nos. 4, 4A
55. Paterson Colt Pistol Variations, R.L. Wilson, Page 23, Plate Nos. 5, 5A
56. Paterson Colt Pistol Variations, R.L. Wilson, Page 25, Plate Nos. 6, 6A
57. Paterson Colt Pistol Variations, R.L. Wilson, Pages 29-35, Plates Nos. 8A through 11A
58. Paterson Colt Pistol Variations, R.L. Wilson, Pages 37-45, Plates Nos. 12A through 16A

development of any of the production models. Hence, this must have been a developmental concept early on by either Pliny Lawton or Harold Crosby.[59]"

The Hand-Grip

Part of the perceived problem in accuracy would be the shape and size of the hand-grip of the proposed Colt537. However, for the Pocket and the No. 2 Belt Models, little help could be envisioned, since the grip would be so small, there would be a limited ability to control their accuracy. Also, it may be that no one would be concerned about it. That might be the case for the No. 1 and No. 2; but for a No. 3 Belt model, and/or the No. 5 Holster or Texas model with calibers ranging from a .31 to .36 caliber. These revolvers are entering the category of deadly weapons. And, this might be the reason Colt, Lawton, or Crosby revised the design of the hand grip of the proposed Colt537 experiment. This was the birth of the flared heel of the hand-grip; and must have improved the accuracy.

Various Sizes of Hand-Grips & Associated Characteristics Among Models

Colt537	**Pocket**	**Belt**	**Belt**	**Holster/Texas**
Experimental	**Production**	**Production**	**Production**	**Production**
Hand-made	Model No.1	Model No.2	Model No. 3	Model No.5
Type of Grip				
Flared Heel	**Straight Heel**	**Straight Heel**	**Flared Heel**	**Flared Heel**
Large	Small	Larger	Larger	Largest
Size of Frame				
Large	Small	Medium	Medium	Largest
Colt537 Caliber	**Pocket Caliber**	**Belt Caliber**	**Belt Caliber**	**Holster/Texas Caliber**
.31 cal	.28 cal	.31 cal	.31 cal & .34	.36 cal
Cylinder Type				
Elongated Cylinder	Regular. Cylinder	Regular Cylinder	Regular Cylinder	Regular Cylinder

It was found that the shooter was more able to get his hand around the grip for a more firm hold, consequently, providing the shooter greater stability. Whatever improvements there were; they must have been the best they could come up with. Colt and Company

---

59. Paterson Colt Pistol Variations, R.L. Wilson, Page 121, Col 1, Par 1, L 16

chose to continue with roughly the same flared hand-grip design, well onto models of the present day revolvers. The level of accuracy he hoped for, at that time, remained elusive.

Image 85

Source: R.L. Wilson/M.Desparte

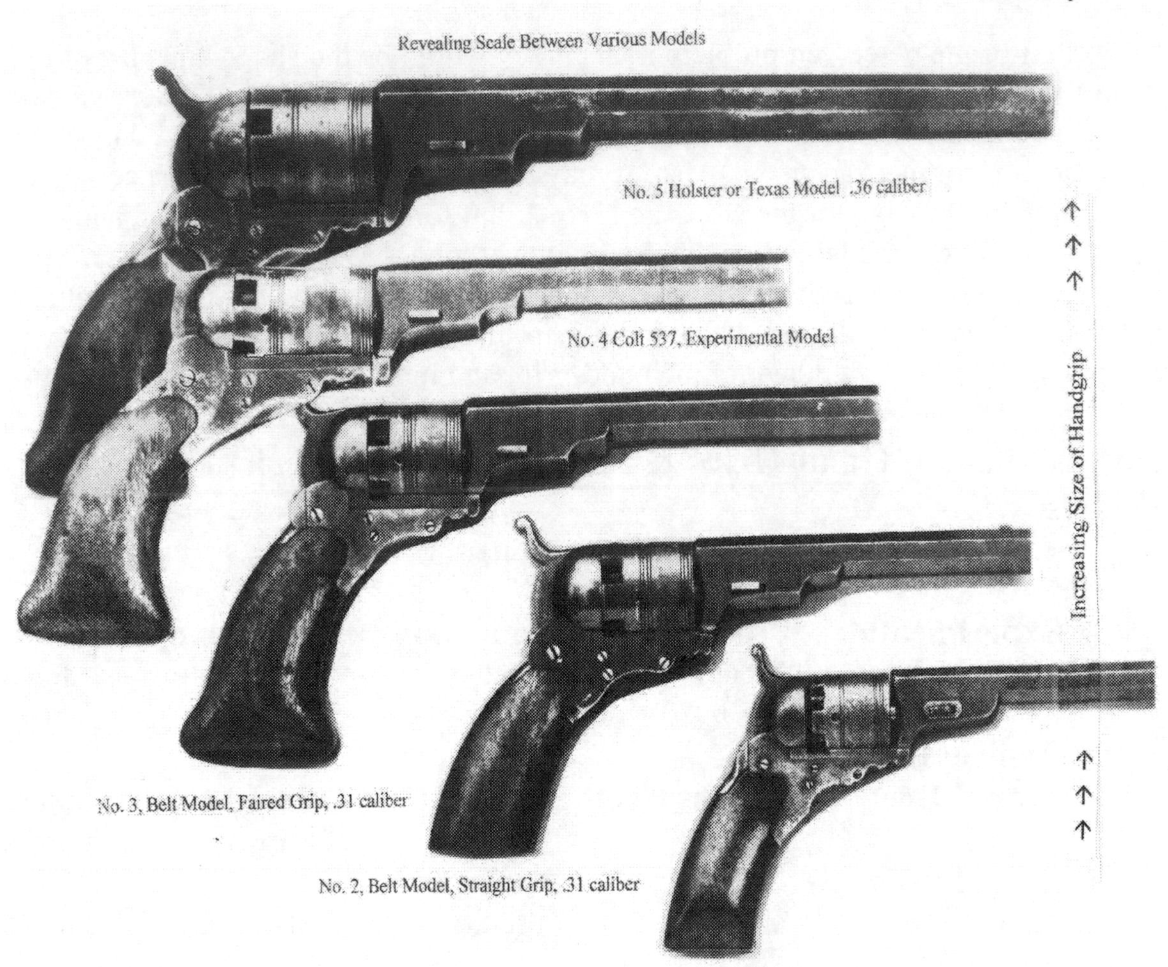

Increase in Size and Shape of the Hand Grip

Observe how Colt537 fits in between No. 3 Belt Model and No. 5 Holster or Texas Model above and on the following page. It seems as though Colt knew what he was doing all the time. The experiment was within a hair's breadth of the final No. 5 size. He knew where he wanted to end up, **Image 85**. Since the intent was to advance the Colt537 Experiment to the .36 caliber level and in doing so, assure the accuracy of this weapon. It would appear that Colt and Lawton made the Colt537 sacrificial device. It had the sized frame as needed for a .36 caliber load/charge. Therefore, utilizing the Colt537 elongated cylinder in the .36 caliber frame without expending additional resources was a very prudent decision

.Sam Colt vs. Dudley Seldon

Pressure to get on with production continued to be placed on Colt and Lawton from Dudley Seldon, the Company Treasurer, and others on the Board of Directors. The following is a quote from a letter Seldon had written to Colt and Colt's response. That pressure could have stifled any further development of Colt537, had it not been for Colt's persistence.

> "April 14th, 1837, Colt sarcastically wrote on his copy of the letter the essence of the conversation he had with Seldon: from D. Selden. Esq. dictating what sample guns to make for (and) to be examined at West Point."[60]

Dudley also complained that too much time and effort had been devoted to samples and experiments delaying the attention necessary to begin manufacture. As late as April 18, 1837 Seldon complained to Colt. It was during this time, the hand-making of Colt537 was begun.

> "Had you developed (disclosed) to the Company all the defects in the original plans the state of its affairs would have been different from what they now are. Seldon was in league with other members of the board, seeking the common goals of success and (quick) profit."[61]

The following are commentary between Colt and Dudley Seldon, Company Treasurer on July 5th 1837 regarding his frustration and annoyance with the actions and attitude of Colt:

> "A different rule ought not to be adopted for you from that which controls business generally."[62]

At issues were the debts of Colt to Seldon and the company, the high cost of making prototypes (really meaning experimental revolvers), and the fact that no machine mass produced guns had yet been completed for the market.

"The Patent ought to be assigned; you so stipulated and I have called your attention to it at least twenty times without any effect.

> "And there should be a penalty to Sam because of the deficiencies in the original plan, and loss of time, and the expense of constructing models

---

60. Paterson Colt Pistol Variations, Page 151, Col 1. Para 1, L 1
61. Paterson Colt Pistol Variations, Page 151, Col 1. Para 2, L 5
64 Paterson Colt Pistol Variations, Page 151, Col 1. Para 4, L 4

proving wholly defective, thereby delaying all the operations of the company, you represented that your instruments exhibited at the time the company was organized were free from all objections, you know how correct (incorrect) the statement was."[63]

The pressure placed on Colt at this time, it is believed, may have caused most of the ongoing experimentation to cease. The design of Colt537, from this point in time on, was reduced to solely pushing on a project which would lead to the development of the .36 caliber No. 5 Holster or Texas Model. This is when the proposal of any, or if any, No. 4 model was dropped.

The additional length of the .31 caliber cylinder of Colt537, in a way, was performing as a substitute for a .36 caliber revolver, Holster or Texas Model, obviously to determine the strength of the larger frame of the Colt537. If there was a failure at this point, it would mean back to the proverbial drawing board. This range of powder loads would also test the strength of the metal, of the cylinder, and internal working parts as well as the frame. There was always the concern of too much powder causing a rupture of the chamber.

This .31 caliber Colt537 experimental frame could, in terms of present-day standards, be considered a Magnum Model. The frame would have the capability of being fitted with any one of the .3l, .34, .36, or .44 caliber firing systems. A .44 grain charge would really be pushing it. This single frame could have been used as an all-purpose frame. If the Colt537 were a counterfeit, would someone have thought through all these possibilities? It is hard to believe that this would have been the case. **That being said, during this era, no other .31 caliber colt Paterson or Paterson Brevete cylinder with a ratio of length to width, close or similar to that of the Colt537 cylinder configuration have been found.** There is one exception, the Prototype experimental six-shot version of the No. 2 Belt Model revolver found on Page 80 *of Paterson Colt Pistol Variations*.[64] Also, in Image 6 on page 8 of this manuscript. **The ratio of No.3, Belt Models is 0.83. The average ratio among Paterson Brevetes is 1.14, the ratio for Colt537 ratio is I.41**, This is 24 % greater than all others, meaning that no other .31 caliber Paterson type revolver was able to pack as much gunpowder into a firing chamber as that found in the Colt537.[65] And, this may indicate that the design of the cylinder for Colt537 was, actually the first .31 caliber Magnum

63. Paterson Colt Pistol Variations, R.L. Wilson, Page 151, Col 1, Par 4, L 13
64. Paterson Colt Pistol Variations. R.L. Wilson, Plate No. 53, P 80
65. Research performed by the author

Clearly, the term that would be used today is that Colt and Pliny Lawton, were thinking outside the proverbial box. Time and financial resources limited how far outside of the box they could extend themselves.

> "Pliny Lawton and Colt took their largest size pistol (at that time) the Colt537 Experiment out to the firing range and tried their skill at shooting. They discovered that, with the front sight on the barrel, and the rear sight on the hammer lip, five shots could be fired at a mark with the same point of aim, and all grouped as well as the holding of the shooter. Then, with the barrel removed, the cylinder reloaded, the barrel replaced, and another round of five shots was fired, the shots would group as well but in an entirely different part of the target. In the smaller pistols, the very grips had not been large enough to hold the gun (revolver) well for accurate shooting. And this inherent inability to hold a point of aim had not gone unnoticed. Now it was evident in all of its horrible reality the Colts just wouldn't shoot! And, this was the sort of thing with which they had been trying to revolutionize warfare?"[66] **These are Sam Colt's exact words**!

It was hard to dismiss the association between each loads grouping, i.e., five shots at one location of the target and the next five shots grouping at another location on the target. But, be that as it may, Colt believes that the problem was with the rifling of the barrel and not the hand-grip, or anything else, for that matter. Colt exclaims,

> "***Why bother to even rifle the barrels, It was just a waste of labor***!"[67]
> **Again, Colt's exact words!**

But he had to check it out. This is a very important point which will eventually be discussed in the following pages. Colt and Lawton, rather than destroy any future factory made product, appear to stick with the Colt537 Experiment.

It is highly suspected, by me, the author that, euphemistically,* this is the "Smoking Gun."** ***The revolver was, in fact, the Colt537 Experimental, handmade in the Colt factory, under the supervision of Pliny Lawton, the plant manager. Better to use an experimental revolver than to try to rectify any problems after the production model has been developed. It was this Experiment in which the problem of accuracy resided. Colt and Pliny Lawton were determined to resolve the issue. In attempting to eliminate the accuracy problem, they inflicted a significant amount of damage to the bore of Colt537 Experiment. It started out as a hand-grip problem, and then shifted over to a rifling issue. There is evidence that the bore of Colt537 originally

66. The Story of Colts Revolver, William Edwards, Page 78, Col 1, Para 2, L. 1
67. The Story of Colts Revolver, William Edwards, Page 78, Col 2, Para 1, L. 12

had five lands and grooves. All the following manufactured revolvers, i.e., No. 1, No. 2, and No. 3 models had eleven lands and grooves. So what was so different about the Colt 537 Experimental, the five lands and grooves? That is not all; the cylinder was one-half inch longer than the regular No. 3, .31 caliber Belt Model. The longer cylinder had longer firing chambers. Hence, greater capacities of black powder in each of the five firing chambers could easily be employed for greater power. Larger capacities cause a stronger explosion, greatly increasing the velocity of the bullet. However, there exist diminishing returns; too much powder can also reduce the ball velocity. The above observation fits in with what was originally a phenomenon, discussed in the **second paragraph on page 107**. In addition, having less lands reduces the chance of gun explosion.

Colt Removes the Rifling in Colt537

Colt or Lawton may have incorporated a safety valve, so to speak, by establishing five lands and grooves in the bore of the barrel, and at the same time, by doing so, increased the effective distance and velocity of a shot by taking advantage of the extra powder capacity of the elongated cylinder. This is to say nothing regarding improvement or reduction in accuracy. It was a crossroads for both the inventor and the plant manager. It seems as though the rifling was still suspect. Additional concerns regarding excessive powder charges may also affect the accuracy in some way. The reader may recall that Colt being so frustrated with Colt537 Experiment's limited accuracy, he exclaimed,

"Why bother to even rifle the barrels, it was just a waste of labor."[68]

Colt537 originally had five lands and five grooves. Inspecting the revolver recently, I realized that the rifling of Colt537 Experiment had been removed. Colt or Lawton apparently had the rifling removed to determine if there really was some validity to this issue. The thought being, if there was no difference in accuracy, then why waste all that cost of labor in rifling the bore, if there was no payoff in doing so. There is evidence, in the bore, that this actually occurred. It can be seen that ninety-eight percent of these five lands were removed from the bore of Colt537 by some type of scraping or drilling, one can still see powder stains in the five grooves, as seen in **Images 86, 87, and 88 on the following pages.**

Colt537 Experiment as a Smooth Bore

It would appear that Colt537 had run its full course. And, there was no reason to publicize the fact. Hence, Colt537 Experimental model had no reason to be mentioned again.

[68] The Story of Colt's Revolver, William B. Edwards, Page 78, Col 2, Par 1, L 12

Since the rifling of the barrel had been reamed out, the diameter of the bore is now larger by a few hundredths of an inch. This requires a larger lead ball. However, since the cylinder has a larger powder capacity, which is due to the elongated firing chambers, the additional safety, that a rifled barrel provides (in its ability to release expanding gasses) had been eliminated, through the elimination of the rifling. The ignition of the larger powder capacity would have no channel for any excessive pressure to escape, if too much powder were used with a larger sized ball. This could possibly cause, as discussed previously, a rupture of the firing cylinder or the barrel. It would appear that Colt and or Lawton realized the danger and had a single groove run the length of the bore to serve as a channel to allow for escaping gas. Altering Colt537 in this manner completely exhausted its usefulness for any further purpose. It is not known if this final adjustment made any difference.

The Evidence!!!

When I obtained the revolver, the rifling in the barrel was missing. In addition, there was a deep groove running along the roof of the bore of the barrel. Logic tells us Lawton had the rifling removed from the barrel, to determine, once and for all, if it improved the accuracy. Upon inspection of the bore, traces of the rifling can still be seen. **Image 86** is a photographic image of the bore minus the lands, which can be faintly seen below. Observe the five darkened areas running the entire length of the bore. They appear to be the remains of the five grooves after the lands had been removed. The lighter areas are assumed to be where the lands once existed. Where the lands had been removed exhibits fresh surface, **Images 86, 87** and, **88** indicate the composite of locations of these grooves. If one were to shine a light down the bore, the deep cut groove on the roof of the bore would be visible. The cut of this groove is quite poor and reflects sloppy workmanship. This may be exhibiting the level of frustration within the Colt, Lawton and Crosby design and development team. The line in image 86 is pointing to the remains of one of the five lands in the bore.

Image 86

Source: M. Desparte

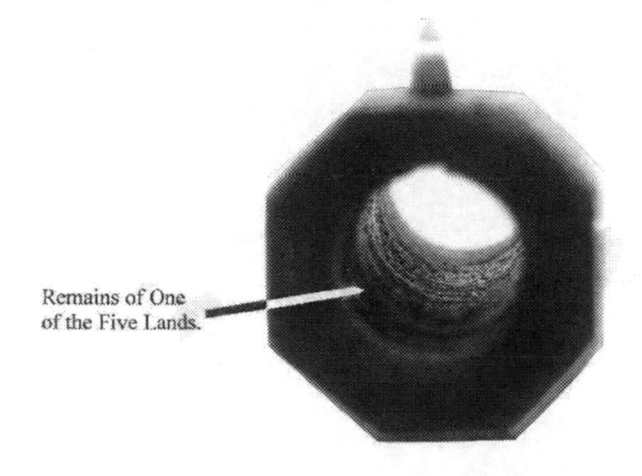

Bore of the Barrel – Lower Left
jpg.
Image 9

Image 87

Source: M. Desparte

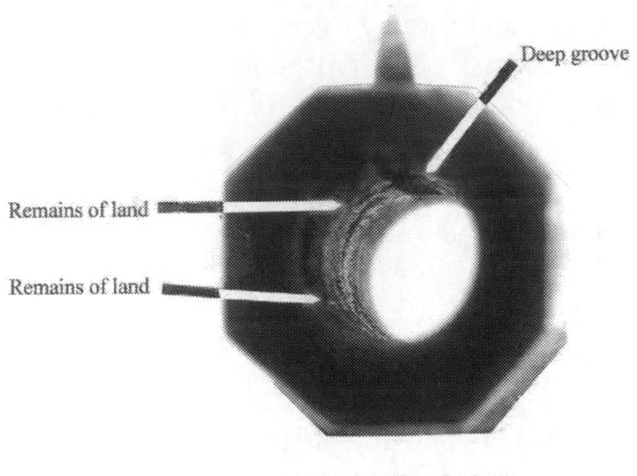

Bore of the Barrel – Left
jpg.
Image 9

Image 88

Source: M. Desparte

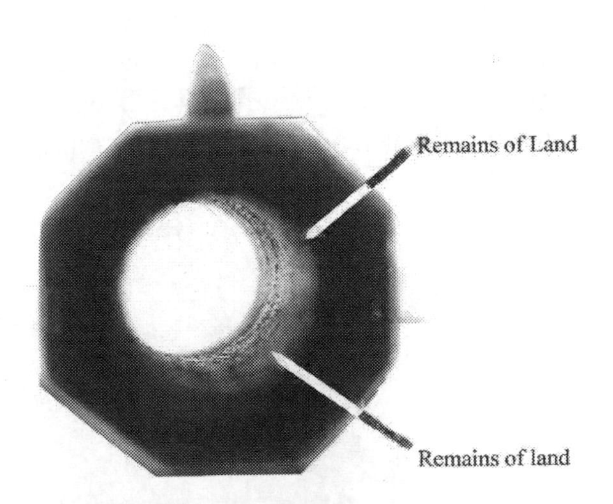

Bore of the Barrel – Right
jpg.
Image 9

Why Was the Rifling Messed With?

The dark areas could represent powder burns or stains of the grooves. One can also see some deep striations, which indicate that the lands had been scrapped away by some sharp instrument, leaving a relatively brighter smooth bore.

Apparently, this removal of the lands didn't bring any satisfaction for either Colt or Lawton. There may have been a concern regarding the capacity for excessive pressures generated by the greater amount of gunpowder used in the elongated cylinder. It is repetitive, but it is important to recall that the Colt537 Experiment cylinder was one half inch longer than the regular Belt Model cylinder at 1.22" in length. The longer cylinder has a longer firing chamber, a greater powder capacity. Consequently, the additional one half inch extension, now, has the possibility of rupturing the cylinder by carelessly loading the chamber to capacity. However, more than likely, cast steel was used in the cylinder due its extra capacity. Combining that with the fact that Colt's rifling was now nonexistent, there was no mechanism to reduce the excess pressure resulting from an overloaded powder charge when the ball is a shade within the size of the bore. Also, now with the removal of the lands, the size of the bore increased to somewhere between .310 and .314 diameter developing, say a .314" caliber smooth bore, possibly, the same caliber of the ball. If the ball were a smaller size, the ball could rattle from side to side as it sped along the bore when fired, further reducing accuracy.

One can observe that the caliber of the ball would have to be increased to snugly fit the bore of the barrel. This then would recreate the previous problem, i.e., a snug ball/bullet with no rifling, would be setting the stage for an excessive buildup of explosive pressure upon ignition. It was then, presumably, agreed between Lawton and Colt that again they had to provide a way to release excessive pressure. The one possible way was to develop a deep groove along the top of the bore from the breech to the muzzle, so as to function as a pressure release. Apparently, there must not have been any improvements to the accuracy of Colt537 Experiment, following this action. The following statement was taken from the text:

> "It must be something other than stability. In fact the remedy was simple. The hole bored (in the cylinder) to receive the cylinder arbor was drilled with a straight drill, which bored a hole slightly oversize but more or less slightly ovoid. The arbor, too, was also basically ovoid, and when the two mated, there was no fit at all. Had the barrel been part of a drill press and the arbor the tail of a drill holder, an apprentice would have suspected that with this state of affairs their axes would never coincide. Each time the barrel was replaced on the arbor and the wedge tapped in to draw it up tight, the minute irregularities on both arbor and inner bore surface of the cylinder would cause the pieces to miss match, and so the barrel naturally pointed in a slightly different direction. Observing the concentric wedging

effect of two mating tapers led Lawton to change the arbor-barrel boring and wrote to Colt, after an afternoon of good shooting, "and I think we can make each (No. 5) as accurate, good shooting followed."[69]

All this was occurring while, it was suspected, Dudley Seldon, was in his office, wringing his hands wondering what Colt was doing.

If one were to remove the barrel of Colt537, looking straight down at the cylinder on the arbor, one can see a slight amount of space between the arbor and the cylinder hole. This is just another highly suspect occurrence of Colt537 features that coincide with discussions found in any one of the source materials. **When does the plethora of circumstantial evidence validate the fact that Colt537 is the authentic Colt Experiment?**

This has been an effort to describe the difficulties surrounding the development of the No.5 Holster or Texas Model, through the experimentation conducted on the .31 caliber Colt537 Experimental revolver. It is felt that these last series of issues seriously limited any further experimentation with Colt537. I assume the gun was set aside, consequently languishing its existence in some corner shelf in the Colt Factory Supply Room. What future use or level of importance it could claim is unknown at this time.[70]

.

It now had a defective arbor, defective cylinder, altered rifled bore, i.e., a smooth bore, and finally a groove along the top of the barrel. What else could they have done with the Colt537 Experiment? The deep groove on the upper inside of the bore provides the escape route for gasses bypassing a tightly fitting ball.

What Colt and Lawton failed to recognize was they had, for a short period, developed the first Colt Magnum revolver. It took over a century and a half before the Colt factory recognized the potential, shown in the present day Colt537 and/or the Colt 44 Magnums. This is based on a lesser mass, flying at a greater velocity, and having a similar impact as that of a larger mass, traveling at a slower velocity, producing relatively the same amount of energy. It is not known if the elongated cylinder may have needed additional attention. The other factor was Dudley Seldon's insistence that Colt get on with the manufacturing the .36 caliber Holster or Texas Model. Had there been greater financial resources, what would the future have given them? Colt and his genius employees assisted in developing and expanding this great nation through further enhancement of his revolvers, there was always the concern of too much powder causing a rupture of the chamber of a pistol, be it a single shot musket or one of Colts revolvers. The story goes that one would be able to determine the length in time in service of a Cavalry Trooper by the number of fingers he had remaining on his shooting hand.

---

69. The Story of Colt'sRevolver, Wm. B. Edwards, page 78, col 2, par 2, 1 1

70. See Appendix 4, Letter describing years the Colt537 was kept as a family heirloom.

Chapter Nine
The Genesis of the No. 5 Model

Colt537 is the Genesis of No. 5 Holster or Texas Model

The development of Colt537 Experiment progressed as far as a .31 caliber revolver, with an extra-long cylinder, mounted on an enlarged frame. What is unique about Colt537 is that it is the hand-made predecessor of each of the four manufactured/production Paterson models. The Colt537, although being handmade has the finial markings of the No. 5 Holster or Texas Model. It is difficult to understand what their intent was in doing so, other than possibly setting it as the goal.

Colt realized he had some distance to go before he could reach the specific requirements of the military. His recent completion of the .28 caliber and .31 caliber Nos.2 and 3 models were deemed, by the military, as not having the stopping power the military was seeking. Colt's hope was that the production of the future .36 caliber Holster model would be something they would be interested in.

After building the Colt537 and the first three production models, Colt Lawton and Crosby moved on to the development of the more powerful revolver by taking the same well thought out, incremental steps, they extended their experimentation by rigorously checking the revolver's ease of recycling through all five chambers of the cylinder, first, by dry firing the gun multiple times. And then, loading and firing it in multiple cycles, using ball bullets. It is believed that a more powerful caliber concept utilizing Colt537's elongated cylinder with its greater gun powder capacity than needed, and its enlarged frame would assist in defining the path necessary in reaching their goal of a light and powerful .36 caliber revolver that could meet the military's needs.

Colt and Lawton also were thinking they could go beyond this goal by taking advantage of the removable recoil shield, similar to the one used in Colt537. This recoil shield was a separate part, separate from the frame with the advantage of eventually being reinforced for use in making one or two future production models. The design of which was left for the future. Apparently, they felt they could start with improvements to make Colt537 an ultra-powerful ,31 caliber magnum, Using the same elongated cylinder, they could have four levels of power for this magnum, a .31, 34 .36, and 44 powder loads, all using the .31 caliber ball, from .31 caliber firing chambers and through a .31

caliber bore. All that is really needed was strengthening the recoil shield, use cast steel in the cylinder and slightly increase the thickness of the frame. What flexibility!

After having the military realize that the .54 caliber revolver that they at first thought they wanted was too cumbersome and impractical, Colt felt certain the future .36 caliber Holster model revolver would be their eventual choice. The Colt537 Experiment was the stepping stone to that goal, but first, he needed to test out the capabilities of his new recoil shield, enlarged frame, cylinder, barrel, and its accuracy. More than likely, Colt and Lawton, determining that Colt537 was meeting the mechanical perfection they had sought, and now need to plan a pathway for the development of the production model, the .36 caliber Holster or Texas Model. If they jumped too far ahead, and if a complex problem were to arise, they would have to again refer, so to speak, back to the drawing board

More than likely, Lawton, Crosby, or one of the other members of his team needed to determine the amount of black powder required to obtain a specific amount of penetration on a wooden board at a specific distance. That distance would be the average distance from an enemy combatant during particular types of battle conditions. Once that was determined, the amount of black powder could be calculated. Knowing the diameter and weight of the ball, the next step would have been to determine the volume of the chamber that would hold the specific amount of powder plus the diameter of the ball. Also knowing the thickness of metal needed between the chamber walls would complete calculations for the .36 caliber cylinder. Considering the volume of Colt537 experiment's firing chambers, it was definitely designed to test the power and the function of the new enlarged frame. There were a few more needed steps concerning the redesign of the firing system that was not previously mentioned, but for simplicity purposes, the above description is close enough, as they say, "for government work." During this time, the Board of Directors and Dudley Seldon were wringing their hands, wondering when Colt would provide them with a product to sell.

The frame, having a cylinder gap of 1.72 inches, was more than enough length needed to house a .36 caliber cylinder. Rather than jump to the development of the .36 caliber cylinder, Colt and Lawton took a more cautious approach and developed a .31 caliber cylinder with a length of 1.72 inches. That length produced more than enough of a volume needed for varying velocities and impacts. It also reduced the amount of time it would have taken in making a .36 caliber barrel, a .36 caliber recoil shield, a .36 caliber cylinder, and the .36 caliber frame. That is to say nothing about the redesigning of all the internal working parts.

The parts for the construction of Colt537 were taken from various sources, some new and some old. There may have been parts found in the small gunsmith shop the company was using for other experiments prior to the completion of the Colt Factory. Once put together, Colt had the ability to utilize the extra capacity of the elongated cylinder (more than likely made of cast steel) to test the more powerful .31 caliber charges, and even going beyond a .36 caliber, and onto something close to the .44 caliber level, in terms of power. I was able to fill one of the chambers of Colt537 with 25 grains of black powder. That is enough gunpowder for a .44 caliber revolver, including the ball. It wasn't fired. This compilation was to determine how powerful one could make this revolver before it became dangerous to the shooter. A .36 caliber revolver would require a black powder load of approximately 15 to 18 grains, with a maximum of 20 grains; **see Image 32 on page 60,** for Colt Black Powder Pistol Loading Data.

Upon completion of testing, Colt would eventually use the design of the Colt537 to construct the .36 caliber Holster model. It would be a fairly easy thing to do, if it were accomplished in the Colt factory. The recoil shield, as mentioned previously, was a separate part that could be easily removed from the Colt537 Experiment's frame. The process could have been accomplished in steps. The recoil shield and cylinder arbor, attached to the recoil shield could be detached from the Colt537 frame and replaced with a larger recoil shield having an elongated cylinder arbor which would have the diameter of a .36 caliber cylinder. A .36 caliber cylinder would replace the .31 caliber elongated cylinder. It would also be necessary to replace the .31 caliber bore/barrel with a .36 caliber bore/barrel with eleven lands and grooves. The most difficult part of transitioning from Colt537 Experiment to the Holster or Texas Model would be making the internal firing system, i.e., internal working parts, including the hammer, hand, sear, trigger extension arm, and a sundry of other small parts, i.e., screws and flat springs. They would require a rescaling to the needed size and possibly slightly altered shape. Pliny Lawton might have been able to get away with only lengthening the hand for a longer cylinder rotation and re-synchronize the operation of the bolt.

> "No other gunsmith, outside of the Colt Factory, except for John Pearson, who wasn't working for Colt at this time, would have had the expertise, in redesigning these internal working parts. They would have a difficult time getting the mechanism to work correctly, by making exact copies of the same parts found in the .31 caliber Belt Model, or for any of the other models. Tolerances among these pieces are, 1/1000 of an inch."[71]

The firing system of the original .31 caliber No. 3 Belt Model would not be compatible with Colt537 Experiment or the No.5 Holster or Texas Model frame. For that matter, both the No. 3, and the No. 5 Holster or Texas Model design, may not have yet been on paper. It may not have gotten further than a figment of Colt's, or Lawton's, or Crosby's imagination, at this point in time (early 1837). Logic dictates that the Colt537 Experiment, in its early stage, would have been called the .31 caliber experiment, and it would have been up to the U.S. Military on how to motivate Colt into manufacturing a .36 caliber No. 5 Holster/Texas Model.

---

71. Paterson Museum, Paterson, New Jersey, Curator, Mr Bruce Balistrieri

Colt537's Experimental Frame

Here is a little back history to more or less set the stage for the development of a more powerful revolver. Colt knew he wasn't going to get anywhere trying to sell low caliber revolvers to the military. Many of the officers were interested in something more substantial. They were thinking of something like the .53 caliber level. This is a ball/bullet that was the same size as those used in that era's musket rifle, the mini-ball. This is the same sized ball that inflicted such terrible damage to soldiers on both sides during the Civil War. A sample of this pistol was ordered from the Colt factory for test purposes, by the U. S. Navy. It was the massive .53 caliber. The rifling was of seven lands and grooves. Eventually, it was determined to be impractical. One may recall that Colt537 Experiment originally had five lands and grooves. The production models Nos.1, 2, 3, and 5 had eleven lands and grooves. This appears to be a brand characteristic for Colt[72]. As was discussed there was a specific purpose for having specific number of lands and grooves.

As time went on the majority of the military minds were beginning to accept the theory that a smaller caliber with a greater velocity could do as much damage as a lumbering .53 caliber shot. In addition, this revolver was massive, in size and weight. More and more practical minds were thinking less mass and greater velocity. In today's terms, Colt was trying to match the foot pounds of energy produced by the .36 caliber bullet with that of the lumbering .53 caliber mini-ball. Example: 16lb. cannon ball at a velocity of 100ft per second vs. a 32lb cannon ball at 50ft per second. Both create the same amount of foot pound energy. The concept is illustrated below.

16lbs. x 100ft/sec. = 1600lbs energy, vs, 32lbs. x 50ft/sec = 1600lbs energy.

There were more accepting of the smaller caliber concept, i.e., the coming down from the .53 caliber size, while Colt was attempting to come up in size. Where would they meet? Between 1836 and 1837, Colt and Pliny Lawton initiate a strategy. Develop one test revolver, get it to function perfectly. Then use it as the design to make a series, of say, four or five revolvers differing in scale, and caliber. I called that test revolver the Colt537. Colt, on discussing this strategy with the P.A. Mfg. Co.'s board of directors, (this is assumed) a proposal was presented.

> "(the) First was (to be) the No. 1 Ring Lever rifle, followed by the No. 1 Pocket revolver. With the obvious importance of sales to government, the No. 1 rifle was an understandable product, but why the Pocket Revolver? It would appear that P.A. Mfg. Co. felt the diminutive arm would have a good market, and that the relatively small size meant a relatively small investment. Breaking in the workmen on the diminutive arm also allowed for Pliny Lawton and Colt to improve the manufacturing process

72. Paterson Colt Pistol Variations, RL Wilson, Plate No. 37, Page 74

and possibly develop details which would lead to more imposing larger-sized pistols. Furthermore, the Navy Commissioners had asked (February 24, 1836) for a sample pocket pistol, a suggestion that a market for such an arm existed even with the services."[73]

This experimental frame was unique in concept. It was composed of three-pieces. Consider the composition of a pocket watch. It has a back plate, a central piece and a front plate. The frame of this experimental revolver has a left plate, a central piece and a right plate. Both the pocket watch and the revolver have the central piece, in which the operating mechanism resides. Thinking ahead, Colt's new frame could utilize a number of different calibers without changing the frame size. The reason for the three-piece frame was to determine precisely where the internal parts of the firing system would lie. What ledges and voids would be needed to be milled to allow sufficient room for these internal parts to operate properly without decreasing the strength of the frame? Due to the nature of building something for the first time, there is a lot of guess work involved. The parts are attached to any one of the three pieces. The frame is assembled, but the mechanism does not function as desired. The three piece frame must then be dismantled. An assessment is made. Adjustments are employed and the frame is reconstructed. This process goes on until a satisfactory operation is achieved. Once accomplished, the three pieces of the frame can again be put together, without the internal mechanisms. Now having the knowledge of where ledges and void areas are located, a single piece frame can be milled out. Each new frame design would go through the same process in accommodating various calibers ranging from .28 to .36 caliber. One begins to acquire the impression that Colt could obtain unlimited derivatives from this concept. And in the years to come, this is exactly what he did.

This new experimental revolver with the larger frame was designed to handle powder charges from 15 grains to 25 grains for the .36 to .44 calibers, **see images 68 and 69 on pages 84 and 85**. Employing his incremental step philosophy, Colt's first model was this .31 caliber with a greater charge capacity than needed. This frame was designed to incorporate a 1.72" cylinder gap. Various calibers of cylinders could be employed on this frame, provided that a recoil shield and frame were capable of handling the shock produced by igniting the charge in the corresponding firing chamber. Hence, the .31 caliber recoil shield with an elongated cylinder of 1.72" and a .31 caliber barrel, along with the need for some of the other parts associated with the new frame.

The Colt537 Experiment was originally built as an enlarged experimental three-piece lock frame. Intentions were to eventually make more powerful .31, .34, .36, and even .44 caliber revolvers sitting on this enlarged frame, each only a step or two away from a transition to a single piece .36 or .44 caliber frame, ending that phase. It more than likely would be called a Holster Model, ready to be used as a template to copy in the

---

73. Paterson Colt Pistol Variations, RL Wilson, Page 96, Col 1, Par 3, L 3

manufacture of a salable product. It would be using relatively the same .36 caliber frame design as that of the Colt537 Experiment. But the prototype would include a single piece frame. The first model would arrive as a .36 caliber, No. 5, Holster or Texas Model.

Actually, this frame was designed to be used for a multiplicity of different calibers; the detachable recoil shield is the key. See the series of steps allowing the interchangeability of some of the key parts for this purpose, found in Appendix 2. After the completion of the No. 3 Belt Model the development of the No. 5 frame (now single piece machine produced) was initiated. This time the .36 caliber cylinder was developed and fitted onto a roughly, inch and a half, cylinder gap. Any slight adjustment would be accomplished by snugging up or relaxing the length of the cylinder gap, through the adjustment of the recoil shield. This adjustment is needed for the placement of the .36 caliber cylinder on the (now machine produced) single piece frame. This can only be accomplished after the barrel was attached to the frame. The correct alignment of the .36 caliber firing chambers (yes, now machine produced) to the .36 caliber barrel was essential. Now the remaining parts needing resizing or rescaling would also be made by machine within the factory and hand filed where needed to be able to interact effectively with the rest of the firing mechanism. It is believed that this revolver was called the No. 5 or the Holster Model. It was not until a later date that the name of the model and was changed to the "Texas Model" when the news got out about the battle of Bandera Pass: The name change was made by Colt to reflect the revolver's effectiveness in the following gun battle with the Comanche Indians.

> "In an engagement with seventy to eighty Comanche Indians, who after an engagement of a few hours of intense fighting made a hasty retreat (leaving) thirty to forty dead bodies on the field, only two of Captain Hays of a squad of fourteen Texas Rangers were badly speared, but recovered.[74]

The significance is that the Colt537 Experiment is the Genesis of the No. 5 Holster or Texas Model revolver. Simple logic tells us that there would not have been a No. 5 Holster or Texas Model if there had not been the Colt537 Experiment.

The large three-piece, Colt537 Experimental frame with its advanced internal firing mechanism, coupled with the company's recent experiences gleaned during the development of the No. 1, 2, and 3 production models, and their interactions with Colt537, all aided in making the No. 5 Holster or Texas Model the gun that started the, "**Winning of the West**."

---

74. Paterson Colt Pistol Variations, L.R. Wilson, page 188, Col 1, Par 4, L 4

The Transition of Colt537 to the Mass Produced No. 5 Holster or Texas Model.

1. The profile and other factors associated with the design of the Colt537 Experiment were transformed from being a hand-made pistol to a production line and machine made .36 caliber, 5 shot revolvers.

2. The Colt537 Experimental markings transitioned to the production No. 5 Holster or Texas Model Barrel, the Patent claims, Address, and Model designation finials.

3. The Colt537 Experiment enlarged three-piece frame was redeveloped into a machine made single piece frame. This new frame, generally, retains its large size, shape, and internal platforms for rescaled internal parts of the No. 5, Holster or Texas Model.

4. During the transition, the Colt537 Experiment's .31 cal. recoil shield was able to be removed and replaced with a production type .36 cal. recoil shield.

5. The Colt537 Experiment .31 cal. barrel could be removed and replaced with a .36 cal. barrel.

6. The Colt537 .31 cal. cylinder and recoil shield, with Arbor/Pin, was replaced by a normal sized .36 cal. Cylinder and recoil shield.

Other factors leading to the completion and development of a new .36 cal. No. 5 Holster or Texas Model have not been found in any of the resources reviewed for this document that addresses the following needs.

1. Calculate the length of the hand needed to rotate the circular ratchet/toothed rack, encircling the arbor, and attached to the breech of the cylinder, so as to perfectly align each one of the five firing chambers with the bore of the barrel. See diagram of the composition of the No. 5 Holster or Texas Model Schematic Drawing, **page 48** of this manuscript, and the rest is assumed.

2. Establish the number of teeth, and the distance between each tooth, on the toothed ratchet to assist in the perfect alignment of each one of the five firing chambers with the bore of the barrel.

3. Calculate the distance required for the cylinder to rotate for perfect alignment with each of the five firing chambers.

4. Set the timing of the bolt so as to have it lock the cylinder in place, once the alignment of the firing chamber is completed.

5. Determine the size of the rotating half disc attached to the lower forward face of the hammer so as to rotate the exact distance needed to have the hand move the ratchet or toothed rack the exact distance needed to assist in the rotation of the cylinder in performing task 1 to 4 above.

6. While at the same time as the hammer is performing task 5, the firing ledge of the hammer is placed in the exact location on the forward face of the lower part of the sear, so as to release the hammer when the trigger is depressed allowing the hammer to swing forward onto the percussion cap and fire the revolver. The process is repeated four additional times.

It is important to note that R. L. Wilson refers to the first of "factory production models" as prototype, (but not experimental). I consider the Colt537 an experimental. Experimental because, although the frame is similar, only similar, to production models in design and size, The Colt537 was first proven, to be a compilation of thought, having a three-piece lock frame. In other words, the frame is correct in terms of design and size, but the internal system, at that time, was yet to be tested and modified to assure continuous service.

Thinking back, why were the two .31 caliber revolvers labeled as No.2 and No. 3 Belt Models? Because one had a straight hand-grip and the other had a flared hand-grip? The only difference between the two was the shape of the hand-grip. The shape of the hand-grip determined the difference between No. 2 Belt Model and No. 3 Belt Model? That was all? Later on in production, the No. 3 was also developed as a .34 caliber. Carrying this logic a step further, if that was the only difference between the two models, then the increased length of Colt537 Experiment's, .31 caliber cylinder, could be easily justified in assuming that Colt537 Experiment could also be the No. 4 experimental revolver. Or, Colt537, a .31 caliber could have been one of two No. 5 models, with Colt537 being a .31 caliber magnum type revolver, and, the other, the No. 5 Holster or Texas Model being the second. Colt 537 could not fit this nitch, it wasn't a production model.

Looking at the history of the development of the Belt Model, Model No. 3, and Colt537 Experiment, are .31 caliber revolvers. Some may be thinking they were built at the same time. Therefore, the Colt537 Experiment could keep its present makeup as a more potent .31 caliber revolver, by improving on its primitive Experimental frame, and elongated cylinder. However, this thought runs into trouble because Colt537 is comprised of handmade parts and a three piece main frame. All would have to be redesigned.

Historical Significance of the Colt Paterson Experiment

"R.L. Wilson, in defining one model of Paterson from another, he indicated that Colt made no reference to the barrel length, type of grips, or caliber. He believes that Colt refers only to frames and cylinders. There are two sizes of frames and cylinders, in the factory production models produced prior to the eventual development of the No. 5 Holster or Texas Model,"[75]

By virtue of this comment, he is not including experimental revolvers. All that was really needed was to case harden the cylinder, replace the.31 caliber barrel, place the address with the star and snake finials on the barrel, and perform other internal enhancements to meet the requirements of factory machinery and enable Colt537 to be a production No. 4, .31 caliber magnum, but that didn't happen.

The Three-Piece Frame

Image 89 **Image 90**

Source: M. Desparte Source: M. Desparte

View of Three-Pieces or Plates of Colt537 Experiment Frame

Fore-grip section of middle plate, i.e., the fore-grip extension

Right Plate, plus visible portion of the middle plate, i.e., the fore-grip

75. Paterson Colt Pistol Variations, P.R. Phillips and R.L. Wilson, page 7, Para 3, L 13

In spite of the pros and cons associated with this issue, work continued, on the development of the .36 caliber Holster model, using the design of the Colt537 Experiment frame, but, converting it to a single piece frame and keeping the basic design of the firing system, i.e., internal workings to eventually produce the No. 5, Holster model.

Images 89, 90, 91, and 92 depict the three-piece frame of Colt537 Experiment. The three plates/pieces of the frame being sandwiched together.

The No. 5, Holster model frame and the Colt537 Experiment frame look very similar, in spite of the fact that one is a single piece and the other is composed of three-pieces. The three-piece frame is a telltale sign that it was the original frame makeup. No other Colts of this size are found with a three-piece frame.

Image 91

Source: M. Desparte

Underside of Colt537 Three-Piece Experimental Frame

In order to house the internal firing system, the milling must meet an extremely precise configuration. The cavity, produced by such precision milling, is irregular in shape. It will be larger in some areas and smaller in others, and may have minute platforms on which springs and levers will be attached. Given the type of machinery available at that time, milling out the interior of the frame would have been next to impossible without, first milling out platforms and other irregular cavities on each of the three-pieces/frame plates. I wonder how many pieces of a reproduced plate were thrown out because of over milling or other misjudgments.

Image 92

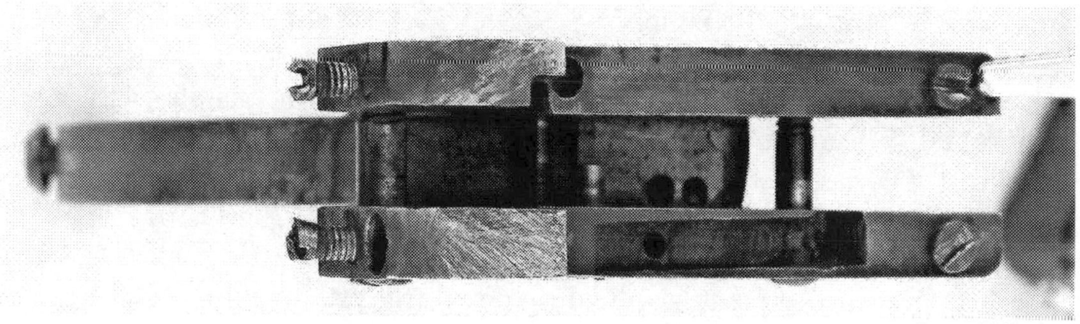

Source: M. Desparte

Top of the Three-Piece Frame and Required Milling

View the comparison between the Colt537 Experiment, **on page 48, Image 17 Item 11** and that of the No. 5 Holster model, **Image 90, page 121**, then review the location of Bolt Screw and the Actuating Bar Screw on both revolvers.[76]&[77] Their positions indicate the frame is similar to that of the Colt537 Experiment, and the later No.5 Holster or Texas Model, indicating that they both have similar, and almost exact, internal firing systems. The No. 5 Holster model exhibits a more refined version of the Colt537 Experiment. The three-piece frame of Colt537 indicates it is the first cut at making a frame from scratch, an experiment. It is next to impossible to make a solid one piece frame and be able to precisely locate where each individual part would sit. The question arises as to who fabricated the revolver? Based on my research, it is believed that most of the design work was accomplished by Samuel Colt, Pliny Lawton and Harold B. Crosby, (Crosby by one source was considered the gun designer in the Paterson factory). The proof lies in the fact that the barrel has the correct address with the new finials for the Holster or Texas Model. Rolled forms of engraving were produced in the Colt factory. The fact that Colt537 Experiment has the finial designation, *~~~~~~, in its address, indicates it was factory produced. Other experiments used by Colt, possibly not having the address placed on them, were, more than likely, designed and built by John Pearson and his assistants. Brash and Cummings spent most of their time in their Baltimore shop prior to 1837. Although not mentioned too much in this paper but an individual having significant expertise in the Colt plant was H. B. Crosby. He was deemed as a highly respected craftsman and more than likely had a hand in developing the Colt537.

---

76. Appendix 2, Pages 1 and 2
77. Appendix 2, Pages 2

To nail down that this enlarged frame was produced by Colt, Lawton and Crosby, it is necessary to review the following quote from R.L. Wilson's book on Paterson Colt Pistol Variations which speaks to the issue.

> "Features shown and subsequently adopted in Paterson pistols (varied and improved in various degrees) include automatic drop-down trigger (when cocking the hammer), "V" type mainspring, stop slots on periphery of cylinder, and basic construction of lock frame, cylinder, and barrel."[78]

The Colt537 Experiment has the drop down trigger, stop slots on the cylinder, and a basic three-piece lock frame. The complete revolver is composed of thirty six (36) pieces. Colt537 Experiment does not have a one piece frame, and the "V" type mainspring. However, previous experimental models produced by John Pearson or Colt Patent Arms had single leaf mainsprings, including the Colt537 Experiment. It was a .31 caliber, having internal parts enabling the rotation of the cylinder to accurately stop and lock for firing. It was designed, geared, and built for the functioning of the .31 caliber on a .36 caliber frame. In essence, the .36 caliber No. 5 was completely designed from the lessons learned in constructing the .31 caliber Experiment with the enlarged frame. The .36 caliber frame in the No. 5 Holster or Texas Model now had a .36 caliber barrel, cylinder, and recoil shield, hammer and all the necessary internal parts geared with the proper sequencing of activities and lengths. Once completed, the No. 5 could be called the prototype. From this point on, patent drawings were made of appropriate parts for approval. Also from this point, the prototype could be used as a template from which other No. 5 Holster or Texas Models could be manufactured, sold, and finally generate a profit for the company.

I am stating this once again, it is extremely important and must be understood, the one piece frame is next to impossible to mill out for an exact configuration of the internal area, for the attachment of internal moving parts, without knowing the exact dimensions of each part (within one thousandth of an inch) and the exact location of where these internal parts will reside. The ensuing trial and error process would require continuous access to the installed mechanism in order to identify which of the pieces require some slight or major adjustment, or even reshaping to enable the part to function adequately. All it would take is a one-thousandth of an inch in the wrong location to render the revolver inoperable. It may even require more than one of the internal parts to receive additional attention since more than one or two pieces interact with each other. This three-piece frame is unique, it is the mother design. Colt537 Experiment's new enlarged frame became the No.5 Holster, and later called the "Holster or Texas Model", having the same designed, enlarged frame. Slight adjustments were made to accommodate machine manufacturing. This statement needs to be repeated again and again.

---

78. Paterson Colt Pistol Variations, P.R. Phillips and R.L. Wilson, page 7, Para 3, L 13

Historical Significance of the Colt Paterson Experiment

When viewing all of the models pictured and their descriptions in detail in all of the books available to me, i.e., including *Colt Brevete Revolvers*, *The Paterson Colt Book*, *The Folding Trigger Paterson Colt*, *The Story of Colt's Revolvers*, and *Paterson Colt Pistol Variations* among others, none were found having a three-piece or plate frame. The three-piece frame will be found, only on the experimental versions of the individual model. The design is similar to that of a pocket watch. A pocket watch is also made up of three plates, a front, center and back plate. The center plate houses the working parts. Front and back plates provide protection and access to the internal parts.

Chapter Ten
Differences in internal and external Parts

Internal and External Parts of No. 3 Belt, No. 5 Holster or Texas Model, and Colt537

Can the Colt537 Be Replicated?

When the hammer is pulled back to a cocked position, there are three distinct operations taking place at the same time.

As the hammer, **Item 29 on page 48,** is being cocked, it forces the hand, **Item 28**, which is attached to the hammer to move upward. In doing so, the upper tip of the hand catches the teeth of the toothed rack, **Item 7**, which rotates around the cylinder arbor or pin, **Item 9**. Attached to the toothed rack is a cam which fits in a groove in the central part of the cylinder **Item 3**, causing it to rotate around the cylinder pin. The hand rotates the toothed rack a specific distance so that one of the firing chambers aligns itself with the bore of the barrel, **Item 1**.

While the above is happening, the bolt, **Item 12,** disengages from the cylinder's cylinder stop, slot allowing the cylinder to rotate its prescribed distance, mentioned above, upon completion of the cylinder's rotation; the bolt re-engages with the next cylinder stop and locks the cylinder in place.

Concurrent with the two above activities taking place, the sear assembly, **Item 15**, is pushed forward by the base of the hammer which forces the trigger (**Item 16**) to rotate downward. This sets the revolver in a ready to be fired position.

Upon squeezing the trigger, the sear assembly is pulled forward by a flange at the upper end of the trigger. This disengages the sear from its locked, cocked position. The hammer, being released by the sear, enables the head of the hammer to rotate forward and slam onto the percussion cap, which is sitting on the nipple tube, **Item 4 on page 48,** attached to the breech of the firing chamber. The cap is ignited, sending a spark down the nipple tube to the firing chamber, igniting the powder, sending the bullet on its way.

Historical Significance of the Colt Paterson Experiment

Consider the mental exercise needed to identify and determine the following:

1. The beginning of a shooting sequence of activities. When the hammer is pulled back the cylinder will rotate a specific distance, and align a firing chamber with the bore. of the revolver.

2. Now that cylinder, in order to keep that alignment, must have a locking device. The firing chamber must be locked by the bolt to maintain this perfect alignment.

3. How will this locking device unlock and lock itself in thc rotating cycle?

4. How will this cylinder rotate?

5. How will the trigger extend itself?

6. How will all these things be accomplished by the mere pulling back of the hammer?

7. How will this chain reaction be accomplished?

8. How many pieces and what are they in order to build a Colt No. 5 Holster or Texas Model?

A gunsmith wishing to make a revolver just like Colt537, who doesn't have any of these parts, is taking on a monumental task. He must somehow acquire a No.5 frame. Oops, can't find a No. 5 frame, the No. 5 frame is made of one solid block of metal. Thc Colt537's frame is a three-piece frame. One would have to split the No.5 frame into three flat plates, to make one similar to the Colt537 Experiment, that is to say, similar to what is shown in **Images 89, 90, 91,** and **92, pages 121 and 123**. The alternative would be to acquire three plates of metal to make an exact copy of the Colt537 Experiment frame. It seems to me that the gunsmith would stop right there, and think to himself," How will I accomplish this without having an exact copy of this spccific revolver?"

Hmm, there is only one revolver exactly like this in the world. It seems that this would be an excellent place to stop since all the internal parts found in the Colt537 Experiment would be larger, smaller, or slightly different in design, than the Colt No. 3 or the No. 5. This is due to the fact that it was a .31 caliber revolver, having a .31 caliber recoil shield, causing a smaller diameter of cylinder, smaller bore in a barrel and slightly re-sized internal firing system. That would include an altered angle of attack on the smaller or larger hammer, a recalculated length of the hand, sear assembly, sear lever and trigger. In addition, these internal parts had to be hand filed and manipulated to enable thc revolver to function smoothly. Tolerances are as close as one thousandth of an inch are needed.

There would be no reason to make this Colt537 Experiment revolver, say 50, 100 or 150 years later than its era. What would have been the purpose? It is highly unlikely that the person would find a .31 caliber recoil shield, with all of its integral parts, and then have to make an elongated .31 caliber cylinder; there are none of these around. Then make and place recoil shield and the cylinder on a three-piece frame, which would also have to be made. Then bore out the barrel of a perfectly good .31 caliber barrel having 5 lands and grooves. It is highly unlikely that you would find one. Then you would have to fire the revolver, say more than 200 times (estimate) to cause a staining of the metal caused by burning gunpowder. After this, scrape the lands and grooves out and make the barrel a smooth bore, but yet retain the stain of the grooves. And, then place another groove along the top of this inner now smooth bore, to release the excessive buildup of pressure, resulting from using a larger than .31 caliber ball. Then realizing one needs to enlarge the diameter of the firing chambers in the cylinder to match up with the larger than normal .31 caliber smooth bore. It doesn't make sense, does it?

Replacements, Worn Out Parts, and Scrap

In some cases, a gun may be found that is composed of a collection of parts, from other guns, not necessarily from the Colt factory. However, it is also important to mention the eventual replacement of parts, usually, was due to heavy use and improvements. As parts wore out, they were replaced with used parts from other cannibalized revolvers, and new pieces were added as the situation dictated. Hence, in these cases, serial numbers or shop numbers found on these replaced parts would not, of course, match those of the original. Colt537 Experiment has sets of differing identifying numbers throughout the revolver; however, most are in the right locations. This lends credence to the fact that many of the pieces of Colt537 Experiment were thought to have been taken from the factory's faulty parts bin, or miscellaneous parts found in the plant's gunsmith shop; realizing that many faults, due to a needed purpose, may have been negligible. In fabricating this experimental pistol, it is hard to determine if some parts came from the gunsmiths' scrap pile or some other source of replacement parts. See Standard Location for control numbers and misused serial numbers, **page 94**. The significance is: differing identification numbers in correct locations indicate a Colt product may have been scrapped or discarded for some unknown reason.

The parts, where did they come from?
It was important as to what parts these numbers were found on:

The hammer	No Numbers
The recoil shield	No Numbers
Trigger Actuating bar	No Numbers
Hand	No Numbers
Cylinder Ratchet	No Numbers
Cylinder Pin	No Numbers

Part	Numbers	Notes
Recoil Shield	No Numbers	
Sear	No Numbers	
Trigger Extension Bar (lever)	No Numbers	
Bolt	No Numbers	
Trigger	No Numbers	
Mainspring (leaf)	No Numbers	
Barrel 714, 58 large, 6, 0,	Numbers,	* Too many Nos. used on different experiments
Wedge 7?4, ? = unclear	Numbers	May have been a spare part
Back Strap 71	Numbers	Had the appearance of being reshaped
Frame Plate 771	Numbers	May have been a spare part
Cylinder 571	Numbers	Probably made at Colt Factory
Frame Front Grip Strap	Numbers	Could be gunsmith's control Number 771

*Barrel was 1/16 of an inch short of 5", would be enough to file off numbers on the breech side or lug side of the barrel. Barrel had the No. 5 address on it, but reversed.

Summing up my thoughts regarding the source of the parts found in Colt537. It is my belief that the main piece of this revolver is the frame. The frame has a number on it. It cannot be a serial number, because the frame is a three-piece frame. Therefore it is an experimental piece. The number on the center plate of the three-piece frame is a workshop job number, not a serial number. No one has ever figured out how their number sequencing was conducted.

It becomes apparent that some pieces of Colt537 may have been taken from a defective parts bin. Actually the part may not have been defective, meaning inoperable for the job it was intended to perform. It may have been an over-cut on some corner or deep file markings that destroyed whatever was being made. Hence, it may or may not have had a job number on it, in the experimental workshop.

In summary, all of the major pieces where numbers were found, the numbers were attempted to be eradicated, All of the numbers were different. Therefore eliminating someone claiming this revolver was a prototype, a few numbers were still visible, while others were visible under a microscope. The numbers found were not consistent, almost random in nature. Consequently, It is believed that all parts were either made by Colt workers, and the remainder came from the Colt's Parts Bin.

Chapter Eleven
Conclusions

The Largest Paterson Production Model Revolver Made

The largest pistol made by John Pearson for Colt was a .54 caliber made in 1835 or1836.[79] There were other samples ranging in size and caliber that were ordered by the Navy for test purposes, but the .54 caliber was the largest. It had seven lands and grooves, and was identified as Serial No. 1 on the butt strap, back of the barrel, frame plate; back of the cylinder and internally.

To the Navy, it seemed as if Colt was ready to continue to make these on a grand scale, if the military were so inclined. However, that was not the case. After looking at the cost of ammunition, i.e., black powder and lead for ball or bullet, and its unwieldiness, thinking began to trend toward a philosophy of greater velocity, less weight, and more economical opportunities.[80] The gun was so massive that it eventually disqualified itself from use by most of the military and naval officials that sought to sponsor it.

The Colt537's .31 caliber bore had rifling with five lands and grooves, and five firing chambers. Each chamber could accept as much as 25 grains. This amount of powder would be more than sufficient for a .36 and enough for a .44 caliber revolver.

Considering the lesser number of lands or grooves, in the barrel, i.e., five; it becomes apparent that the capacity of this cylinder was used to find the optimum amount of powder for the greatest penetration. Based on the army standard of 59-foot pounds of energy, the minimum amount of killing power needed in a bullet, and a .36 caliber using 15-20 grains of black powder would amount to enough bullet energy needed in stopping a moving human target.

All of the other manufactured models, i.e., the No. 1 Pocket Model, the No. 2, and the No. 3 Belt Models, having eleven lands and grooves, must have also gone through

79. Paterson Colt Pistol Variations, R. L. Wilson, Page 59, Plate 25, L 1
80. Paterson Colt Pistol Variations, R. L. Wilson, Page 59, Plate 25, L 5

similar experimentation to determine optimum amounts of powder usage prior to designing the cylinder with its firing chambers. And, the depth of these chambers was set at the optimum. Here again, a significant amount of experimentation had to take place. The time taken for this activity was a continuous frustration to those seeking immediate profit from sales.

> The thought-"that guns shoot less well with less force and penetration, when overcharged, and that there is one charge which may prove best all around."[81]

This thinking may be part of the problem with the accuracy of a firearm. Experimentation on accuracy may not have taken into account undercharged or overcharged firing cylinders.

Colt537's Travel through Time is Not Exactly Crystal Clear, But Close

Colt537 was purchased at an auction held at the:

> "Rushmore Civic Center, Rapid City, South Dakota in 2011[82]"

At the time of this author's purchase of Colt537 Experiment the revolver was owned by a Mr. Frederick, of Montana. *(The person is real, the name is fictitious)* The ad stated the revolver was an,

> "Early copy of Colt Patterson belt pistol, was the only marking" i.e., Pat. Arms Mg. Co. Patterson NJ-Colts PT", is on the top of the five-inch barrel. It also has nickel a silver blade front sight, a 3I caliber bore, fitted with walnut grips. The revolver displays a natural silver gray turning brown patina, with a smoothly functioning tight action. The only known history relating to this gun is that it was purchased many years ago from an elderly couple at a Baltimore gun show. No FFL."[83] **See Appendix 1, page 140.**

The seller of the pistol was a Mr. Frederick, who purchased the revolver from a Mr. Gunnerson, *(The person is real, the name is fictitious)* of Sioux Falls, SD. Upon receiving a letter from Mr. Gunnerson, he indicated that he bought the subject Paterson revolver in question, which he called the Experiment No.4, from an elderly couple (husband and wife) during a gun show, in Sioux Falls, South Dakota, in February 1998. Gunnerson indicated he was very interested in the history behind the gun. The elderly

---

81. The Story of Colt's Revolver, William B. Edwards, Page 55, Col 1, L 20
82. Paterson Colt Pistol Variations, R.L. Wilson, Page 7, Par 3, L 3
83. Rushmore Civic Center, Rapid Center, South Dakota in 2011

couple told him the family story about how they received the gun. Their great, or great, great-grandfather had worked for the Paterson Company in Paterson, New Jersey. When the company went bankrupt, the subject employee's wages were not paid; instead, the employees not receiving recent pay were permitted to take their wages in guns or gun parts. According to the elderly couple, Colt537 was the revolver their great-great grandfather was working on at the time, so he completed it and took it home. The couple also relayed that it had been in the family since the time of the plant closing, that date would be sometime in 1842. However, the elderly couple was not willing to give him the family name, and he dropped the issue. Mr. Gunnerson also indicated that he eventually sold the gun to a Mr. John Frederick.

When comparing the Gunnerson letter to the auction statement made by Mr. Frederick, his statement was, “he purchased Colt537 from Mr. Gunnerson at a Baltimore Gun Show”. This appears to be a disconnect between the two. Gunnerson states the exchange took at a gun show in Sioux Falls, S.D. That raises a red flag. In addition, Mr. Gunnerson's discussion with the elderly family and their reluctance to provide him with their last name diminishes what could have been a great story. That raises the second red flag. The failure to provide a receipt, for the cash exchange of $1,750.00, for the pistol, in 1998, seems highly suspect. That amount, in that year, would have been a small fortune. That's the third red flag.

The fact that the revolver exchanged hands between Mr. Frederick, and Mr. Gunnerson has been verified. If Mr. Gunnerson’s sale took place at a Baltimore gun show, it would render more credence to the story. John Pearson’s gunsmith shop was in Baltimore. But then the question would be, did the relative actually work in the Colt factory or did he work for Pearson. But then again, the revolver, based on information gleaned from the book, had specific attributes that are solely Colt markers, i.e., “The Colt Address and respective finials proving the gun was made at the Colt factory”[84], &”[85]. Consequently, it was a Colt worker. A receipt would have provided Mr. Gunnerson with the exact information needed to prove the accuracy of the transfer as well as lineage.

The transferring of the revolver from generation to generation for three or four generations seems very plausible; it makes sense, and is a good story in itself. The time span seems to fit. But, the fact that the great whatever, grandfather, the employee at the Colt factory, was working on this particular model of the revolver doesn't fit. If the great grandfather had worked on the gun and then took it home as payment for his labor, then who or how did the reaming out of the rifling in the bore occur? And, who placed the additional groove in the bore? The plant officially closed in 1842. It is believed the employees were released long before that. Because of its unique characteristics, this revolver is proving to have quite a story, in spite of its contradictory aspects when

84. Paterson Colt Pistol Variations, L.R. Wilson, Page 17, Item C
85. The Story of Colt's Revolver, William B. Edwards, Page 53, Col 2, Par 3, L 5

comparing auction notes with the Gunnerson letter, reamed out rifling, hmmmm? deep groove along the roof of the bore, hmmmm?

With regard to the statement made by Mr. Frederick, found in the auction notes, there are additional conflicting issues that need to be brought to light. It is stated that the revolver is a copy of a Colt Paterson Belt Model. This is not true. The image, of the right side, of the frame, indicates the revolver is not a Belt Model. The right side of the frame has a screw arrangement that reflects the contrary. The bolt screw is forward of the actuating bar screw or sometimes called the sear screw. Belt Models have that bolt screw rearward of the actuating bar or sear screw. On further analysis, the frame of the revolver is larger than that of the normal Belt Model revolver. The cylinder of Colt537 is the close to the same length as that of the No. 2 Experimental Belt Model shown in **Image 7 on page 8.** In fact, the frame is close to the same size as a Holster or Texas Model revolver. The revolver also has barrel markings which indicate it is a member of the Holster/Texas Model family. Those markings include the star and snake finials, before and after the address. This is a very good indication that the revolver may be an experimental version of the No. 5 Holster or Texas Model. **See pages 51 and 96** to view the complete address with finials. The truth is, that Mr. Frederick didn't realize what he had.

I reflect back to Pliny Lawton in February of 1836. He spoke of breaking in the workmen on the diminutive arm, which would allow himself and Colt to improve the manufacturing process and possibly develop details which would lead to more imposing larger sized pistols. It is my belief Pliny Lawton was talking about the development of, or the use of, the template/sample/pattern/design of the Colt537 Experiment to be used as the guiding design in making the No. 1 Pocket or Baby Model Paterson, the Nos. 2 and 3 Belt Models and finally the No. 5 Holster or Texas Model. The three-piece lock frame is proof of being the template for a more substantial single piece frame of approximately the same size as Colt537. The associated parts support that theory. The composition of parts included rudimentary coil springs rather than the flat springs used in the four production models. The flat or leaf type mainspring was another rudimentary piece which was replaced with the "V" type mainspring. The list goes on.

With the above proof in mind and considering all of these features found in Colt537, it is safe to reiterate that Colt537 is the Genesis of the four Paterson Model revolvers. Based on the above observations, it is reasonable to believe that the story may have changed over the years as the gun passed from generation to generation, even from person to person in each of the related families. Colt537 has a barrel that does not reflect all of the normal construction parameters identified in the four production models. That is to be expected. Its barrel does not have eleven lands and grooves, it had five of each. How can the deep groove along the upper portion of the bore be explained as a normal construction trait of a production model? There are too many file marks throughout Colt537 to call it a production model

Historical Significance of the Colt Paterson Experiment

It is believed that Mr. Gunnerson was the recipient of the original handmade model experiment and prototype for the four Paterson production models. There are more features, than one might expect in an experiment.

- Colt537 Experimental and Prototype, handmade revolver was developed in 1837.
- First developed No. 1 Pocket or Baby production model revolver, early fall 1837.
- Second developed No. 2 Belt production model straight grip, mid fall 1837.
- Third developed No. 3 Belt production model flared grip, late fall 1837.
- Fourth developed No. 5. Holster or Texas production model flared grip, spring 1838.
- Developed Patent No. 1304, August 29, 1839.

"Soon after the issuance of the August 29, 1839, patent, and the signing of the contract with the Republic of Texas Navy for 180 Holster Model pistols, i.e., Holster or Texas Model pistols, Sam Colt became anxious to go to Washington again. But, first, he had to have something to sell. For the next three months, he assisted Pliny Lawton in getting the largest size pistol ready in some quantity. This arm was the No.5. Although it was not definitely known what sort of a belt scabbard, or to use; the modern term, which eventually became, a "Holster" and was made to carry what is now called the No. 5 Holster or Texas Model."[86]

> "Of a mechanical pattern identical with the other three sizes i.e., models in production, this largest pistol was a powerful and hard shooting gun, capable of really serious work. However, "Lawton and Colt discovered that, with the front sight on the barrel, and the rear sight on the hammer lip, five shots could be fired at a mark with the same point of aim, and all grouped quite satisfactorily, but at a different location on the target. Then with the barrel removed, the cylinder reloaded, the barrel replaced, ending another round fired, the shots would group as well but in an entirely different part of the target. In smaller pistols, the very small grips had not been large enough to hold the gun firmly for accurate shooting, and this inherent inability to hold a point of aim had gone unnoticed. Now it was evident in all its horrible reality, the Colt just wouldn't shoot (accurately)! And this was the sort of thing with which they had been trying to revolutionize warfare. Why bother to even rifle the barrels, it was just a waste of labor."[87]

86. The Story of Colt's Revolver, William B. Edwards, Page 77, Col 2, Par 2, L 4
87. The Story of Colt's Revolver, William B. Edwards, Page 78, Col 1, Para 2, L 5

The above statement directly correlates with the condition of Colt537 Experiment. The bore of the barrel shows that the lands of the rifling had been scraped away, but not completely, enough remains to see that prior to the lands being removed, the revolver had five lands and grooves rather than the characteristic eleven found in the No.5 Holster orTexas Model. **See page 109 and 110.**"[88] After a bit of consternation,

> "…the cries stopped as they discovered why. The hole bored to receive the fore part of the cylinder arbor was drilled with a straight drill which bored a hole slightly, oversize, but more or less cylindrical, i.e., slightly ovoid. The arbor, too, was basically cylindrical, and when the two mated, there was no fit at all. Had the barrel been part of the drill press and the arbor the tail of a drill holder, the veriest apprentice would have suspected that with this state of affairs, their axes would never coincide. But Colt, too much in a hurry, had overlooked this little detail. Each time the barrel was replaced on the arbor and the wedge tapped in to draw it up tight, the minute irregularities on both arbor and inner bored surface would cause them to match differently, and so the barrel naturally pointed in another direction. Observing the concentric wedging effect of two mating tapers led Lawton to change the arbor-barrel boring, and he wrote to Colt, after an afternoon of good shooting. He wrote to Colt this extraction "and I think we can make each (revolver) as accurate." Things were good for Colt."[89]

The Colt537 Had Given It's Full in Service to Its Master – Who really put their heart and soul into that its design?

In effect, its mission was complete. Instead of being located in a place of honor for its contributions, it is believed its honor and distinction were relegated to some innocuous position on the shelves in the office storage room of the Colt plant, probably destined never to ever see the light of day again. At least not until that fateful day when someone, possibly Colt, Pliny Lawton or Henry B. Crosby, any one of them, more than likely, entered the storage area looking for misplaced samples of revolvers past or parts thereof. The need was to gather enough parts to, in his mind, equal an amount for services rendered to the company that he had not been paid for. The company was entering receivership and had no resources with which to pay its last remaining workers. Since he was one of Colt's trusted workers, more than likely he had contributed significantly to the development of Colt537. He recognized the revolver, and being a forward thinking individual, realized its future historical value. Something not to sell, but to save within the family, pass on for generations. Someday it might be a valuable family heirloom. Basically, that is exactly what happened to Colt537, except the elderly couple, Mr.

88. Three images of Colt 537's bore; remnants of removed lands are seen.
89. The Story of Colt's Revolver, William B. Edwards, Page 78, Col 1, Para 2, L 1

Gunnerson spoken of earlier, fell onto hard times, and had a need to sell the gun. And this is where the story can make a full circle. Who was he? Colt? Lawton? Crosby? Or, was it one of the workers who hid guns under coal pile? The one or two workers who secreted a gun in their lunch box as they left work at the end of the day? Colt would not have taken it. If so, it would be in one of Colt's Museum's.

Laughton was a company man, had the keys to the plant. He was always doing things to make Colt look good in Dudley Seldon's eyes. Pliny was always self-sacrificing, always found doing something for the betterment of the company.

Henry Crosby was known to have taken twenty-five sets of parts, made revolvers out of them, then sold them for a handsome profit. In later life he became a businessman entrepreneur.

Workers who placed revolvers under the coal pile must have been taking finished or close to finished revolvers. They probably would not have had an opportunity to get a hold of this revolver.

The workers who took a gun in their lunch box also probably looked for the best guns to take, high caliber production models, of course, Colt Nos 3 and 5.

Doing a Short Analysis of the Suspects

As the company was getting close to its demise, the workers would be able to tell that the plant would be closing shortly. It is suspected that they took the best and some parts in exchange for wages. Therefore I would discount the factory workers.

Pliny Lawton, Plant Supervisor, was the right person for that job level. Colt needed an individual that was looking out for the company, and its boss, always making the supreme sacrifice. At one time he was working so hard he began looking like a ghost of a man. All realized he was really sacrificing himself for the betterment of the company.

Henry Crosby, it seems as though Henry was somewhere in between the supervisor level and the common worker/gunsmith. It also seems that his transaction was exchanging lost wages for twenty-five sets of revolver parts. It was well known that he assembled these twenty-five sets, sold them and made a handsome profit. He later started a grocery enterprise. It seems like Henry was the entrepreneur.

Samuel Colt, all of the Revolvers Sam would have kept, would principally, be in a museum such as the Armsmear Museum in Hartford, Connecticut; the Wadsworth Athenaeum of Art, also in Hartford, Connecticut; or the Woolaroc Museum in Bartlesville Oklahoma.

What Would Be Some of the Eliminating Factors?

The factory employees were released on May 1, 1841. It was the same date the accounting books were closed. That should also be the date the majority (approximately nine) of the workers were released. They probably were lower level workers, some may have been those that stashed recently fabricated revolvers etc. under the coal pile including those that may have taken a revolver or two in their lunch boxes. The source of this information comes from: A History of Industrial Paterson, by L.R. Trumbull.

When did the factory close?

The accounting books were closed on May 1, 1841.

Was the date of closing of the Paterson Arms Mill the same date the workers were released?

It is assumed that approximately nine employees were released on May 1, 1841. Some of the employees may have remained in the plant to finish up their revolver or rifle.

When did the local Sheriff take an accounting of the mill's assets?

That was, more than likely, just before May 1, 1841, the closing of the books.

When did the Public Auction of Gun related items take place?

December 9, 1841.

When did the Public Auction of Machinery and Tools take place?

May 14 and 15, 1845.

When was Colt537 designed and made?

Early to Mid-1837. Best estimate

What products were taken in exchange for wages?

Completely finished revolvers, unfinished revolvers, and parts of revolvers

What type of products were stolen from Paterson Arms Mill prior to the Sheriff's accounting of the Plant's Assets?

Mostly revolvers and rifles

Who, among the employees, would have taken what, in terms of revolvers and rifles?

They, more than likely would have tried to take the best they could of either a revolver or rifle. They would have bypassed the Colt537 for lack of its perceived value at that time.

It would now be appropriate to determine who would be the most likely person to have taken Colt537 from the storage room, in the office section of the Paterson Gun Mill.

Was it any one of the nine workers? Information from above states that approximately nine of the thirteen workers were let go before, or on May 1, 1841. That was the day the accounting books of the Plant were closed. If any one of them had taken any guns (revolvers or rifles) they would have been production models. Low paid workers would not have access to the storeroom in the office area of the plant where, it is assumed Colt537 was being stored, i.e., stored along with the sixteen to twenty-six Pre-Paterson revolvers developed by John Pearson. The guns were taken prior to the Sheriff's arrival. Colt537 was made in early 1837. Experiments on it were later on in 1837 and early in 1838. Many of the factory workers on the mill floor would have had no knowledge of Colt537's existence.

Was it Henry B Crosby? It would be hard to think that Crosby would have taken Colt537. He more than likely had the keys to the plant, but it was widely known that he had taken twenty-five complete sets of parts, sufficient to assemble twenty five Colt Revolvers. It is said he made a handsome profit from the exchange of wages for the gun kits. Later on in life he was a local businessman. Crosby is judged to be an entrepreneur. He more than likely knew about Colt537 but passed it up for profits. Colt537 in the condition it was in at that time had relatively no significant value.

What about Pliny Lawton, the plant supervisor? Pliny Lawton was a company man, a self-sacrificing man. The plant and its workers were his family, Sam Colt included. He was so involved with his work at the plant that he neglected his health. At one time, some were saying he looked as gray as a ghost. Too much work, and too little sleep. When Colt537's experimentation was completed, Pliny would have been the one that placed it on the shelf of the office storeroom, next to the Pre-Paterson revolvers. Pliny would have been the one who understood the latent value of Colt537, if not to society to his family. It could be kept within the family with instructions to pass it on (within the family). It was passed on for three, maybe four generations. Instructions for maintaining the condition of the revolver, and cautions regarding what time and neglect could do to it may also have been passed down. For an old gun, it is in great shape.

I believe, if I were to attempt to follow up on finding the name of the family, it would be Pliny Lawton's family. Any genealogist out there who is wants to take the challenge?

Contact me, Michael Desparte at baraga@aol.com

Appendicies

Appendix 1, Page 1

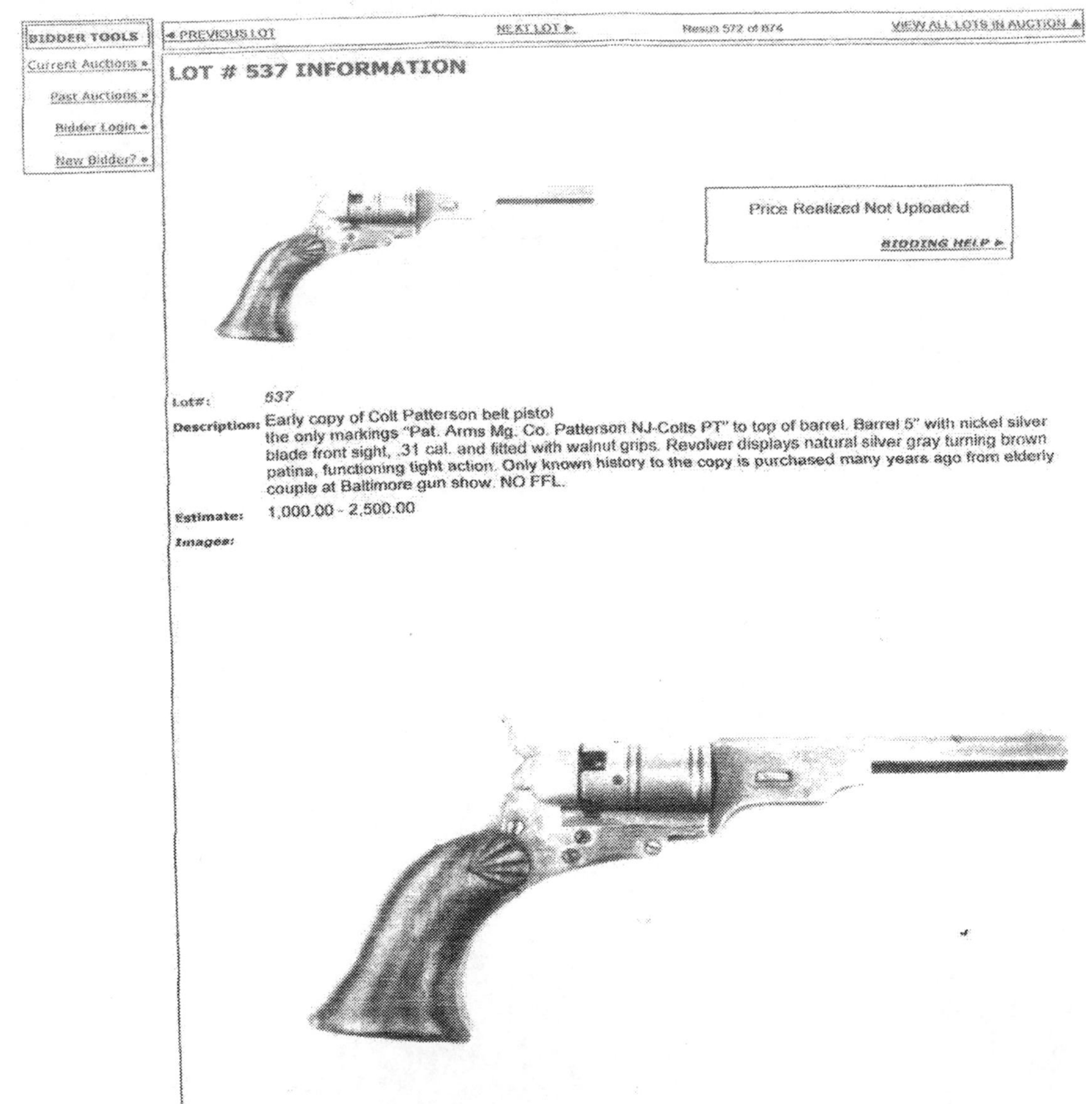

BIDDER TOOLS
Current Auctions »
Past Auctions »
Bidder Login »
New Bidder? »

◄ PREVIOUS LOT | NEXT LOT ► | Result 572 of 874 | VIEW ALL LOTS IN AUCTION ▲

LOT # 537 INFORMATION

Price Realized Not Uploaded

BIDDING HELP ►

Lot#: 537

Description: Early copy of Colt Patterson belt pistol the only markings "Pat. Arms Mg. Co. Patterson NJ-Colts PT" to top of barrel. Barrel 5" with nickel silver blade front sight, .31 cal. and fitted with walnut grips. Revolver displays natural silver gray turning brown patina, functioning tight action. Only known history to the copy is purchased many years ago from elderly couple at Baltimore gun show. NO FFL.

Estimate: 1,000.00 - 2,500.00

Images:

Appendix 1, Page 2

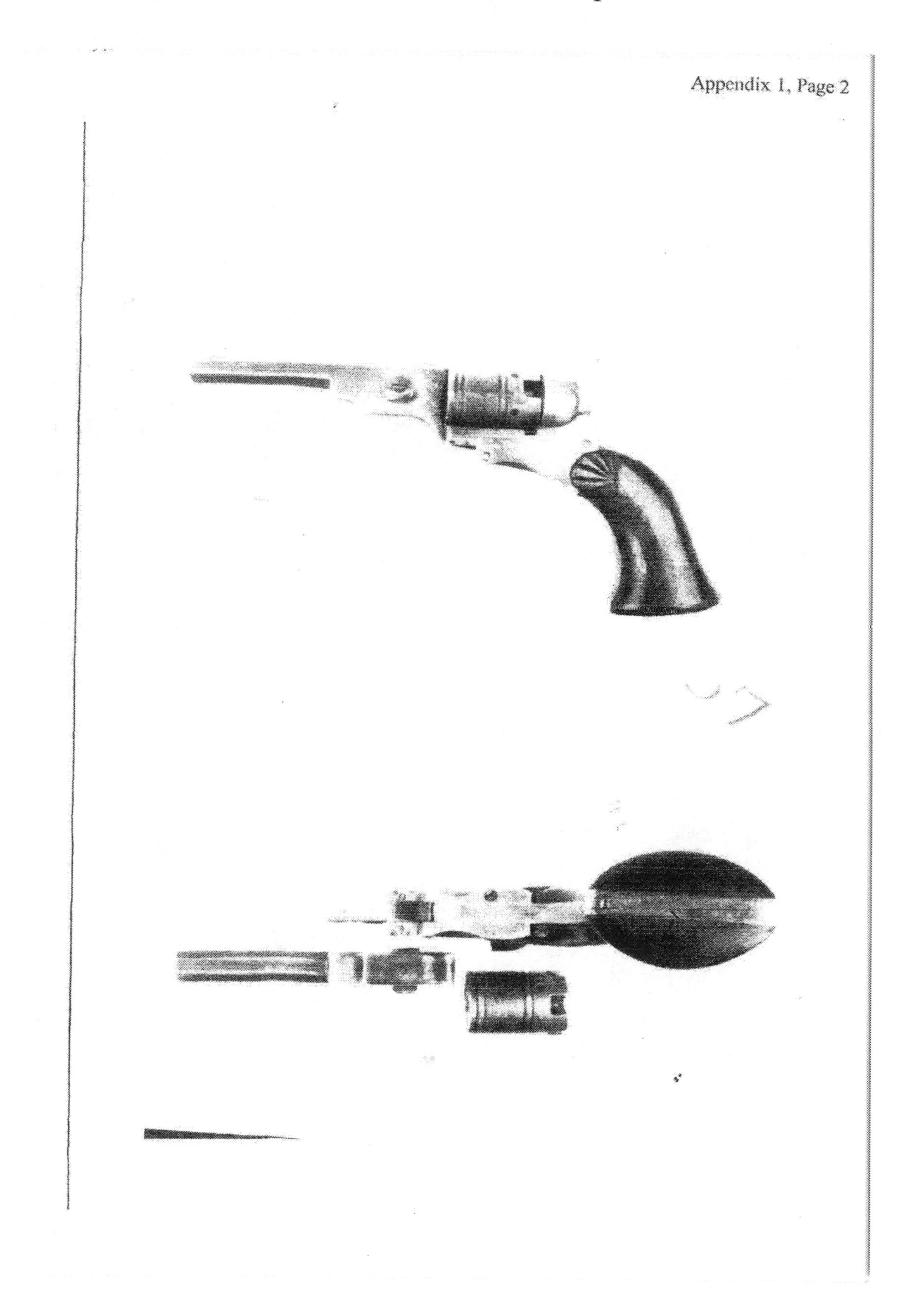

Appendix 1, Page 3

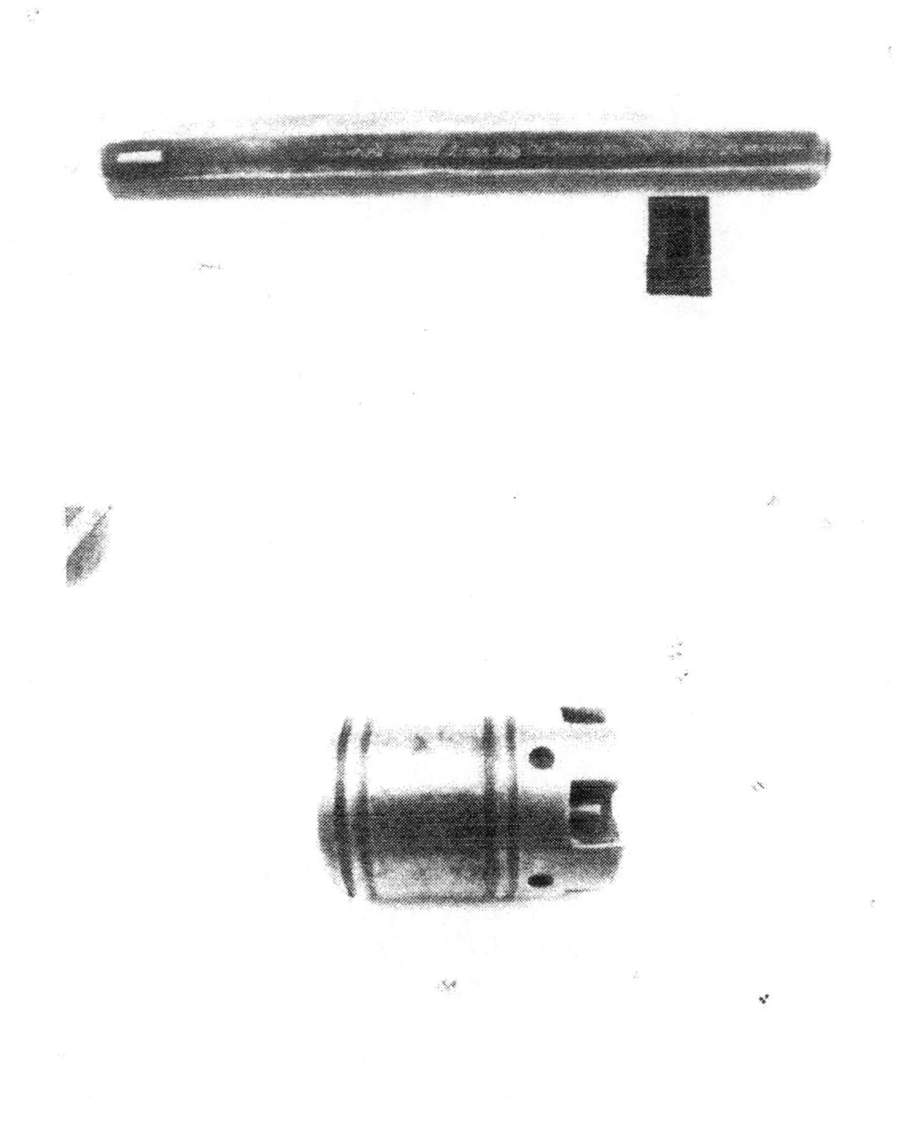

Appendix 1, Page 4

AUCTION INFORMATION:

Name	2 Day Fall Antique and Firearms Auction
Date(s)	12 Nov 2011 - 13 Nov 2011
Location	Rushmore Civic Center LaCroix Hall Rapid City, SD
Buyer Premium	15% (faxed/mailed bids show as floor bid
Print Catalog	Click here for printer friendly catalog.
Terms and Conditions	Click here to view terms and conditions.

Powered by Auction Flex

Appendix 2, Page 1

Scale Images of the Belt Model above the Holster or Texas Model

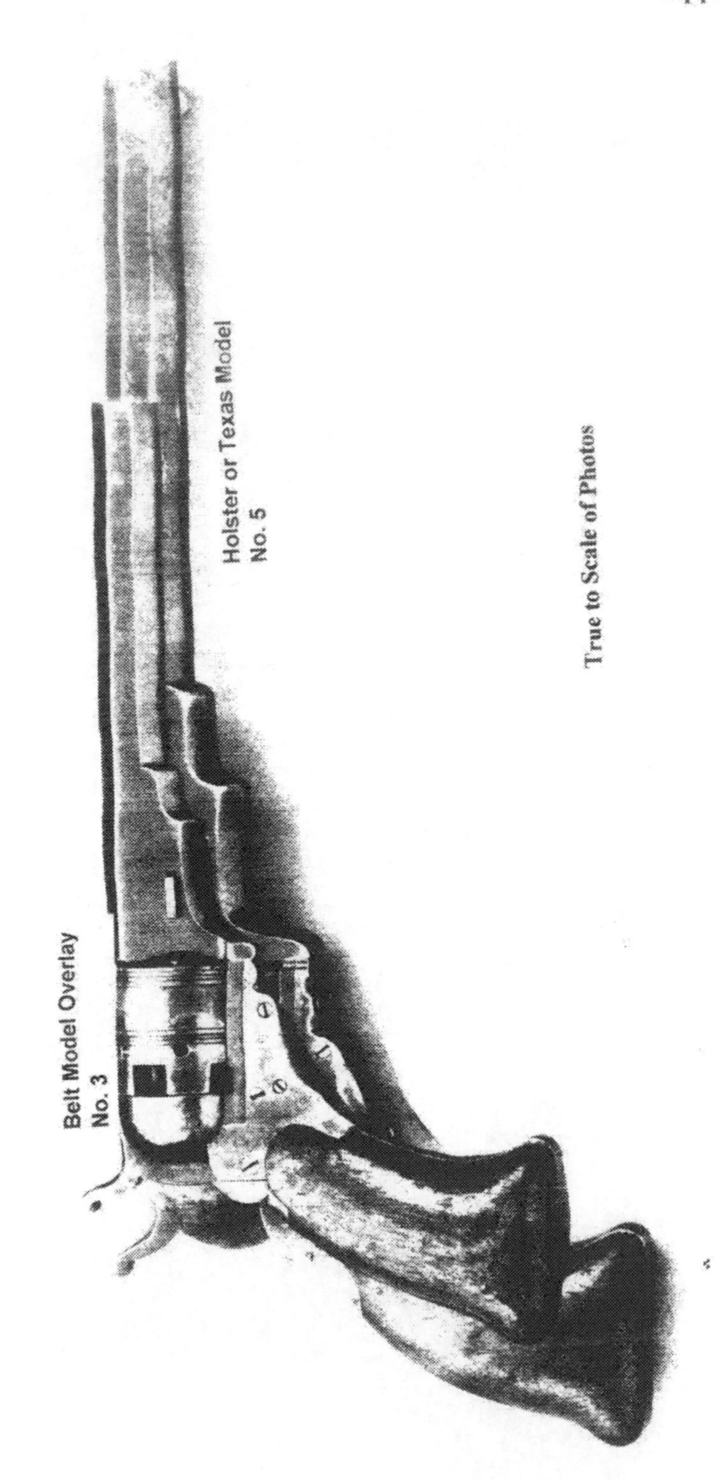

Source: The Paterson Colt Book, R.L. Wilson, Pages 100 and 101, Para 1, Line 1

Historical Significance of the Colt Paterson Experiment

Appendix 2, Page 2

Separate Images of the Belt Model and the Holster or Texas Model

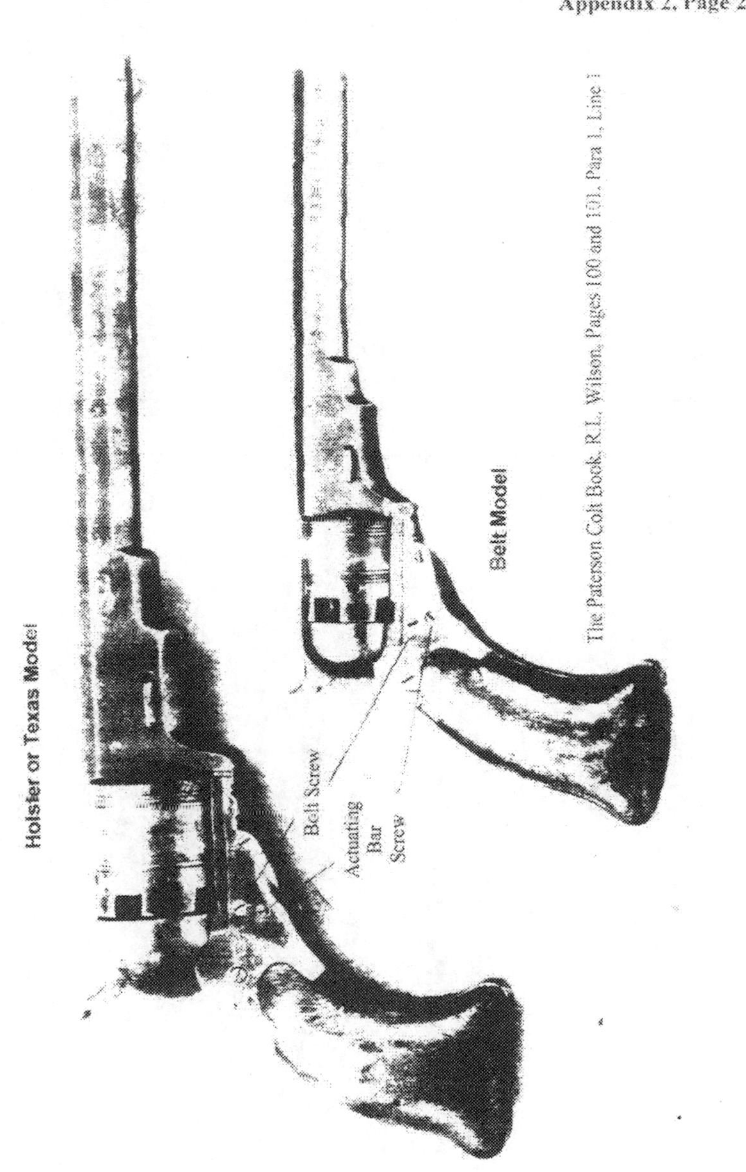

The Paterson Colt Book, R.L. Wilson, Pages 100 and 101, Para 1, Line 1

154

Appendix 2, Page 3

Belt and Holster or Texas Hybrid
Exploded View

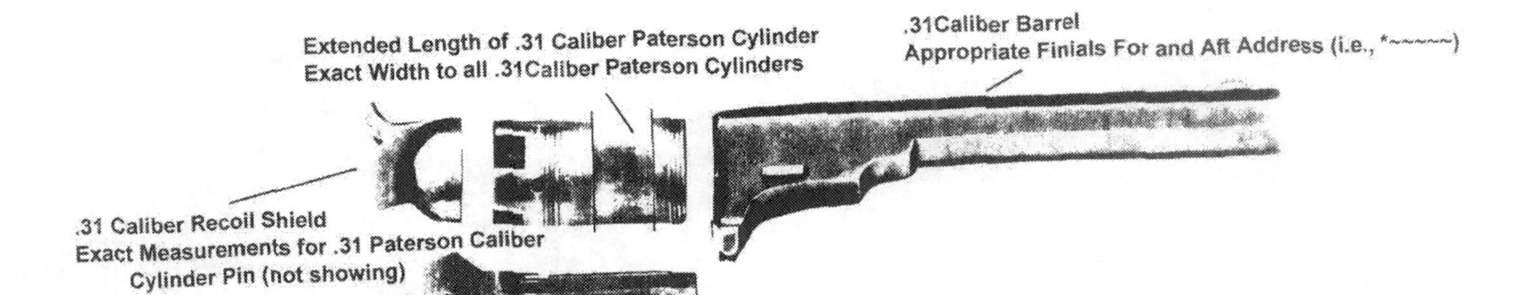

True to Scale of Photos

The Paterson Colt Book, R.L. Wilson, Pages 100 and 101, Para 1, Line 1

Appendix 2, Page 4

The Making of a Hybrid

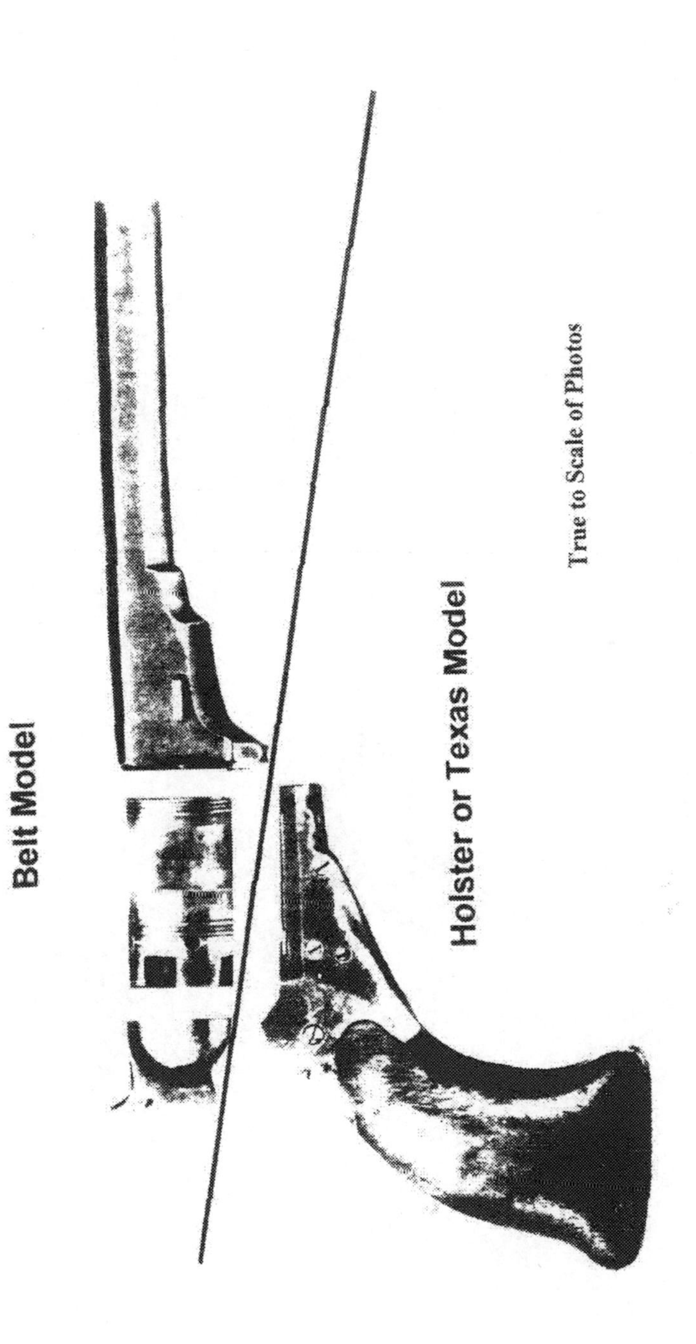

True to Scale of Photos

Source: The Paterson Colt Book, R.L. Wilson, Pages 100 and 101, Para 1, Line 1

Appendix 2, Page 5

Belt and Holster or Texas Hybrid

Assembled

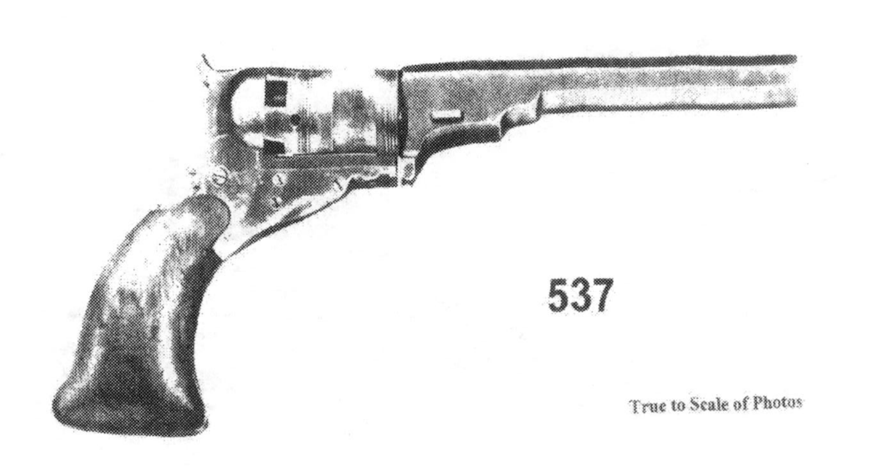

Source: The Paterson Colt Book, R.L. Wilson, Pages 100 and 101, Para 1, Line 1

Appendix 3

Summary of Twenty-Three Unique Characteristics, or Features of Colt537

1. Unique frame of Colt537 is too large for a Belt Model. The frame is just right for a .36 caliber, but not for a .31 caliber revolver.

2. Colt537's unique cylinder, too long for a normal Belt Model, it has a sufficient volume for a .36 caliber, but it is a .31 caliber.

3. Colt537 is so unique that it has a .31 caliber on a .36 caliber frame.

4. Colt537's unique barrel, had 5 lands and grooves.

5. Colt537's unique barrel, had only one groove on upper portion of bore, running the full length of the barrel.

6. Colt537 is so unique that its handmade model, had coil springs, rather than flat-springs.

7. Colt537's is so unique to the production model that it had straight, or flat, or leaf mainspring.

8. Colt537 is unique in that it is a handmade revolver.

9. Proof of being a Paterson, almost all internal parts are similar to production model parts.

10. Squared shoulder on breech of cylinder, therefore made prior to 1840.

11. Nipple shoulders are missing therefore made in late 1837 or early 1838.

12. Reverse address on top flat of the barrel, excellently done, however it is in reverse. Could be, there was no policy at this time on which way it was to read.

13. Barrel lacking its lands and grooves.

14. Barrel has faint workshop or other type numbers, some large, some small.

15. The hand's flat spring shows improvements in production models.

16. Cylinder has a flaw in one of the partitions.

17. Hammer was spliced together.

18. Thickness of the neck of the hand-grip is the first flared grip preliminary design, mostly to accommodate the mainspring.

19. Mainspring similar in design to the first Lawton-Colt Revolver page 80 variations book.

20. Colt537 has a three-piece lock frame, indicates it as being the original No. 5 frame Workshop numbers throughout the gun, in Colt locations.

21. Address on percussion models seem to be cut rather than a roller imprint.

22. Ratio of cylinder length to width is similar to first Lawton-Colt Experiment on page 80 variations.

23. Flat springs replace coil springs on production models. Colt537 has all coil springs with the exception of the hand and mainspring. Of particular note is the flat spring embedded in the Colt537's hand. This similar design resurfaces in the Colt 1851 Navy and continues on in other Colt models. The fact that it originally shows up in the Colt537 is another bit of support for Colt537's authenticity.

Appendix 4

A Chance Encounter

This is a summary of what was discussed with an individual that claimed he was the previous owner of Colt537. This individual indicated that Ccolt537 was purchased at a Sioux Falls, South Dakota Gun Show in the late 1990's He said he purchased it from an elderly couple for approximately seventeen hundred dollars. This couple indicated that they had the gun in their family for several generations. He also said that the original owner worked in the Colt factory at the time of closing. The family story was that this person had been working in the plant for a while and had not been paid his wages. Since the factory was closing, and the workers had not been paid, they were allowed to take a gun or gun parts with which to make a gun, in lieu of final wages. Colt537 was the one this person was working on at that time, and when he finished building it, he took it home. And that was two or three generations past. He said he was not able to get the individuals name.

It seems like a good story, but several issues do not mesh with what Mr. Frederick had said as to where he purchased the gun. Mr. Frederick, the one that put the revolver up for auction indicated that he purchased the gun from Mr. Gunnerson at a Baltimore gun show.

Since the revolver is a handmade, it would not be one that the subject worker was working on when the plant closed. Those revolvers were production models, having machine made external and internal parts. Many of those parts, although similar in design were not like the parts that are found in Colt537.

In the text of this research paper I have used factitious names for the subject individuals to protect them from unwanted communication.

What I think is happening is that over time the original owners story changed, much like a telephone game. Where one individual starts a story and it is transmitted through a number of other individuals. By the time the story is received by the final listener, the story has completely changed.

The fact that the original family name was not received, lends the story incredulous, but there is enough here to make one wonder.

Appendix 5

SPIRIT OF THE TIMES

See page 31 and 32 for additional information.

Source: Colt Firearms, James E. Serven

SPIRIT OF THE TIMES.

NEW-YORK: SATURDAY MORNING, JULY 7, 1838.

Aware of the difficulty of bringing our government to entertain the idea of any change in the implements of warfare, unless spurred on by the necessities of actual service, Mr. Colt resolved to look exclusively to the spirit of private enterprise for giving efficacy to his invention. He obtained a charter from the legislature of New Jersey, for a Patent Arms Manufacturing Company, with a capital of three hundred thousand dollars. The stock has been taken by several of our wealthiest citizens. An armory is already built at Paterson, N. J. When all its arrangements are complete, this armory will employ five hundred artisans. Upwards of one hundred are now constantly at work there, not only during the entire day, but even through a portion of the night.

At the recent fair of the American Institute, specimens of these ingenious weapons were exhibited in public for the first time. They attracted universal admiration. A committee of learned and practical mechanics pronounced upon their merits. After the most rigid scrutiny, they were accorded the highest and unqualified praise. The inventor was elected a member of the Institute. He was also presented with the greatest distinction in the power of the Institute to bestow—a golden medal.

To give our readers a better understanding of the principle upon which these Firearms are constructed, the following diagram is submitted of a Pistol, which is manufactured, and acts upon the same principle as the Rifle, with this exception, that the Cock of the Rifle acts horizontally, and is concealed beneath the Sight:—

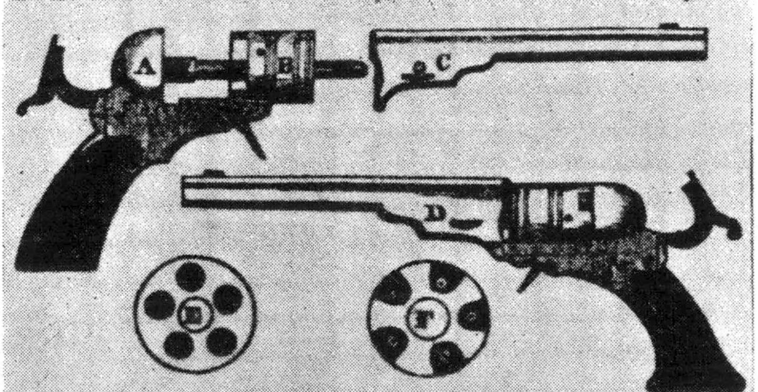

The *upper plate* represents the pistol in three detached portions as thus:—

A—the Stock, including the Hammer or Cock, and the Cylinder on which the Receiver B revolves, and to which the Barrel C is fastened.

B—the Receiver or Chamber, prepared for five charges.

C—the Barrel, which is fastened to the Cylinder, on which the Receiver revolves; to the left of the letter C is the wedge, which fastens the Barrel to the Cylinder.

The *lower plate*, D, presents the Pistol complete, cocked ready for firing. When discharged, the trigger, by a spring, may be closed into the Stock; the act of cocking throws the Trigger out, and turns the Receiver one charge each time.

E represents the inverted end of the Receiver, adjoining the Barrel. The five black dots denote the Chambers for charges, and the white ring (enclosing the letter E) the hole or aperture through which the Cylinder runs.

F represents the inverted end of the Receiver, next the Hammer, the small white dots denoting the Cones on which the percussion Caps are placed.